D0977552

In the Words
of
Great Business
Leaders

JULIE M. FENSTER

JOHN WILEY & SONS, INC.

NEW YORK · CHICHESTER · WEINHEIM · BRISBANE · SINGAPORE · TORONTO

For friends at *American Heritage* magazine—

Richard Snow
Frederick Allen
Catherine Calhoun

This book is printed on acid-free paper. ♾

Copyright © 2000 by Julie Fenster. All rights reserved.

Published by John Wiley & Sons, Inc.
Published simultaneously in Canada.

No part of this publication may be reproduced, stored in a retrieval system or transmitted in any form or by any means, electronic, mechanical, photocopying, recording, scanning or otherwise, except as permitted under Sections 107 or 108 of the 1976 United States Copyright Act, without either the prior written permission of the Publisher, or authorization through payment of the appropriate per-copy fee to the Copyright Clearance Center, 222 Rosewood Drive, Danvers, MA 01923, (978) 750-8400, fax (978) 750-4744. Requests to the Publisher for permission should be addressed to the Permissions Department, John Wiley & Sons, Inc., 605 Third Avenue, New York, NY 10158-0012, (212) 850-6011, fax (212) 850-6008, E-Mail: PERMREQ@WILEY.COM.

This publication is designed to provide accurate and authoritative information in regard to the subject matter covered. It is sold with the understanding that the publisher is not engaged in rendering legal, accounting, or other professional services. If legal advice or other expert assistance is required, the services of a competent professional person should be sought.

PHOTO CREDITS: Page 2: IBM Archives; Page 28: Photograph DN-0856338, William Wrigley Jr., Chicago (IL), 1928, photographer—*Chicago Daily News*; Page 50: Carnegie Library of Pittsburgh; Page 78: UPI/CORBIS-BETTMANN; Page 92: The Mary Pickford Foundation; Page 108: Courtesy of Polaroid Corporation; Page 126: UPI/CORBIS-BETTMANN; Page 144: Western Reserve Historical Society, Cleveland, Ohio; Page 174: Courtesy Ford Motor Company; Page 194: A'lelia Bundles/Walker Family Collection; Page 206: Corporate Archives, Bank of America; Page 226: Bridgestone/Firestone, Inc.; Page 250: UPI/CORBIS-BETTMANN; Page 268: Copyright 1976—GM Corp. Used with permission of GM Media Archives. All rights reserved; Page 290: Reproduced with permission of the Hewlett-Packard Company Archives; Page 312: Southwest Airlines, photo by David Woo; Page 328: UPI/CORBIS-BETTMANN; Page 342: UPI/CORBIS-BETTMANN; Page 352: UPI/CORBIS-BETTMANN.

ISBN 0-471-34855-4

Printed in the United States of America.

10 9 8 7 6 5 4 3 2 1

CONTENTS

INTRODUCTION

If all of business is a school, as some people say, then it is wise to have the best teachers.

That is the purpose of *In the Words of Great Business Leaders*. It is the chance to hear the most useful ideas directly from America's best. Their topic is business and the result is keen insight and advice too valuable to miss.

The book offers not just one voice on the subject of real business, but nineteen. And from leaders who don't dwell on business the way it could be or ought to be, but business the way it is, day in and day out, with all the turning points that build an important career. The quotes herein, taken from a wide variety of sources including letters, speeches, interviews, and memoirs, add up to something more than nuggets of advice. The pages are lined with those, without nonsense or preaching, and with humor and real-life examples. But taken together, these quotes, these impressions from plain experience, these nuggets of advice do more: They reveal the overall direction in thinking on the part of each of the great business leaders. Dare one say "philosophy"? Some unspoken shading

in outlook gives each of those profiled an utterly unique bearing. It is a book of mentors, and no two readers will ever read it
quite the same way.

The people who fill this book were, or are, real leaders in
business. They had to be: making something more than mere
money and leaving a path to follow. That point might not matter if the book were merely the sum of hundreds of quotes and
anecdotes; but as the book is also a reflection of underlying
philosophies, it made a vital difference. The leaders had to
leave a path worth following.

That's a dangerous admission to make, because nobody is
perfect and some of the people in this book sagged quite a bit
in that department at certain points in their careers. Wherever
relevant, I have pointed out those places, but overall, each of
those included made the cut for being, in a single word, progressive: creating business rather than merely benefitting from
it, innovating or pioneering in the best sense of risk-taking, and
leaving some distinct advancement in their industries, not only
in their own companies.

If none of the foregoing accomplishments are of interest
to you—if you only want to make a lot of money with your
time in this world—these people should still be of keen interest to you. Their net worth, added together and translated into
today's dollars, is close to $300 billion. Only one person in the
whole list was never a millionaire, and that was adamantly by
choice: A.P. Giannini, the founder of the Bank of America,
would not allow his net worth to reach $1 million and gave
away about half his fortune every time it neared that figure.

On the other side of the coin, you ought to note that three
of the people in this book started major companies with less
than $50—totaled together, in today's dollars or any other dol-

lars. They are William Wrigley Jr., who started his gum company with $32, Madame C.J. Walker, who founded a national beauty company with $1.50, and Margaret Rudkin, who started Pepperidge Farm with the cost of ingredients for twelve loaves of bread. David Packard seems flush by comparison, having cofounded Hewlett-Packard with $538.

Two of the people in the book started from even less than zero: Ted Turner inherited a bankrupt company from his father, while Henry Ford II inherited one on the verge of collapse from his grandfather and namesake. Two of those found in the book had no such incentives toward success: Both William S. Paley of CBS and J. Paul Getty were rich young playboys who surprised nearly everyone by settling down (or perhaps not settling down) to become workaholic businessmen.

As to the actual demographics, there are only three women on this roster, which doesn't come close to either the proportion of women in the population or the percentage who have had careers in business. Minorities, with one of nineteen, aren't properly represented, either, against those criteria. However, it is worth considering that both percentages, as reflected in the book, are far greater than the numbers of women or minorities commonly asked for their business advice, even up to the current time, or regularly asked to speak on that subject. Without a fair collection of opinion and anecdote, it was impossible to include an otherwise vivid person.

Because the book includes all different types of business leaders, by design, the quotes vary in nature. Harvey Firestone, of tire fame, and Thomas Watson Sr., longtime president of IBM, were at ease giving direct, pinpointed advice. Some of their epigrams probably ought to be engraved on the faces of wristwatches as constant reminders. Others make points with a more circumspect or narrative cast.

The secret strength of *In the Words of Great Business Leaders* is that each reader who has looked over the chapters so far has told me with steady candor how clear and succinct certain of the business leaders are—and how opaque some others are. Of course, the readers' favorites are never the same. No one person in business has all the answers, but the right roster will come close.

This group of great business leaders, already pressed to represent a full range of backgrounds and points of view, also reflects a balance of industries and regions in America. Without too much overlapping, the pattern was supposed to be that there is no pattern. That may be a fetching theory, but a table of contents is supposed to have a pattern, and these nineteen could go in practically any order. Alphabetical order seemed timid under the circumstances, and chronological order seemed unoriginal. People of action should be placed in action, and so I placed the great business leaders in sections according to their strong points. Don't take the sections too seriously: the mavericks are also good bosses; the self-made successes are hard workers—and all of them were good in sales.

To give *In the Words of Great Business Leaders* a little more in the way of a plot, and perhaps a trifle more suspense, than the average quote book, the profiles included with each chapter are stories from the lives of the great business leaders. No person in this book is chiseled in stone, but sometimes that is easy to forget when their words are. In fact, these leaders are not so very different from anyone reading this now, except that they got into and out of some of the same business situations first. I hope you can see them and hear them toughing it out in their own ways and in their own words.

PART I

Talk About Convincing:
SALESMEN

William Wrigley Jr. considered the matter carefully and couldn't name even one person in business who wasn't ultimately in sales. At any level and in any industry, sales is the word behind business. It is also the word behind growth.

"I've never recognized any elevation above that of salesman," boasted Thomas Watson, IBM's first president.

The men in this section—Watson, Wrigley, and steelmaker Andrew Carnegie—were veritable strongmen of sales. Not many people ever started out lower in business: two door-to-door salesmen and a bobbin boy. Of course, few ever ended up higher, and each knew firsthand the catalog of problems that could arise from within or without to test a person in the business of sales. That is to say, to test a person in business. Flashes of brilliance don't contribute in the long run. Sales is an attitude made up of details that beg to be overlooked, of habits that seem so forgiving.

All of the men in this chapter were engaged in selling every hour of the business day. So is everybody, as a matter of fact. The only difference is that some people don't forget it.

Thomas Watson Sr. welcomes IBM salesmen to a company convention in 1924. Watson was a familiar figure to most IBM employees, and knew a remarkable number of them by name.

Thomas J. Watson Sr.

1874–1956

Thomas Watson Sr. was not the founder of International Business Machines, but he was in every sense the spirit behind it. In 1914 Watson took charge of the faltering conglomerate of manufacturing companies and presided over it until 1956. By then, IBM was among the nation's ten largest manufacturers, poised to lead the business world into the computer age. Though Watson was not technically oriented, he guided IBM into an overwhelming dominance of the field of data processing. The company's ultimate sales manager, he emphasized education and results, turning his ever expanding staff into a sales engine for IBM. One of the most famous businessmen of his time, Thomas Watson was a hard-driving man whose grandest ambitions were realized on the corporate level; yet he never lost an overt sense of respect for each individual employee. In Watson's eyes, IBM was a family—an old-fashioned attitude that somehow suited the ultra-modern company.

$\mathcal{E}$very summer, the National Cash Register Company hosted a celebration of its top salesmen called the Hundred Point Club Convention, named for the fact that every invited guest had completely filled his annual quota. It was a week off from work to talk about how exciting it was to work—at NCR. At the culmination of the 1913 convention, an assistant sales manager named R.H. Grant delivered a typical speech for the Hundred Pointers. It was followed by a truly rousing speech by the company's popular sales manager, Thomas J. Watson, who concluded to a burst of noisy applause from the salesmen in the audience. Before the applause could even crest, though, the president of the company, John Patterson, hurried to the podium and quieted the audience. He wanted to use that moment to say how very much he had enjoyed the speech made by R.H. Grant. But Grant had spoken before Watson: For the audience, it seemed a quirky oversight, a bit of confusion. To those onstage, though, there was no confusion, only shock. Patterson had just let Thomas Watson know that his career at NCR was at a close.

At forty, Watson had been working at NCR for eighteen years. His attachment to the company had an almost Dickensian cast: NCR had picked him up when he was a veritable orphan of business and he had proved himself deserving of every opportunity offered, every chance to learn from the company and improve himself toward its model. He knew the company could be cruel, but that fact had never scared him—until the end of his speech at the Hundred Point Convention in 1913.

Before arriving at NCR, Thomas Watson had made his start in sales by peddling pianos door-to-door in the farm district near his hometown of Painted Post, New York, where his father was a lumber dealer. As a young man, Watson was both honest and industrious, two qualities he felt sure would bring him a fortune as a salesman. After a series of setbacks, however, he began to realize that there was even more to it.

While returning a cash register left over from yet another failed business—a butcher shop—Watson managed to talk himself into a job at NCR's Buffalo sales office. He soon talked like an NCR man, he thought like one, he dressed like one, and what is more, he succeeded as one. At twenty-eight, he was named to an executive post at the home office in Dayton, Ohio. John Patterson rewarded Watson's loyalty with a swank Pierce-Arrow car and, later on, with the use of a house adjacent to his own.

But Patterson, for all his brilliance, was like some mythological creature who gave life to heroes only to destroy them when they grew to equal him. He nurtured a strong roster of executives through the years, and clashed with any who became too powerful or charismatic. Those who did either were cut or left under fire. As sales manager at NCR, Thomas Watson did an excellent job. That ought to have worried him.

Early in 1913, twenty-two NCR executives had been found guilty of violating the Sherman Antitrust Act. Both Patterson and Watson were among them, each facing a sentence of one year in jail.

Eventually Patterson welcomed a deal by which sentences would be waived for those executives admitting culpability. All but three joined him in signing; one of those who refused was Thomas J. Watson. Maintaining that he had done nothing wrong, he chose to pursue an appeal, with the specter of jail time if he lost. Such bravado did not please John Patterson.

On one occasion, Patterson fired an executive by sending him out on an errand: When the man drove back up to the building, he noticed that his desk and chair were on the front lawn. On cue, the desk burst into flames. The man simply drove away. In Watson's case, Patterson was openly insulting in the months following the Hundred Point Convention in June 1913, and then in November, he came right out and demanded a letter of resignation. Watson was no longer an NCR man. At forty, the most vivid possibility in his future was jail time.

For months, Watson did not work at all. The authors of a 1960 biography simplified the crucial juncture almost to the point of unintended pathos: "Other than a vision of greatness, Watson had no concept of what he wanted to do." The same could be said of many job seekers, but Watson had far better credentials than most. He still believed in Patterson's sales methods — but believed he could better them. He still believed in John Patterson, too, but was ready to outgrow his former mentor, however unwillingly at first.

Thomas Watson was lanky in build. Disdaining sports of any kind, he carried himself with more dignity than vigor, remaining unmussed whatever the conditions and however long the day. His face could be severe, his thin features and small, dark eyes bearing down sharply. In fact, he had an engaging personality, not necessarily through humor, which colored his outlook only faintly, but through his very earnestness. His seminal traits — temper and warmth — might have come from the opposite ends of some personalities, but not in such an earnest man. Often compared to a minister or a deacon, he consistently exuded the impression that he cared. He cared about his work, he cared about his workers as individuals, he cared about the whole world. The job Watson needed was one that required a management executive with the instincts of a mother dog.

Charles Flint, the financier who credited himself with inventing the conglomerate, had patched four vaguely related businesses into the Computing-Tabulating-Recording Co. (C-T-R) in 1911. Three years later, the company was foundering, barely able to carry its own massive debt. After a three-day interview, Flint hired Watson to lead C-T-R, overcoming the objections of at least one board member who inquired testily as to who would run the company while Watson was in jail. Watson had his opportunity, though a wobbly one: The job agreement contained the humbling provision that he could not officially become president until his criminal charges were settled. Only months before, he had been second in command at the one of the nation's champion companies.

C-T-R made a pale comparison. It was small and obscure, a pile of jagged shards getting along neither within themselves nor among themselves. The similarity between it and NCR lay in the product lines. Each were pioneers in commercial control: NCR registered sales. C-T-R registered time (International Time Recording Co. and Bundy Manufacturing), bulk inventory (Computing Scale Co.), and information (Tabulating Machine Co.). The tabulating machine sorted punched cards that stored data and kept track of that data at the same time. Punch clocks may have been of intimate interest to Watson, a man who devoted hours to contemplating the word *minute,* but the tabulator was the most potent of all the company's products. It didn't count minutes, but saved them, and Watson knew from his contemplations that in his age, in any age, saving time is where the money is. One of Watson's long-term missions would be to fit tabulating machines into ever smaller businesses.

As the nominal president of C-T-R, however, Watson did not fit into his own company very well at first. For a year, he served the strange sentence meted out by his antitrust case: a presidency paled by uncertainty regarding his future. Finally, in May of 1915, Watson received a telegram saying that his guilty verdict had been set aside. Within days, he was named president, fully and officially.

Upon arriving at C-T-R, Watson had been expected to duplicate NCR's approach, and he did, especially in basic sales methods and in his cultivation of international operations, an emphasis that resulted in the company's 1924 name change to International Business Machines. As at NCR, employees were expected to enhance the company's reputation by leading respectable lives. Watson viewed himself and every other employee as ambassadors for IBM, not merely during work hours but all the time. Conservative dress became symbolic of the company's prescribed image: Even machine oilers at the main factory in Endicott, New York, felt compelled to wear white shirts and ties to work, changing into overalls only within the building. Watson also expected IBM employees to marry well, live in good neighborhoods, drive late-model cars, contribute to their communities, attend church, and conduct themselves soberly at all times. In fact, drinking was prohibited on company time and smoking was banned in most company offices.

Most employees responded to the policies the way Watson had responded to NCR: They were glad to belong to an organization they considered worth belonging to. At its worst, however, Watson's imitation of NCR's uniform image resulted in a prejudice against hiring salesmen, in particular, of differing ethnic backgrounds.

As Watson shaped his new company, pulling it together and pushing it forward, he reverted to his own basic instincts, those of an upstate piano salesman who was honest and industrious—callow, but determined to learn. Watson created an educational complex underscored by his own edict: Serve, don't just sell. Watson's attitude was that IBM should have the better product and the better sales technique: if it did not, then the other company deserved the sale. That didn't happen often: Throughout most of its history, IBM controlled on average eighty-eight percent of the market for punch card tabulators.

Singed, and almost consumed, by Patterson's heedless emphasis on growth, Watson created IBM as an equally aggressive company, but one with a sense of perspective about success. He wanted it to be decent, at a time when many companies were rapacious. Executives and salesmen were encouraged to believe that the company would not let them down or lay them off.

If Watson's response to prosperity was expansion, his response to adversity was expansion on an even grander scale. In the worst days of the Great Depression, when IBM's sales drooped, Watson didn't fire salesmen—he hired them, by the hundreds. "You know," he said at the age of fifty-eight to a businessman who mocked his response to the downturn, "when a man gets about my age, he always does something foolish. Now some men run to playing poker and others to horse races, some to ladies and one thing and another. My hobby is hiring salesmen."

During World War II, Thomas Watson's support was instrumental in creating one of the first practical computers, the Mark I, a navy project developed in partnership with Harvard University. After the war, though, Watson regarded the computer as nothing more than an interesting but impractical and unremunerative advancement on the tabulator. His son, Thomas Jr., proved more visionary. As the only junior executive who could—occasionally—win an argument with Thomas Sr., he was responsible for IBM's slightly delayed entry into the commercial development of the computer in 1948. Blunt-spoken and amazingly clear-sighted, Thomas Jr. would lead IBM through its greatest era of growth from 1952 through his gradual retirement in the early 1970s. Even more impatient than his father, "Young Tom" succeeded as a manager because he was as honest about his own limitations as he was about everyone else's. Thomas Sr. was no less successful, yet he could not quite see limitations. Or at least he kept his eyes from looking.

Advancing IBM's growth through the 1950s, Thomas Watson Sr. expanded into a public figure, almost a statue of American enterprise, with a marblelike polish. Early in his rise as a public figure, he became known for his liberal outlook, as one of the few industrialists to wholeheartedly support Franklin Roosevelt and his New Deal business controls. Watson also worked intensively for world peace.

As it turned out, IBM benefited magnificently from Roosevelt's New Deal, receiving the contract to supply data processing equipment for the newly formed Social Security Bureau in 1935. As for world peace, it was—if nothing else— noticeably profitable for IBM, a company with operations in seventy-nine countries by 1940. But those are cynical attitudes. Had Thomas Watson Sr. been a cynical man, he would have pleaded guilty in 1913 to something he believed he did not do. But then, IBM would not have existed at all if Thomas Watson had been a cynical man.

In the words that follow, Thomas J. Watson Sr. comes through with some of the gusto he must have imparted at his favorite events, IBM conventions and sales meetings. The points he makes spark individual potential without compressing anyone into a set pattern. Watson knew how to be an employee—he'd dealt with his own share of difficult bosses—and he knew how to be a boss as well, but what he mostly liked to speak about was salesmanship. He credits enthusiasm as the most important asset in sales, and shows how to cultivate it step by step. One step in the process became Watson's most famous dictum of all: "Think."

IN THE WORDS OF

Thomas J. Watson Sr.

Perspective

In any job, there are two things to learn: first, the routine methods to be gone through; and second, the reason for it all. Many men fail, because they never learned the mechanics of their work properly. But a greater proportion fail because they never truly find out what their jobs are all about, and how their day's work ties in with the big plan of what their company is trying to do.

Character

Character should never be confused with reputation. It is not a matter of externals.

Leadership

The farther we keep away from the "boss" proposition—of being the "boss" of the men under us—the more successful we are going to be. If a man cannot be a real assistant and furnish assistance to the men under him he has no business being over men at all. That is not one of our problems [at IBM], but it does exist in many places throughout the country, where a man, because of his impressive title, assumes the attitude of a "boss" and tells people what to do, instead of helping them to do it.

Really successful men are pushed up, not pulled up.

Goals

Whatever is the best thing for the business is the best thing for the men in it. Let us keep that in mind—what is the best thing for the business is the best thing for everybody in it.

Outlook

[*In 1932, when Watson was fifty-eight, he made a differentiation between actual age in business and heart-age.*]

When we reach forty years of age, we find seventy-two percent of all people younger than we are. It doesn't make any difference how many here tonight are over forty. We won't discuss that in detail, but I want to leave this thought—that we cannot afford to let our hearts get more than forty years old if we are going to contribute anything to this civilization, because we have to be in a position to make contacts and make those contacts count with that seventy-two percent of the world's population which is under forty.

Management

My duty is not the building of this business; it is, rather, the building of the organization. The organization builds the business.

It does not take executive ability to discharge a man, but it does take it to develop men.

Motivation — Enthusiasm

[In 1915, one year after Thomas Watson joined C-T-R, he made a speech at one of the company's divisions, International Time Recording Co. (ITR). Watson's talk was typical of his motivational style, and is quoted at length.]

It is easy to say "Work," to a man, but you must give him something besides that. There is something which makes a man want to work. It is enthusiasm. You never saw a lazy man in your life who was enthusiastic. You never saw an enthusiastic man who was lazy. If we have enthusiasm, we want to work. As we are talking about success, let us apply it to the ITR business; if we work we know we shall be successful. We know that if we have the enthusiasm, we shall want to work, and that will make us successful.

What is it that gives us enthusiasm? It is not something that you can go out and buy. It is not a condition that just happens to you as you go through life. We have to do something to create enthusiasm within ourselves, that will make us want to work. There is only one thing on earth which will do it and that is knowledge. Knowledge creates enthusiasm. It is the only thing that will. Why are some of you here enthusiastic about baseball? Because you have a knowledge of the game. You played baseball when you were boys in school and you know everything about the scores, the errors and all the rest. There are times when you would walk miles to a good baseball game and sit out in the hot sun and yell yourselves hoarse. You know whether the players are doing it right or not. You have enthusiasm. . . . The same thing applies to business. If we have a knowledge of this business and apply it, we will then have the proper amount of enthusiasm; we will do the proper amount of work to make us all successful.

M o t i v a t i o n — K n o w l e d g e

[*Watson explained in his speech how to acquire the type of knowledge that leads to enthusiasm.*]

How are we going to get that knowledge? There is only one way—through study. That is the only way we can get knowledge. Right there is where most of us fall down. We say to you, "Study." Yes, study and get the knowledge that will give you enthusiasm which, in turn, will cause you to work and be successful.

First, we must study by reading, then by listening, discussing, observing and thinking. We must study in those five ways. When we read we must always keep in mind that we are not reading just to get to the conclusion of the writer, because if we do that we are just getting one man's view. We must read and keep in mind the fact that we are reading to stimulate our own thoughts; we should take the points and the ideas and the suggestions that we get from this reading and apply them in our own way and in our own work.

Listening is one of the best ways in the world to learn. Sometimes we don't take time to listen to the other fellow. That sometimes applies to the man when he is a supervisor. His manager is trying to tell him something, but he doesn't listen, he doesn't have his mind open. Sometimes you reverse that. Sometimes the man up above does not take the time to listen to other men, the men below him. Then he often loses a whole lot of knowledge and misses one of the greatest opportunities to study. We must therefore listen to each other . . .

Discussion is one of the greatest mediums in the world by which people learn and that is why we are all here this morning. . . .

Observation. We can always study through observation and to the salesman, perhaps, that applies more than to anybody else, because as you go about in your daily work calling on the different institutions you are studying by observation. You may not have analyzed it just like this, but you have been doing it just the same.

Motivation — Thinking

[*Watson went on to explain what was, perhaps, his favorite theme.*]

But thinking is the most important point of the whole proposition. Think! Sometimes we read and listen and discuss and observe and then we don't take the time to sit down and think it all over and arrive at a proper conclusion that is our own. Anything that is our own is strong to us. If a man has a strong selling point, if it is strong in his heart and he believes it, when he passes that to me, it is strong to me. I might try to take the same idea and put it up in the man's own way and it wouldn't be effective at all, because a part of its strength would be the personality that originally went with it. We must all take time to do enough thinking to formulate our own conclusions.

[Thomas Watson traveled tirelessly to spend time in IBM offices throughout North America and Europe, speaking with employees informally or in the banquet atmosphere so familiar within the company culture. Even as an elderly man, he maintained the rigorous schedule, often visiting two or three different offices a day for weeks on end. His own unceasing motivation obviously had a great deal to do with enthusiasm, as was revealed in an impromptu remark he made at the end of speech in 1929.]

I am sorry I cannot talk to you all day. The IBM means so much to me that I could stay here for twenty-four hours and talk about it.

Innovation

[Watson expected every employee to stay alert for chances to help the company.]

When you get suggestions, as you must, from the manufacturers and the merchants with whom you come in contact, and they say, "If you had a Time Recorder that would do so-and-so —," and the idea sounds absolutely ridiculous and foolish to you, make a note of it and send it to the factory. Let our talented inventors decide whether it is impossible or not. That is their business. That is why we keep them here, and we are willing to keep twice as many as we have here now; if you will furnish the thoughts, we will let them work out the ideas. We must progress and we can't do it in any other way.

Time Management

You carefully count and check your dollars, but do you count and check with equal seriousness that indispensable possession that is so necessary for the acquisition of dollars—time?

After a clock has ticked off sixty seconds a minute is gone, never to be brought back. It is impossible for us to put forth extra effort and make up for the loss of that minute. We have all said to ourselves, after realizing that we have wasted a certain number of minutes, hours, days or months, perhaps, that we will brace up and "pull ourselves together." We say we are going to make up for lost time. When you say that you are simply fooling yourself, for such a thing cannot be done.

Check up each day the amount of time you spend in your prospects' stores or with merchants in your office. It is the length of time you stand up in front of a retail merchant who needs a scale, talking and demonstrating scales to him, that constitutes your work . . .

Keep check on yourself by jotting in a little memorandum book the actual time you spend talking scales. At the end of the first week you probably would say to yourself that you are ashamed of the record, of the small number of hours actually put in in the sort of work that earns commissions. Soon you will double your efforts and your income will grow accordingly.

That doesn't mean you will be working harder—only more systematically. It means you will have learned how to organize yourself.

Investing

I suggest that you pick out five successful companies with good earnings. See what each of them has been doing in the way of building up its business and building up its earning power during the past seven years. Then make up your mind that just as soon as you can get money enough you are going to buy shares of stock in one of those companies. Then add to this as you can, keep on buying in one or more or all five of those companies, and say to yourself that you are not going to sell those shares when their value increases.

Do not be tempted to sell out and take a profit as long as the company in which you have invested your money is increasing its earnings.

Diligence

I don't want any of you to go away feeling that we are urging you to work too hard. We do not advocate that. We simply want you to use good judgment. We don't want any man to do anything in the interest of this company that would in any way interfere with his health or comfort or personal privileges. We simply ask for an honest effort.

Efficiency

[*At IBM, Watson banned smoking and drinking on company time, and he often made mention of the connection between healthy habits and job performance.*]

Whether we are trying to increase our efficiency in selling or along any other line, one of the most important things we have to consider is our health. And in this consideration we have five essentials to remember: Fresh Air; Exercise; Sleep; Food; Drink.

Taking Orders

I can recall many times when I resented supervision from my superior officers. That cost me money. It will cost any man money. A good thought for anybody who is being supervised to bear in mind is that the man who cannot accept supervision profitably will never find himself in a position to supervise others. None of us can escape supervision. The president and general manager of every concern are supervised more closely than the salesmen. Keep that in mind when you get a criticism from any of the executives of your company. Instead of resenting it, analyze and turn it to your benefit.

Giving Orders

Men in the field, as well as men in the office or factory, should be given every opportunity to solve their own problems and overcome their difficulties. If they make a mistake and admit it, forgiveness should be automatic. But the same mistake must not be made a second time.

You should always be fair with your salesmen because they are always alone in their field and meet people who have a great habit of saying "No." Let them discuss matters with you and try to help them.

Self-appraisal

You often hear men say, "Well, my record is as good as the average." When a man says that he is paying himself no compliment at all.

Salesmanship

If a prospect asks about some other make of machine tell him that you know very little about it. Tell him that Mr. Blank over on Main Street is the agent, and should be able to answer questions, because he sells that product. You are there to talk International.

Think of the effect which that will have on the prospective customer. He will feel that you are a reliable businessman talking business in an honorable way. You have something to talk about and know how to do it.

I wish I could get that thought firmly into your minds today. All you have to do is go into your territories and talk International. Do not allow anyone to lead you astray by discussing something else. If you do you will lose your point of vantage. Just as soon as you start to criticise or depreciate some other product you start weakening your case. On the other hand, by concentrating on your own goods you are constantly strengthening your own case.

※

Whether we are selling scales, time recorders or tabulating machines, we prove our case by getting the prospect to figure out the actual savings that we can effect.

※

Very often it is one single word used in your approach that opens up the proper contact between you and the prospect. If a Dayton Scale salesman introduces himself with the words, "I represent the Dayton Scale Division of the International Business Machines Corporation," it makes the merchant think beyond our scale division . . .

Human nature, you know, is the same the world over. We all like to be identified with important things.

※

Cover every point of your equipment in talking about it. Don't dwell on any one thing. Explain the entire subject to the prospect.

Personality

Always remember that your personality is your big asset. Do not try to emulate another person. Present your proposition in your own natural way, always keeping your personality *behind your product.* Some men get their personalities between their product and the prospect by dressing flashily or doing something unusual to attract attention. Such conduct only kills business. Real personality comes from the heart. Many salesmen fail because they strive to do something unique to make people look at them when they come in. This may attract attention but it is detrimental to the proposition they are coming to present. When you talk in an unusual manner or try to imitate someone else, you are not acting naturally and the prospect feels that at once. He begins to think about you, wondering why you introduce yourself in such fashion. Then he forgets about the wonderful accounting aid you are bringing him. So forget yourselves and become enthusiastic about your product.

Persistence

It does not require a genius to find the people who need these machines. Walking and talking are all that is necessary. These are the two things we must do. Most of us can talk, but some are a little shy on the walking. Whether you use a motor car or your feet, the main thing is to cover ground and keep moving from the time you start out in the morning.

🌾

My manager used to say: "There are only two classes of people who never change: fools and dead people." That is pretty true. Keep track of those fellows who say "No," today, because next week, next month or next year they are going to say "Yes," to somebody who is selling our kind of goods.

Sales Challenge

That word "why" is one of the strongest words in the selling language. When some man tells you that he doesn't want the machine you are selling, ask him why, and let him answer before you start telling him why he ought to have it.

Let him tell you why he doesn't want it. I think the answer nine times out of ten will be that it costs too much money. Then you present your real selling argument, which should sound something like this:

"If I can't show you where this machine will save you money in your business, I don't want to sell it to you."

First of all, show him that he is going to save money . . .

Duty

You sometimes hear people criticize various sales methods. They object to the so-called strong-arm method of selling or to what they call high-pressure salesmanship. Do not listen to that. What they really mean is that you have a group of salesmen who hang on to their prospects until they get the order and bring it home. That is what you employ them for. If they are selling an article of merit, it is their duty, as salesmen, to use every conceivable argument they can that is honest to convince the prospect that he ought to sign the order. That is the only way your business can run. . . .

I know that kind of selling means harder work, staying a little longer with the man, walking a little farther every day to find the man who will say yes. But it gets results.

Working

If you do not enjoy your surroundings and associations, my advice is to change your work. Some years ago, a man who was rooming with me remarked that I was very happy in my work and that he wished he were happy in his. I told him that if I could not be happy in my work, I would not work.

Success

Never think of this business as being a successful one. It is not. It is merely succeeding, going a little farther each year in its endeavor to succeed. Whenever an individual or a business decides that success has been attained, progress stops.

Self-development

When you learn to supervise yourselves, you attract favorable attention and are ready to supervise others. "Self supervision is the best supervision." Develop your initiative—do something that no one else has done. Think of something that should be done in our business and tell us about it. Spur us on to do more in the way of developing better machines and better men in IBM.

Hiring

There was a time when I thought I could look a man over and decide from his appearance, personality and conversation whether he would be a success or a failure. That theory was exploded years ago.

Education

Teaching is of no value unless somebody learns what is being taught.

Business Viewpoint

Early in our work we learned that business is a vast school, parading its problems before our eyes and waiting for an answer.

Promotions

When a man is given a promotion his responsibility has been extended, and the first thing for him to do is to worry over it instead of taking a great deal of pride in his new power. His first duty is to sit down and to think seriously about his responsibility and how he can aid his co-workers who in time will be doing bigger things in our business. It does all of us good to worry a little about how we are going to take care of our jobs.

Priorities

I started as a salesman and they call me "President" now; but I call myself "salesman," and I will never let my thoughts get away from selling and from the conviction that my duty is selling. When any man in any business moves up from the selling to other positions and loses sight of the importance of selling, advertising, and sales promotion generally, he is going the other way—he isn't going up; he is going down. He may not know it but he will soon find out.

Character

If we have anybody in any department—sales, factory or office—who we discover is a man of real character but does not display good manners, we must get rid of him and give the job to somebody who does possess those qualities. Then we will have a real organization. Of course, we must always set the right kind of example all the way along the line as to character and good manners. Then you can teach the men anything, because they are with you, they will listen to you; they are not trying to show off or be smart. They get right down to business.

Integrity

Just be honest with yourself and you will not have to worry about being honest with anybody else.

William Wrigley Jr. prepares to throw out the first ball at Chicago's Wrigley Field in 1928. As owner of the Chicago Cubs, Wrigley flatly refused to make any business appointments on afternoons when his team was playing.

William Wrigley Jr.

1861–1932

William Wrigley Jr. never lacked for self-confidence, a quality that was knitted to a sense of humor in his broad personality. Both as a salesman and as head of the gum company that he founded, Wrigley set his standards carefully and let results follow. A vocal champion of long-range thinking, Wrigley spent money liberally in order to accomplish worthwhile business goals, and for a time, he was responsible for the largest advertising budget in the world, in his effort to make the name of Wrigley's Gum familiar. He succeeded in that. Through the gum company, William Wrigley amassed a fortune that allowed him to make outright purchases of the Chicago Cubs baseball team and the resort island of Santa Catalina—and to operate both according to his own ideas. Wrigley had the advantage of knowing exactly what he wanted for each of his separate businesses, but it was never anything as mundane as mere profitability. That came later, in Wrigley's enterprises, only after the real sense of accomplishment.

*W*hen William Wrigley Jr. was eleven, he ran away from home. He boarded a train in his hometown of Philadelphia and, a few hours later, arrived in New York City his own man. As he told the story later, he wasn't unhappy at home, where he was the oldest of nine children. William Sr., a soap manufacturer, was an indulgent father in many ways, but he was naturally sober in demeanor. His oldest son was naturally buoyant. Skipping out at the beginning of summer vacation in 1872, William Wrigley Jr. was less a runaway than an adventurer, impelled by the certainty that he could take care of himself.

If Wrigley hadn't been able to take care of himself, he would have found out soon enough in New York. He arrived with only a few pennies, but found his first job within hours, signing on as a newsboy. Forced to sleep in the street, he made the best of that, too, and found a grate near the *Tribune* building that gushed heat all night, while the presses below turned out papers. Unlike a typical runaway, he sent postcards home to assure his parents of his well-being, and for their part, they didn't try to come after him. Before the school year started that fall, Wrigley returned home, the adventure having been won.

During a summer of odd jobs and free accommodations, Wrigley had proved a vital point: He was equal to the world. Even as its smallest and poorest particle, he'd stood up for himself, earning a lasting sense of power—the right to give in to enthusiasm.

Seven years later, in 1879, Wrigley exercised that right again when he and another nineteen-year-old decided to become silver barons in Colorado. Having stashed their rail tickets inside his hat for safekeeping, Wrigley made the mistake of sitting down next to an open window on the train. The hat was whisked off somewhere in Missouri, followed shortly by the two boys, who were whisked off in Kansas City. Wrigley managed to find jobs for himself and his fellow silver baron as waiters in a hash house, a particularly bleak one. "I'd rather starve than work there," remarked his friend.

"I wouldn't," William said and started carrying dishes. He later sold rubber stamps door-to-door in Kansas City. That was all he saw of the Wild West, but at least he earned enough money to go home—and to make his appearance in a new cowboy outfit.

Wrigley reverted to selling his father's soap, the job he'd held since the age of thirteen, when he was permanently expelled from school for throwing a pie at the schoolhouse. That had hardly been his first offense. His record also listed frequent absences when Philadelphia's baseball team was playing at home. However, throwing a pie at the school made Wrigley an incorrigible case as far as the authorities were concerned. He talked his father into letting him go out on the road, where he learned most of what he knew about business, taking people as he found them and then figuring out ways to sell them soap.

For all of his success as a salesman, Wrigley had only $32 to his name at the age of twenty-nine, when he took his wife, Ada, to Chicago to start a new soap business. He hadn't saved much money of his own, but an uncle invested a hefty sum— $5,000—in the Chicago venture. Wrigley's father backed him with merchandise, and the business lurched slowly to a start. It accelerated with a sudden jump after the company started giving umbrellas to dealers who placed orders. Wrigley had concluded that if the dealers were motivated, they could move his soap off the shelves even at twice its previous price. The prospect of free umbrellas not only motivated those early dealers, it changed the future of the William Wrigley Jr. Co.

Before long, it was hard to tell exactly what business Wrigley was in, with all the home furnishings and appliances he started shipping as premiums for dealers. As a matter of fact, he changed businesses not long after arriving in Chicago, selling baking powder rather than soap, but it hardly mattered. "Everybody likes something extra, for nothing," he once said, while supplying willing retailers with coffee pots and cuspidors, baby carriages, fur rugs, and boudoir lamps. Somewhere underneath the heap, there was some baking powder, and Wrigley was making money on it.

Stocky and muscular, William Wrigley Jr. had a ruddy complexion, blue eyes, and thick black hair. He and Ada had one child, a son named Philip who would later take over his father's businesses. They were a close family, and Philip would recall that in his early childhood, when the family was not at all rich, he and his father liked nothing better than to spend their evenings listening while Ada read out loud to them from a novel. Wrigley's favorite hobbies were horseback riding and bird-watching; he also boxed, golfed, and earned swimming medals even in middle age. Disdaining religion, he good-naturedly asked people, "What's your superstition?" if the subject were broached. He did, however, have baseball to give him respite from life, and perhaps meaning within it. Even in his hardest working years, when he calculated that he spent more than half his time on the road, he made time on summer afternoons to go to baseball games.

Within the Wrigley company, the sporting proposition was the selection of premiums. Choosing them in advance and in bulk was like picking out a single Christmas present to delight thousands of people. When Wrigley chose wrong, the dealers let him know in their own clear fashion: They stopped ordering his baking powder. After playing the game for a year, Wrigley decided to offer something simpler as a dealer premium. He selected chewing gum, a novelty brought to the market by Thomas Adams in the 1860s.

Chewing gum was an uncertain product when Wrigley decided to try it out. To his surprise, the new premium sparked instant excitement: Dealers began to ask if they had to order baking powder just to get the gum. Turning the whole company over to chewing gum, Wrigley started production of his own brands in 1892; included among them were Spearmint and Juicy Fruit. From the first, he wanted to enhance sales with a premium (deciding against possibility of offering a can of baking powder with every order of gum). Wrigley offered a wider array of appliances and sundries than ever, so that his Doublemint gum would double a retailer's revenues, first from the gum and second from the sale of the premium. The effort was so successful that by 1932, the Wrigley Co.'s order of electric clocks filled twenty-nine train cars. The razors filled fifty.

As distribution of the gum expanded, advertising for it exploded. Wrigley was the world's leading advertiser in the decades before and after World War I. From city squares to newly constructed highways, the landscape was littered with the company's billboards; one of them, along a railroad track in New Jersey, stretched for three miles. During the 1920s, every single bus, subway, or elevated train car in the country—62,000 in all—carried at least one card touting Wrigley's gum. For years, it was a tradition that every toddler in the country received two sticks of gum from the company on his or her second birthday. On two occasions, the company mailed four sticks to every person listed in every phone book in America. Others called Wrigley a "plunger," and said that he was wasting his money, oversaturating the country with his message. But he wasn't wasting money: By 1922, William Wrigley was selling ten billion sticks of gum per year.

William Wrigley never diversified his company: The business at hand was chewing gum. However, with an income that exceeded $5 million per year after 1917, he did diversify his own business interests. In 1919, he purchased Santa Catalina Island, off the Southern California coast. The same size as Bermuda (twenty-seven miles long and as much as eight miles wide), Catalina had been little improved by previous attempts at land speculation. Wrigley paid $3.5 million for it. "I'm going to spend a lot of money there in the next several years," he told the Los Angeles *Express,* referring to a total that would reach $7 million during his lifetime.

Having entered a business, Wrigley was uniquely oblivious to making money. According to the formula he used over and over again, expenditures needed only contribute toward a tangible goal, such as the enhancement of Catalina as a resort for all classes of people. Profitability did not interfere with Wrigley's goals, but rather was presumed to follow them at a distance. "Eventually," he said of Catalina, "I'll make up the cost by taking the smallest possible profit from an increased number of visitors."

In the case of the Chicago Cubs baseball club, of which Wrigley took control in 1919, the goal was a perfect day at the ballpark. Wrigley had been to enough stadiums around the country to know that most were brusque in atmosphere, and that all were plain dirty: The Cubs' field was both. Furthermore, all of baseball was smudged in another way: The "Black Sox" game-fixing scandal (perpetrated by Chicago's other team, the White Sox) had shocked fans in 1919 and seriously undermined enthusiasm for the game.

On taking control, Wrigley had the Cubs' stadium completely renovated—and scrubbed. "Mr. Wrigley was fanatic about the beauty and cleanliness of the ballpark," recalled Woody English, a shortstop on the 1927 team. "The floors along the refreshment stand were so clean if you dropped a sandwich on the floor, you could pick it up and eat it." The business at hand was baseball, and the new owner did not lose sight of that fact, even though he was—in another sphere—the nation's leading advertiser. He banned billboards from the stadium outright, because they would distract from the game.

Attending nearly every home game (and most of the Cubs' away games), Wrigley wanted to see all kinds of people at the stadium, renamed Wrigley Field in 1924. Particularly successful were Ladies Day and free admission for schoolchildren, brought in by the thousands through an ongoing arrangement with the city school board; had Wrigley's grammar school offered such a program, he might not have thrown a pie at it.

"Every Chicago baseball fan owns a controlling interest in the Cubs—in his own mind," Wrigley wrote. A perfect day at the park includes winning, too, as those fellow owners were quick to remind him, and Wrigley paid high salaries in trying to assemble a championship team. It cost him $500,000 just to sign Rogers Hornsby, but Hornsby was more than a hitting star. He was cold and he was stubborn, but he was utterly incorruptible and the fans knew it.

Philip Wrigley good-naturedly recounted a day when he and Hornsby were about to climb into an experimental airplane for a ride. Suddenly, William Wrigley protested. "Wait a minute, Rog, you can't go," he said, "you're too valuable."

The real benefits of Wrigley's expenditures unfolded between 1929 and 1938, when the Cubs won the pennant four times. Wrigley lived long enough to celebrate only one of those pennants; he died in his sleep in 1932, at the age of seventy. Though the team did not win the World Series during his tenure as owner, it did return strong profits starting in 1925. In 1927, the Cubs became the first major league team to pass the one million mark in attendance, drawing 1.2 million fans. When Wrigley bought the club, they couldn't even draw 200,000.

"I have never seen Mr. Wrigley worried," a company executive said, in a description not disputed by any other, ". . . never without a smile and an optimistic word. In crises that would have crushed many men, that had me running around in circles, he remained as calm, as cheerful, as if he were on a Sunday picnic. I have never seen him angry. He makes all his decisions instantaneously. If his business were smashed to smithereens, he'd pick up the pieces with a smile and start building them over again."

In the words that follow, William Wrigley makes it clear that those who don't like selling shouldn't be in sales. He loved to sell, relating stories and tips about tough customers, discouraging days, and trying to make an impression. Believing in hearty salesmanship, Wrigley embraced advertising in the same spirit. He shows a few of the ways he used advertising effectively in turning Wrigley's Gum into a worldwide brand name. In one sly coup, he didn't advertise at all and received a priceless amount of publicity in return.

IN THE WORDS OF

William Wrigley Jr.

Make a good product at a fair price—then tell the world.

Potential

Many men who are worth not over five hundred dollars at the moment this is printed will be millionaires in less than five years. That prediction involves no risk. It will happen. Who they are, by name, I do not know. But I know what they are. They are salesmen.

Persistence

Sticking is one of the big things in salesmanship—one of the biggest. Nearly all buyers say "No!" at first. Real salesmen stick until the buyer has used up his last "No!" . . .

I tackled my first merchant with the resolve of selling him

an order of soap if it took a week. He was located in West Chester, Pennsylvania. He put me off and put me off, but finally broke down; he admitted he would either have to give me an order or kill me, and he didn't want to kill me. The amount of that order was one dollar and eighty cents. Every man who ever made good with me as a salesman has been a sticker.

Salesmanship

The art of salesmanship can be stated in five words: *Believing something, and convincing others.* That is easy to say. But selling is not easy. A salesman has to master himself; he has to know human nature and like people; he has to be able to stand up and take it on the jaw; he has to stick when they call him a fool for sticking; he has to work hard, late, and long. Success is not easy. But it is worth the price.

Visibility

When I was travelling among the tall-grass towns of Pennsylvania selling soap for my father, I used to drive a four-horse, six-spring wagon painted bright red, with a collar of sleigh bells on each horse. One horse would have been plenty to haul me. The bells were a great nuisance, for they chafed the horse's necks, and if it was six or eight miles between towns, I always took them off. But when I put them on again and drove jingling up to a store, everybody inside would rush out to see what the circus was; most of them had never seen a six-spring wagon before. Nobody sold more soap in those parts than I did.

Bunk? Yes! Sleigh bells had nothing whatever to do with selling soap. They got me a chance to tell my story.

[*As a successful businessman in Chicago, Wrigley rode in imported limousines—which were always bright red.*]

Long-term Thinking

I have sometimes been asked what single policy has been most profitable in our business, and I have always unhesitatingly answered, restraint in regard to immediate profits—going a bit further with the restraint than we might have gone. That has not only been our most profitable policy, it has been pretty nearly our only profitable one. It has been the inspiration of every distinctively successful method we have used . . .

By a sort of paradox, however, it has not been in prosperous times that we have been able to exercise this restraint most profitably. . . . If we have been tempted in good times to take the profits immediately available by increasing our price, we have been tempted equally in poor times to take them by avoiding unnecessary expenses. And it is precisely by refusing to avoid unnecessary expenses, when the pressure for doing it was very great, that the business has been able to make its greatest strides.

It was such a refusal that turned us from a comparatively small local business—local to a few of the larger cities—into a national one. That was in the depression of 1907. Advertising of all sorts had fallen off. Everywhere among manufacturers you heard reasons for not advertising, for exercising less than the ordinary selling effort.

The more I thought about the attitude, the more I wondered at it. It was not only that they were not taking advantage of the ordinary opportunities. They were missing something that looked to me tremendously like an extraordinary opportunity, because so few people were advertising at that time.

Expectation

[*William Wrigley Jr. took a minority interest in the Cubs in 1915; he bought the controlling interest in the club in 1919 and held it until his death in 1932.*]

There was a time when the Cubs were in red ink to the extent of almost half a million dollars. It doesn't require much imagination to realize how such a deficit would have affected an owner interested only in the financial outcome of the undertaking. But it didn't faze me, because I didn't go into baseball for the purpose of making money; that motive was so secondary that it was given little consideration. I stuck because I loved the game itself and wished to contribute to its progress and its greater enjoyment by the American people.

It's a satisfaction to me to believe that I have, to a very considerable extent, accomplished this. Not only are the admissions to Wrigley Field 1,000,000 more than they were when I bought the team, but that attendance has come to include all classes of people.

The Public

The only product that the baseball business has to sell is good will. If you fail to furnish the kind of entertainment that results in general public good will, you're out of luck. There's a catch in this business at every turn, because you're playing with tricky, variable human nature, not inert physical commodities and mechanical methods . . .

The trick is to find the star. I spent seven years and $300,000 to learn that the race of big-league stars on third base evidently had been exhausted.

Deal-making

I believe in the other fellow's right to live. I cannot expect to do well in my business unless he is able to do well in his business.

In no deal did I ever figure our own profit first. That's the wrong end to start from. I always mapped out some proposition whereby the dealer or jobber would make a mighty good thing. If their profits were big enough they would do all our worrying for us. They would become our salesmen through the natural desire to reap rewards that would come from a large turnover of our products. . . . Then, if the proposition left even a small profit for us, I knew it was sound.

Individuality

Every human being is a sample: the only one of his kind. Anybody who starts to sell with any other notion is due to have his eyes opened or lose his pants. No patent plan will sell everybody. One of the biggest things you've got to learn is: *Don't treat them all alike.*

Equanimity

Many a man became my good friend and a customer simply because I would not take offense. There was a wild Irishman, I remember, whose main joy in life, it seemed, was to scare salesmen half to death; and he insulted those he couldn't scare.

"You young whippersnapper," he snarled at me, "don't you know there's a danged sight more *outside* of your head than there is *in* it?"

He said it with the intention of starting a row. I only grinned.

"I never thought of it just that way before," I said, "But I'm darned if I don't believe you're right!"

It stopped him. He was as vain as Mamma's only boy. I petted him, asked him to give me advice. And if he is in business today, he probably still has some of the soap I sold him that first trip!

🌿

There was a lesson I learned . . . from Caleb Thornton. Caleb was a Quaker.

It was a rainy day when I first called at Caleb's store, and he had a clerk busy carrying fifty-pound sacks of flour from the back part of the store to the front, arranging them in a neat pile.

"All done!" the man said presently.

"Very well," replied Caleb; now thee may carry them all back and pile them where thee found them."

The man immediately got red around the collar. He wanted to know what was the sense of doing that.

"It's a rainy day," said Caleb, "and there are no customers. I am keeping thee busy. Whether there is any sense in it or not, I pay thee thy wages, and can tell thee to do what I please."

"I'll quit before I'll carry all that flour back," said the clerk. "You can't make a jackass out of me."

He put on his coat, collected his wages, and left. I don't know but I sympathized with him. But Caleb turned to me, quietly smiling, and made his point.

"What good does it do a *poor* man," he said, "to get mad?"

I saw the point; and it was the second thing I learned and never forgot: *Don't let them rile you.* As long as I sold goods, I never got mad at a customer and showed it.

Except once—in a little town in Pennsylvania. The merchant was half drunk. He called me a liar, a particular kind of liar—and meant it. He was big; I was a boy, but husky. I hauled off and hit him as hard as I could.

Supervision

[*An avowed yes-man in selling situations, "on anything that didn't matter," as he said, Wrigley tried to weed out yes-men within the executive ranks of his company.*]

A few yes-men may be born, but mostly they are made. Fear is a great breeder of them. An employer who habitually makes yes-men is a poor sort to be associated with. He doesn't develop men's abilities, likes only his own ideas, is stingy with praise and cash, rules by fear, makes less money than he might.

Self-appraisal

There's something of the crook, I believe, in the man who always agrees with you. He wants to get something by methods not quite straight. Maybe he wants your ideas so he won't have to do his own thinking . . . a brainsucker, lazy! Maybe he doubts whether his ideas are any good . . . lack of self-confidence is a common way of being dishonest with oneself. Maybe he is afraid of you and thinks the best way to keep on your blind side is never to question your wisdom. Maybe he is a flatterer who agrees with you to your face, and picks your pocket when your back is turned!

Veracity

Advertising is our printed salesman. It may not be pretty. Sometimes, they tell me, it is not. But it has to be *true*.

A good many years ago a rival chewing gum manufacturer came out with a grand premium offer. He promised to give what he called a ten-dollar, gold-filled watch with every order for eight dollars' worth of chewing gum. We were no slouches at premium-giving ourselves; to match him, we brought out a similar offer.

"They call it gold-filled," we announced; "really, it is gold-washed, and as little gold as possible, at that. It will run, we think. But don't put it in your pocket and depend on it. *It's just exactly the kind of watch you would expect to get in a raffle, or free with eight dollars' worth of gum!*"

Customers swamped us with orders and said it was the first time anybody had ever told them the plain truth.

Advertising

In 1902 I decided to storm New York with publicity. I spent $100,000 and hardly made a ripple. It was money dropped into a hole, so far as anyone could see. I waited until I had another $100,000 and tried it again with the same result.

[*Wrigley backed away from New York, just long enough to see whether the problem was with the advertising.*]

We saved up another $100,000 and went to a smaller community, or rather three communities—Buffalo, Syracuse, and Rochester—all of which together were much smaller than New York City. There we did exactly what we had done in New York—blew our money as hard as we knew how, and much as on the second occasion in New York. And it made a ten-strike. The three cities were set talking about our products, our sales jumped up, and the campaign quickly paid for itself.

What was the difference? Simply that in the last instance there was less competition for our prospects' attention.

[*Wrigley turned again to advertising in New York City.*]

I tried a third time, after recuperating, and this time with a quarter of a million. I wanted to get the dropped $200,000 back. I did—plus.

We have spent more than $20,000,000 to tell the world about our product. I believe in advertising all the time. There is no such thing as getting a business so established that it does not need to advertise. Babies who never heard about you are being born every day, and people who once knew you forget you if you don't keep them reminded constantly. Dull times are the very times when you need advertising most.

Surprise Element

[*William Wrigley was committed to the value of publicity and advertising: "hit 'em hard and hit 'em often," was his advice on the subject of promotion. His company was the world's leading advertiser from the mid-teens through the 1920s, when the Wrigley name was plastered on billboards and bus cards all over the world. Wrigley was single-minded, but he was also wily. In the early 1920s, he built a landmark office building in Chicago.*]

Did you find my name anywhere on this building? Did you find any mention of Spearmint in its outside walls? People thought when I began to put this up that I would plaster my name all over it in letters big enough to be seen miles away. If you look when you go out you will find it in small letters over the front door—but you may have to look twice.

As a matter of fact it was better advertising not to plaster my name on the building. People talk more about it. It is the unusual thing—the thing they didn't expect me to do.

Loyalty

Office employees are salesmen, in one sense. They have to sell their services to the boss—or find a pink slip in the pay envelope! . . .

The first man I hired when I started selling chewing gum was paid seven dollars and a half a week and pushed a wheelbarrow around town. He never objected to working till any and all hours, if we had to finish up. He has a snug job at the factory now, is foreman of a department, and draws five times the wages you would expect him to receive . . .

Henry could not sell five-dollar gold pieces for seventy-five cents. He just has not got the knack, and would not learn if he lived to be a hundred. But he knew how to be loyal. He knew how to do *his job* and give the best he had. He sold himself to me all right.

Temper

[*Wrigley's jovial personality was an expedient in many difficult sales situations, one that he understood could have a downside, if he were not careful.*]

I managed to control my temper, but I never allowed any man to use me as a common doormat—not for long. People do not buy much from a man who fails to command their respect.

Accessibility

[*Wrigley had a series of meetings with a visitor from England, a sales representative named Hartly, who complained that they were continually being interrupted by employees.*]

We had had plenty of talks. Just such talks as I have with anybody who has business in my office. Both doors wide open all the time. Anybody else who has some business item he must see me about at once is free to come and go, no matter who my caller is. No delay. Walk in, get it done, get out. No important transactions held up for the awful ceremony of seeing the boss—when the boss isn't seeable!

I explained all this to Hartley.

"When these people come in here," I said, "they aren't

doing it to interrupt you. They're carrying on this business. If they hear a word or two of our conversation, that's all right. I have no secrets. We're all here to make this business go, and for no other reason. Every time a man walks in or out, I've made some more money."

Integrity

One of the biggest pests in business is the carbon copy—the fellow who always says:

"Yes, Mr. Wrigley, you're absolutely right."

Perhaps meaning:

"Have it our own way, you old buzzard, what do I care?"

Business is built by men who care—care enough to disagree, fight it out to a finish, get facts. When two men always agree, one of them is unnecessary.

Personality

[*Because Wrigley communicated very effectively in person, he tried to keep his written correspondence just as relaxed, in his own individual style. Jobbers and salesmen looked forward to his periodic letters. For example, one once ended:*]

I am sending you in a tube my picture, done in the latest style and signed by myself. Had to sit up a good many nights to do the signing, but I wanted to make it sort of personal.

P.S.—Busted my hand signing the 12,000 photographs so had to sign this letter with a rubber stamp.

Delegating Authority

When I got back to the office once, after a three-months stay in Catalina, a department head came to ask about a certain policy in his department.

"That's O.K.," I said.

He was leaving the room.

"By the way," I called after him, "why did you ask me about that? It's in your department. You know more about it than I do—"

"Well," he replied, "if you say it's O.K. I know I don't have to worry!"

"I was under the impression," I said, "that we paid you a big salary to worry!"

Commitment

Nothing is so much fun as business. I do not expect to do anything but work as long as I can stand up.

There is no rule in this game except to use the best judgment you have, think hard, act quickly, and remember the other fellow has as good a right to live as you.

Andrew Carnegie, at about age seventy, tours an exhibit of airplanes. Rather slight, at about 5 feet, 3 inches tall and weighing just over 100 pounds, Carnegie carried himself with agility and excelled at many sports.

Andrew Carnegie

1835–1919

Andrew Carnegie built his fortune, perhaps the greatest of his day, by supplying the steel that built America's own burgeoning fortune in the Gilded Age. An early promoter of steel in this country, he was the head of Carnegie Steel from its beginning in 1873 until he sold it in 1901. Carnegie built on his early lead by developing efficiencies of scale, the result of diligent cost analysis and unstinting investment in tooling. An amiable man, but a demanding boss, Carnegie ultimately managed employees by leaving them very much on their own: He spent most of his time far from his offices and sized up results mainly through dispatches. Having learned the right questions to ask of a business, he knew exactly how to interpret the answers he received. In retirement, Andrew Carnegie originated a philosophy of wealth that made some observers label him a radical, but that may in the long run have saved capitalism in America.

One morning near the turn of the century, Andrew Carnegie traveled north from his home in New York to keep an appointment with John D. Rockefeller, who lived about an hour north of the city. Carnegie was fond of Rockefeller, even if he did refer to him as "Reckafellow" behind his back.

Reckafellow certainly hadn't wrecked Carnegie. As the world's leading steel master, Andrew Carnegie often boasted that he had "got ahead of John Rockefeller" in signing a long-term lease on Rockefeller's holdings in the Mesabi Range in Wisconsin, a nearly limitless source of iron ore. Carnegie and Rockefeller were the richest private citizens in the world in the years around the turn of the century: Either one might be considered first, according to different measures. Only in golf was their ranking indisputable. Rockefeller always won, a fact that irritated Carnegie no end. In the first place, Carnegie was from Scotland, where golf originated. And in the second place . . . he liked to get ahead of John Rockefeller.

For company on the train ride from New York, Carnegie brought along an old friend, a diplomat who noted as they approached the door of Rockefeller's house that it was lunchtime; he then made the idle prediction that they would probably have something to eat with Rockefeller.

"Well, we will not," Carnegie countered in his faint Scottish lilt, "The old fellow won't ask us to lunch. He'll give us instead some one of the latest small things that have struck his fancy."

As a host, Rockefeller treated both of his guests genially, even as he and Carnegie dispatched their business. The lunch hour passed and then, just before the two visitors left, he excused himself from the room. "I want to get each of you a very nice thing I have recently discovered," he said, in a murmur of excitement.

Carnegie waited, as did the diplomat.

When Rockefeller returned, he handed each man a paper vest. "Keeps out the wind and is light and warm," he explained. Then he bid them good-bye, and they walked away carrying their paper vests.

Andrew Carnegie did not always know so precisely what to expect from other people—but he often did. Known as the "Canny Scot" for his shrewd dealings, he was just as equally the "uncanny Scot" for honing a reliable sense of events that were about to unravel. Yet there was really nothing mysterious about Carnegie's ability to anticipate. He was not born "ahead." He practiced. He trained himself almost as a habit to lean into the future, so that he could have the benefit of detachment. A born individualist, Andrew Carnegie seemed incapable of making assumptions about what *should* be, in human nature. Instead, he gauged his employees, his partners and his adversaries according to what *could* be, for each one and in developing situations. Always a realist, Carnegie remained unusually optimistic, and he only rarely allowed himself to be in a position to be disappointed.

Disappointment indicates waste and Carnegie was loath to waste anything: not money, not opportunity, not materials— and certainly not hope or his own energy. Known as a keen judge of character, he developed techniques for dealing with people that reduced the risk of disappointment, just as he reduced the risk of waste in money and materials. At the same time, he formed habits that kept his own attitudes supple throughout his career, so that he never boxed in the most important potential of all, which was his own.

Andrew Carnegie was born in 1835 in an industrial town in Scotland, where his father, William, was a hand-weaver and his mother, Margaret, ran the household. By 1848, when power looms had all but completely replaced hand weaving, the Carnegies were rendered destitute. They borrowed just enough money from a friend to emigrate to America, where they settled near Pittsburgh and struggled through years of poverty. Andrew never attended school in America, but started work in a cloth mill at the age of thirteen.

Many biographical sketches of Andrew Carnegie cite his childhood as a handicap that made his subsequent success all the more heroic. Carnegie would disagree vehemently. His self-confidence (which was formidable) was rooted in a single truth: that no one in the world could have had a more fortunate start in life than he. To be Scottish was to be descended from heroes, from self-made kings of destiny, such as William Wallace. To be raised in poverty was to be nurtured by caring parents, with no strangers intervening. To be schooled by relatives was to have teachers who set a lifelong example of learning. And to start from nothing at all in America was to enjoy the fullest benefits of the "Triumphant Democracy," as Carnegie later called his new nation.

Margaret Carnegie's family back in Scotland consisted of working-class intellectuals. Considered radicals, they agitated generally against the monarchy and specifically against capitalists.

Andrew Carnegie was rooted in the egalitarian ideal, just as was his adopted nation. He was a humanist. But, along with the nation, he would develop—and perhaps overdevelop—quite another side during the capitalist stampede of the late

1800s. Rather abruptly, both Andrew Carnegie and the United States came to reflect the very worst elements they had each once despised in Europe's oligarchies. Carnegie was aware of the chasm created by his own Gilded Age, of the permanent change of spirit it seemed to reflect in himself as well as the nation. Alone among the millionaires of his era, he would be haunted by that chasm and would be compelled to bridge it somehow.

The most exciting industry in the nation in the 1850s was railroading, and the best-established line of all was the Pennsylvania Railroad. In 1853, when he was sixteen, Carnegie was offered a job there. He found himself surrounded by a business organization modern for its time and by ambitious men from whom to learn.

Carnegie was also surrounded by opportunity. Even as he developed into a ranking executive with the line, he developed his own interests in some of the most lucrative fields of the age. As his biographer, Burton Hendrick, pointed out, Carnegie had major investments in the sleeping car business before Pullman and in the oil fields of Pennsylvania before Rockefeller.

He entered the ranks of manufacturing by starting a company to build railroad bridges. He later expanded into production of iron, the building material of his bridges, and as steel came into use he would become the dominant producer of it in the United States.

With the outbreak of the Civil War, Carnegie went to Washington to organize a telegraph system for the Union army. He believed deeply in the Northern cause, and allowed himself to become overworked, suffering something akin to a nervous breakdown. His superiors advised him to take three months off in 1862. Without a second thought, he and his mother (by then a widow) returned to Scotland.

Every summer for over fifty years, Carnegie would take a long sojourn in Scotland. Even in his most productive years and at the height of his working life, he spent at least six months of each year vacationing. A minute part of each trip might be devoted to business meetings, but most of the time Carnegie was simply enjoying himself. As one of his friends described him, in a letter written from Europe, "Andy is so overflowing that it is extremely difficult to keep him within reasonable bounds, to restrain him within the limits of moderately orderly behavior—he is so continually mischievous and so exuberantly joyous."

Overflowing may be the one word that describes Andrew Carnegie best.

Vacating the office (as well as the country) for half of each year would seem an unlikely method of building an enormous, highly aggressive company. The schedule had practical benefits, though.

To Andrew Carnegie, a good executive did not hold the reins of day-to-day management. His job was to implement a progressive system, install worthy employees, and chart an accurate course for the company. If he needed to do any work per se, then the system had failed. If he had to watch over the employees in order to get the best out of them, then they were flawed—and so was the system. And if the executive had to make myriad decisions just to maneuver the company through each and every day, then the course must be poorly chosen. Carnegie tested his ability as an executive—by leaving.

Outwardly, Carnegie explained his travels in terms of his

need for self-improvement. He had a fear, expressed when he was thirty-three, that "To continue . . . with most of my thoughts wholly upon the way to make more money in the shortest time must degrade me beyond hope of permanent recovery." He studied art in the museums of Europe (at a time when America did not yet have any great museums) and was current in the theater of the foreign capitals. Most of all, Carnegie was devoted to poetry and memorized long passages as a matter of course. He was especially influenced by the work of Shakespeare.

Carnegie's lifelong study of poetry and literature was more than a hobby. As a magnate who admitted that he "had no shadow of a claim to rank as inventor, chemist, investigator or mechanician," he was quick to acknowledge that the human being was the machine he understood. The only people who understood it far better, to his way of thinking, were the best of the poets.

In the steel business, Carnegie's goal, which was not unique, was to expand production while pushing costs ever downward; that allowed him great flexibility on his own pricing, which brought the company increased control over the market. Many companies have proceeded on the same theory—though few put it into practice so effectively. Carnegie was obsessed with bringing down costs, as just one of his telegram exchanges shows:

To Carnegie from an associate:
No. 8 Furnace broke all records today.
Carnegie's reply:
What were the other ten furnaces doing?

In July of 1892, a labor strike at the gigantic Homewood mill, owned by Carnegie Steel, flew out of control on both sides. Previously, the Carnegie response to strikes had been harsh, but in some sense based on fairness. The company would simply shut down until the workers were ready to accept the terms offered. Both sides would suffer, because, significantly, Carnegie held to a pledge never to employ replacement workers ("scabs") during a strike. At Homewood in 1892, however, the company waited only six days before importing replacement workers. Fifteen people were killed in the violence that followed. And all the while, Andrew Carnegie was in Scotland.

In the immediate aftermath, no one knew quite how to regard Andrew Carnegie's role in the tragedy. Privately, he maintained that he would never have hired the replacement workers who so antagonized the strikers, and that he had tried to telegraph his junior partner, Henry Clay Frick, to that effect. Publicly, Carnegie stood behind the actions of his partner and, as time went on, it was he who bore the guilt for the tragedy. He once said, "My name is sacred," regarding the many invitations he turned down to lend that name to business ventures. After 1892, though, the name of Carnegie was forever blighted by the bloodshed that had taken place at Homewood.

Andrew Carnegie is often grouped with the so-called Robber Barons of the Gilded Age: railroad men such as James J. Hill and Edward J. Harriman; financiers such as Jay Gould and J.P. Morgan; or even his own erstwhile partner, Clay Frick. He was different, though, in a key respect that kept all the others at bay. Carnegie's company was a partnership in which he held the controlling measure. He long maintained a disdainful distance from the stock market and the rampaging of

Wall Street, bragging that he never owned any significant shares of stock in his middle or later years. To him, a "businessman" (a vaunted term in his estimation) made business, not just dollars.

Without having to pander to the emotions of stockholders, Carnegie could guide the company according to his own convictions. One of the seminal reasons the company grew as quickly as it did was that Carnegie Steel always expanded *during* panics or depressions. Even as stock prices fell, taking the market for metals with them, Carnegie would put every penny he could find into building up his facilities. Whenever the market for steel returned—as it always did—he stood waiting for it, or looming over it, with increased capacity and lower production costs.

Bold business strikes, and long vacations, gave Andrew Carnegie an early reputation in Pittsburgh as a rather unpredictable man. He was personally popular, but he hadn't really turned out to be like the business idols of his youth, the somber men of Pittsburgh's main streets, who actually strived for predictability. He was "overflowing," with ebullient salesmanship and surprising gestures. Often, he reacted solely to what he called *the flash*. He would listen very politely to almost anyone with a proposal. If he had to reject it, he'd shrug in reply, "I don't get the flash." But when the flash came, it exploded over him, as he described in relating his conversation with one certain inventor: "He had not spoken a minute before, like a flash, the whole range of the discovery burst upon me. 'Yes,' I said, 'that is something which this continent must have.'" That invention was a sleeping car for trains.

Andrew Carnegie was married to Louise Whitfield in New York in 1892, and they had one daughter. By the end of that decade, Carnegie was telling close friends that he was ready to retire from business. Of course, he had been saying that since he was thirty, but in 1902, he sold out to a group headed by J.P. Morgan.

Morgan went on to organize U.S. Steel around the Carnegie company, while Andrew Carnegie retired from business with over $300,000,000. Before his death in 1919, he gave away ninety percent of his fortune, establishing separate foundations that are still active today in such fields as education and science. He also donated hundreds of well-stocked libraries to communities all over the world. Carnegie did not believe in organized religion, yet he donated many organs to churches large and small. When asked why, he replied with a smile, "To make the sermons more bearable." He also funded serious, permanent efforts to establish international peace, the main cause of his last years. Carnegie's initiatives helped create a model for the League of Nations after World War I, which in turn led to the United Nations a generation later.

Nonetheless, the specific charities that Carnegie chose to endow are not as important as the example he left. In trying to bridge the gulf between his own humanist ideal and the vast power—and money—he acquired through the labor of others, Andrew Carnegie became a very unique American philosopher. In his essay, "The Gospel of Wealth," he argued that America would create millionaires, not in contradiction to the spirit of democracy but in fulfillment of it. Most millionaires, he said, only made their fortunes because American society as a whole never stopped expanding, boosting some people to the crest of its wave. To whom were those millionaires obligated? Not to their children, as in European primogeniture. Rather, they were obligated to the society around them. To Carnegie, those who were best at making money were best at distributing it for the benefit of the American community.

Charity was not a new invention when Andrew Carnegie struck his point. However, it was Carnegie who recognized that the seemingly uneasy union of American democracy and unlimited capitalism had to be cemented by large-scale philanthropy. It was the only way he could survive his own success, and a path he cleared for the country to follow.

In the words that follow, Andrew Carnegie shows how well rounded he was as a businessman and as a person, speaking to a great variety of subjects, from humor to income tax. Carnegie makes practical points on management as related to capital investment, nuances of accounting, and quality control. But he didn't start out as a manager, not remotely, and he also speaks about ambition and self-promotion on a basis just as practical. Many people consider salesmanship to be Carnegie's greatest skill of all, and he unravels the story of one crucial sale he made, with the steps he took to ensure it.

Andrew Carnegie

Appraisal

Show me your cost sheets. It is far more interesting to know how cheaply and how well you have done this than how much money you have made. The one is only a temporary result, due possibly to some special condition of trade, but the other means a permanency that will go on with the works as long as they last.

Principles

[System *magazine asked Carnegie for the rules he considered cardinal for a manufacturing business. He submitted them in his own handwriting, making a last-minute change in order between numbers three and four.*]

For <u>Manufacturers</u>

First   Honesty—no sharp bargains, do more not less than you promise.

Second   If disputes arise give the other party the benefit of the doubt, always a profitable investment—avoid resort to law, compromise.

Third   Subject all product to more rigid tests than the purchaser requires. A reputation for producing the best is a sure foundation upon which to build.

Fourth   Should honest capable contractors need extension of payments from accidents or unusual monetary emergency, be lenient and help them thus making them friends.

Focus

The business man not only risks all in business enterprise, but, if wise, he puts his all into one business—he puts all his eggs into one basket. If he goes into the coffee business he deals in coffee, and if into the sugar business, he handles sugar, and the only time when he mixes them is when he takes sugar in his coffee.

Customer Relations

We always accommodated our customers, even although at some expense to ourselves, and in cases of dispute, we gave the other party the benefit of the doubt and settled. These were our rules. We had no lawsuits.

Capital Investment

It is surprising how few men appreciate the enormous dividends derivable from investment in their own business. There is scarcely a manufacturer in the world who has not in his works some machinery that should be thrown out and replaced by improved appliances; or who does not for the want of additional machinery or new methods lose more than sufficient to pay the largest dividend obtainable by investment beyond his own domain. And yet most businessmen whom I have known invest in bank shares and in faraway enterprises, while the true gold mine lies right in their own factories.

Focus

Whatever I engage in, I must push inordinately; therefore should I be careful to choose that life which will be the most elevating in its character.

Accounting

One of the chief sources of success in manufacturing is the introduction and strict maintenance of a perfect system of accounting so that responsibility for money or materials can be brought home to every man. Owners who, in the office, would not trust a clerk with five dollars without having a check on him, were supplying tons of materials daily to men in the mills without exacting an account of their stewardship by weighing what each returned in the finished form.

Humor

There is very little success where there is little laughter.

Attacking Trouble

The more difficult a problem becomes, the more interesting it is.

Pursuing a Deal

I gave a great deal of attention for some years to the affairs of the Keystone Bridge Works, and when important contracts were involved often went myself to meet the parties. On one such occasion, I visited Dubuque, Iowa, with our engineer, Walter Katte. We were competing for the building of the most important railway bridge that had been built up to that time, a bridge across the wide Mississippi, at Dubuque, a span which was considered a great undertaking.

That visit proved how much success turns upon trifles. . . .

Making a Deal

[*Even after learning that the contract for the Dubuque bridge had been awarded to a rival, Carnegie remained to talk with the directors of the railway company.*]

. . . They were delightfully ignorant of the merits of cast- and wrought-iron. We had always made the upper cord of the bridge of the latter, while our rivals' was made of cast-iron.

This furnished my text. I pictured the result of a steamer striking against the one and against the other. In the case of the wrought-iron cord, it would probably only bend; in the case of the cast-iron it would certainly break and down would come the bridge. One of the directors, the well-known Perry Smith, was fortunately able to enforce my argument, by stating to the board that what I said was undoubtedly the case about cast-iron. The other night he had run his buggy in the dark against a lamp-post which was of cast-iron and the lamp-post had broken to pieces. Am I to be censured if I had little difficulty here in recognizing something akin to the hand of Providence, with Perry Smith the manifest agent?

"Ah gentlemen," I said, "there is the point. A little more money and you could have had the indestructible wrought-iron and your bridge would stand against any steamboat. We never have built and we never will build a cheap bridge. Ours don't fall."

There was a pause; then the president of the bridge company, Mr. Allison, the great Senator, asked if I would excuse them for a few moments. I retired . . .

Closing a Deal

[*Though Carnegie had benefitted from one stroke of fortune in making his sales pitch, he left nothing to chance afterward.*]

. . . Soon they recalled me and offered the contract, provided we took the lower price, which was only a few thousand dollars less. I agreed to the concession. That cast-iron lamp-post so opportunely smashed gave us one of our most profitable contracts and, what is more, obtained for us the reputation of having taken the Dubuque bridge against all competitors. It also laid the foundation for me of a lifelong, unbroken friendship with one of America's best and most valuable public men, Senator Allison.

The moral of the story lies on the surface. If you want a contract, be on the spot when it is let. A smashed lamp-post or something equally unthought of may secure the prize if the bidder be on hand. And if possible, stay on hand until you can take the written contract home in your pocket. This we did at Dubuque, although it was suggested that we could leave and it would be sent after us to execute. We preferred to remain, being anxious to see more of the charms of Dubuque.

Quality

The president of an important manufacturing work once boasted to me that their men had chased away the first inspector who had ventured to appear among them, and that they had never been troubled with another since. This was said as a matter of sincere congratulations, but I thought to myself: "This concern will never stand the strain of competition; it is bound to fail when hard times come." The result proved the correctness of my belief. The surest foundation of a manufacturing concern is quality. After that, and a long way after, comes cost.

Overacheiving

The battle of life is already half won by the young man who is brought personally in contact with high officials; and the great aim of every boy should be to do something beyond the sphere of his duties—something which attracts the attention of those over him.

[*Carnegie was a telegram delivery boy as a teenager . . .*]

Having to sweep out the operating-room in the morning, the boys had an opportunity of practicing upon the telegraph instruments before the operators arrived. This was a new chance. I soon began to play with the key and talk with the boys who were at the other stations who had like purposes to my own. Whenever one learns to do anything he has never to wait long for an opportunity of putting his knowledge to use.

[*Carnegie became a hero in the office when he stepped in for a staff telegrapher in an emergency. He was thereupon promoted to the higher-paying job of telegraph operator.*]

Recognition

The world's civilization started from the day on which every one received reward for labor.

Profit Sharing

I never see a fishing fleet set sail without pleasure, thinking this is based upon the form which is probably to prevail generally. Not a man in the boats is paid fixed wages. Each gets his share of the profits. That seems to me the ideal. It would be most interesting if we could compare the results of a fleet so manned and operated with one in which men were paid fixed wages, but I question whether such a fleet as the latter exists. From my experience, I should say a crew of employees versus a crew of partners would not be in the race.

The great secret of success in business of kinds, and especially in manufacturing, where a small saving in each process means fortune, is a liberal division of profits among the men who help to make them and the wider distribution, the better. There lie latent unsuspected powers in willing men around us which only need appreciation and development to produce surprising results. Money rewards alone will not, however, insure these, for to the most sensitive and ambitious natures there must be the note of sympathy, appreciation, friendship. Genius is sensitive in all its forms and it is unusual, not ordinary, ability that tells even in practical affairs. You must capture and keep the heart of the original and supremely able man before his brain can do its best.

Growth

It may be accepted as an axiom that a manufacturing concern in a growing country like ours begins to decay when it stops extending.

Stock Market Trading

Speculation is the parasite of business, feeding upon values, creating none.

Nothing tells in the long run like good judgment, and no sound judgment can remain with the man whose mind is disturbed by the mercurial changes of the Stock Exchange. It places him under an influence akin to intoxication. What is not, he sees, and what he sees, is not. He cannot judge relative values or get the true perspective of things. The molehill seems to him a mountain and the mountain a molehill, and he jumps at conclusions which he should arrive at by reason. His mind is upon the stock quotations and not upon the points that require calm thought.

Dollar making is not necessarily business.

Charity

I estimate that of every thousand dollars spent in so-called charity, nine hundred and fifty of them had better be thrown into the sea.

Years ago I distributed charity indiscriminately, and in doing so committed perhaps the greatest evil I have committed in my life. Let a multi-millionaire take his millions to the slums and call the people together, saying: "There is a wrong distribution of wealth in the world; you have not got your share; I give to each one of you this share in my millions."

Let that be done in the morning and let the millionaire return at night to see what good his action has done and he will find not happiness but pandemonium. Let him distribute another million every day for a month, and at the end of that time what ought we say to him? We ought to say, "Go on your knees and crawl for pardon. You have done more harm in a month than you can ever undo in all your life."

[*Carnegie believed that support of those who were hopelessly poor and sick was the responsibility of government. Private philanthropy, he believed, should "accrue to those who are yet sound and industrious, and seeking through labor the means of betterment."*]

Income Tax

[*In an article he called, "What Would I Do with the Tariff If I Were the Czar," Carnegie explained what he would do about income tax . . . if he were Czar.*]

There would be no income tax. I know of no statesman or authority who does not denounce an income tax as the most objectionable of all taxes. Mr. Gladstone once appealed to the country upon this subject alone, denouncing it as tending to make a nation of liars. While it is in theory a just tax, in practice it is the source of such demoralization as renders it perhaps the most pernicious form of taxation which has ever been conceived since human society has settled into peaceful government.

Management

[*After distinguishing himself through his work at a Pittsburgh telegraph office, Carnegie's first position of responsibility was as assistant to the superintendent of the Pennsylvania Railroad, Thomas Scott. When Scott was promoted, Carnegie took his place.*]

Being a telegrapher, I took charge of our own railroad telegraph wire when it was constructed and I believe that I placed the first young woman telegraph student at work on a railroad; so I see it stated. In those days the Superintendent had to do everything; there was no division of responsibilities. It was supposed that no subordinate could be trusted to run trains by telegraph or attend to a wreck, and Mr. Scott and I, his successor, were two of the most foolish men I have ever known in this respect.

It took me some time to learn, but I did learn that the supremely great managers, such as you have these days, never do any work themselves worth speaking about, their point is to make others work while they think. I applied this lesson in after life, so that business with me has never been a care.

World Commerce

[*In 1904, Carnegie wrote a humorous playlet in the style of the Greek classics to express his opinion of Great Britain's position as the world's leading economic power—a position that applied increasingly to the United States as well.*]

Chorus: . . . To thee the gods have placed under tribute the nations of the earth; none escapes. Rejoice therefore in the rapid advancement of the world, for upon this, thine own undiminished prosperity assuredly depends. Thou must decline if the world prospers not . . .

S o c i a l i s m

[*"But are you a Socialist?"* Carnegie was asked in 1885. He answered as he walked to the train station with a Pittsburgh reporter.]

I believe socialism is the grandest theory ever presented and I am sure some day it will rule the world. Then we will have obtained the millennium.

[*"You hope that the lion and the lamb will lie down side by side, all things be equal, and that profits will share and share alike," the reporter asked.*]

That is the state we are drifting into. Then men will be content to work for the general welfare and share their riches with their neighbors.

[*"Are you prepared now to divide your wealth?"*]

No, not at present, but I do not spend much on myself. I give away every year seven or eight times as much as I spend for personal comforts and pleasures. Working people have my full sympathy and I always extend a helping hand. I am a working-man and in my young days worked in a cotton mill and ran an engine. In all my life, I suppose I have done more work than any employe I ever had. . . . I believe in advancing worthy employes and I carry out those ideas on all occasions, as is witnessed by the young men I have gathered about me.

[*Carnegie never was a socialist, nor did he ever do anything with his own business that even leaned in that direction. Yet, as can be seen by his comments above, he tried to connect himself to the workingmen and their concerns, and met the threat of socialism with a much more supple response than the typical business leader of his day.*]

Humility

When a multi-millionaire makes money, he should remember the class from which he sprung. I don't recognize any elevation from that of the workingman.

Leaders

It is not the million, it is the individual . . .

Shakespeare tells us that honor passes in a path so narrow that but one goes abreast. So with every advance made by man there is always a leader and then come the millions of the multitude that follow.

Wealth

[*Carnegie turned his thoughts on philanthropy into a book*, The Gospel of Wealth.]

The fundamental idea of "The Gospel of Wealth" is that surplus wealth should be considered as a sacred trust to be administered by those into whose hands it falls, during their lives, for the good of the community. It predicts that the day is at hand when he who dies possessed of enormous sums, which were his and free to administer during his life, will die disgraced, and holds that the aim of the millionaire should be to die poor.

B e q u e s t s

I should as soon leave to my son a curse as "the Almighty dollar."

[*—An autograph, written in a friend's album. Andrew Carnegie gave over ninety percent of his fortune to charitable causes, and left about $30 million for his widow and his daughter.*]

D e t a i l s

He is a bold man who calls anything a trifle.

I n t e n s i t y

While statistics say that 95 percent of all young men who enter business fail, this should not discourage any one. Go out with the spirit "sink or swim," and a person will not sink.

R e p u t a t i o n

The highest title which a man can write upon the page of history is his own name.

PART II

No Stone Left Unturned:
HUSTLING HARD WORKERS

A person who lifts diligence practically to the level of distortion — or even long past it — finds in the fever pitch a sort of perpetual motion of the mind, a flow of energy and ideas that takes less effort, not more, than compact little workdays. In fact, the person who finds it much harder to stop working than to start has the easiest workday of anyone. "In looking over my life, my only regret is that I didn't work harder," Mary Pickford wrote in middle age. According to her colleagues, though, that might not have been possible. The same might be said of Sam Walton, the Wal-Mart founder. William Paley was working sixteen-hour days even long after CBS was established — established, at any rate, in everyone else's mind.

However, completing work isn't what the long hours are all about: improving it is. According to Edwin Land, of Polaroid, a sustained, insistent level of concentration was a formula by which he could generate inspiration almost on command. Inspiration is supposed to be a rarefied thing, but, judging by the people in this section, it's not an unpredictable one. It seems to show up just as soon as everyone who can be exhausted quits for the day and toddles home.

Sam Walton pays off a bet by doing a hula dance on Wall Street. In 1983, a down year in retailing, Walton told Wal-Mart employees that if the company reported a rise in pretax earnings of at least 8 percent, he would dance the hula on Wall Street. The company reported an increase of 8.04 percent, and Walton was as good as his word.

Sam Walton

1918–1992

Sam Walton brought fresh enthusiasm to the front lines of chain retailing with what appeared to be a simple formula revolving around happy employees, low costs, consequently low prices, and even happier customers. In a short time, that formula propelled Walton's company, Wal-Mart, to a wide lead as the nation's largest merchandiser. At the time of Walton's death in 1992, thirty years after his company was founded, Wal-Mart had close to 1750 stores, and annual sales of $44 billion. Sam Walton's philosophy was not especially original, but the zeal with which he implemented it started a revolution throughout retailing. Even while Walton was seen to be leading cheers in stores, though, he was also overseeing the vast complexity lying beneath Wal-Mart's simple formula: the evolution of techniques that enforced lower costs and ensured committed employees. Under Sam Walton, Wal-Mart never stopped changing. His most impressive achievement, however, was intrinsic to his personality and to his success. Whatever happened, Sam Walton wasn't distracted for an instant from his original goals, whether Wal-Mart was a company of one store or thousands.

$\mathcal{T}$he astonishing stories about Sam Walton, the Wal-Mart founder, were not about a rich man, but a parsimonious one. When he traveled, he stayed at budget motels and doubled up with colleagues to save money. He rented only compact cars. In the mid-1980s, a friend with less money—no person in America had more money than Sam Walton—took a close look at Walton's outfit of a dark suit, white shirt, and tie, and exclaimed, "My shoes cost more than everything he's wearing today!" Everything Walton was wearing that day, or nearly any day, had been purchased at Wal-Mart.

Sam Walton drove around his hometown of Bentonville, Arkansas, in a beat-up truck with coffee-stained seats and balding tires. "What am I supposed to haul my dogs around in, a Rolls Royce?" he asked in his defense.

When the stories are viewed in light of the fact that Walton had a fortune of over $23 billion, they are astounding, much more so than those told about any billionaire who tried to amaze anyone by *spending* money. Sam Walton didn't try to amaze anyone. He ate breakfast at the local Ramada Inn coffee shop nearly every morning; he picked up a used newspaper rather than spend a quarter on his own; his offices were decorated in "early bus station" with plastic seats in the waiting room; and the froth in his social life consisted of going to Fred's Hickory House on Friday nights: These items were well-chronicled. The fact that he spent $5 for his monthly haircut merited a two-page spread in *Life*.

For a billionaire, Sam Walton was no doubt parsimonious. But for a small-town retailer, he was exactly right, driving his pick-up and taking his wife out for barbecue. Had he owned only one store (instead of 39 percent of 1,960 of them), the list of his eccentricities would suddenly lose all of its power to astound . . . "Storekeeper Gets $5 Haircut."

Yet to be Sam Walton was to be a storekeeper: a one-store keeper, however extensive the Wal-Mart chain became. Walton's greatest strength lay in the fact that his vision was so very limited that way. Only one person came into his view at a time, and each was unique: not that he was always nice, but he was never impersonal. Walton's capacity to regard people as individuals gave Wal-Mart, in turn, its own greatest strength— motivated employees—as Walton imparted the feeling that everything they did mattered to him. It undoubtedly did.

When he started out in 1962 with just one store, he presided over it like a mother hen; when he had a handful, he drove from one to another; when there were hundreds, he flew himself around in a small plane. "The fences aren't as high for Sam as they are for other people," a colleague once said, but at some point, the number of Wal-Mart stores outpaced even the quicksilver Sam Walton and his twin-engine Cessna.

Starting in the late 1960s, several sharp-minded executives found new ways to build upon the original impetus that everything that happened in the stores mattered to Sam Walton. They depended upon technology, not personal appearances. Walton, a low-tech type of person, might have been the last one to suggest computerization on his own, but he was the first to underwrite it, as Wal-Mart pioneered new systems in the interest of lowering costs through increased control of every phase of the retailing system. From its computerized inventory (1969) to centralized computers (1977) to point-of-sale scanning (1980) to satellite communications (1987), Wal-Mart became a tighter organization, even as it grew to be a much bigger one. Technology made a reality of Sam Walton's basic perception: It was one store and he could keep watch over it, even in almost 2,000 towns around the country.

Sam Walton was born in 1918 in Oklahoma, where his father was a mortgage broker. After college, he took a job as a management trainee at J.C. Penney, where he began his life-long fact-gathering mission in retailing.

Walton had a wiry frame, suited to a man who played tennis about twice a week. One of his vice presidents, Bill Fields, recalled a game in which a Wal-Mart vendor, a fine player, "hit a 'customer tennis' return."

"Sam immediately dropped his racket," Fields continued, "and said, 'If you're not going to play to win with everything you have, I don't think we should continue.' " (Walton ultimately lost the match—but won his point.) Mercurial by nature, Walton rarely hid thoughts or reactions on his face: a homey Midwestern face with a high forehead, wide-set, engaging eyes, and thin mouth.

"I probably have traveled and walked into more variety stores than anybody in America," Walton once said. "I am just trying to get ideas that will help us." In 1960, he took a long bus ride to Minnesota just to visit a new type of variety store: the self-service store. Instead of keeping merchandise behind a counter, the self-service store simply piled it up for customers to take for themselves. He also visited pioneering discount stores in the Northeast and the second Kmart in existence, located near Chicago, before deciding to start his own discount department store in 1962.

The story of opening day at the second Wal-Mart, in Rodgers, Arkansas, in 1962, has become apocryphal, recalling a hot day and a parking lot full of watermelons and donkeys (to be ridden in a circle), all contributing in their own ways to a memorable mess. However, it didn't matter how a Wal-Mart started, because Walton didn't intend for it to remain the same, anyway. His obsession was with improvement, and especially with lowering costs. Of course, he could start by trying to think of his own ways to lower costs, and he did, especially in dealings with manufacturers. "Just ask a vendor," said a longtime friend, "He's as cold as Sunday night supper." But more important, Walton encouraged all of his employees to work on lowering costs—to have it constantly in mind, just as he did. He gave them plain facts about company finances, hiding practically nothing. He gave them incentives, including the stock participation plans that made fortunes for some early Wal-Mart employees. And he let word get around that the boss stayed in budget hotels.

With hundreds of thousands of people looking for ways to keep expenses down, Wal-Mart found itself with operating costs that were half of those of its competitors. Following Walton's model, it was by no means a bad thing to have a good attitude at Wal-Mart. "TGIM—Thank goodness it's Monday," said the sign in Walton's executive offices.

Sam Walton became a folk hero, and his visits to stores usually turned into lovefests, in which he led company cheers and extolled the pleasure of working together for lower costs and better service at Wal-Mart. He loved the associates, they loved him, and they all admitted to loving their work, a situation that made many outsiders conclude that there were just a lot of love-starved people at Wal-Mart. But Sam Walton was not just a folk hero among the folks. And not just among the sentimental. Jack Welch, the chief executive officer at General Electric, was among those who got the Walton charge. "Everybody there has a passion for an idea and everyone's ideas count," Welch marveled of Wal-Mart's Bentonville headquarters in 1991, one year before Sam Walton's death. "I've been there three times now. Everytime you go to that place in Arkansas, you can fly back to New York without a plane. The place actually vibrates."

In the words that follow, Sam Walton reveals some of the observations and tips he gleaned from the decades he spent building the Wal-Mart chain. Nearly all of his remarks seem to refer back to his stated priorities as a retailer: ever lower prices and better customer service. The fact that Walton could not be easily distracted from those goals may indicate why his employees seemed to stay focused on the same issues, on behalf of the company.

IN THE WORDS OF

Sam Walton

Ego, in my opinion, is one of the worst things that can happen to a company.

Self-image

If we ever get carried away with how important we are because we're a great big $50 billion chain—instead of one store in Blytheville, Arkansas, or McComb, Mississippi, or Oak Ridge, Tennessee—then you can probably close the book on us.

Employees

How does Wal-Mart do it? They always ask. The answer is always the same—people. Not only the right kind, but interested, dedicated, enthusiastic and loyal people. That's what makes our company exceptional and what enables us to continually achieve the seemingly impossible.

Learning

Anyone willing to work hard, study the business and apply the best principles can do well. I worked at it. I walked into competitors' stores. And I wandered into more stores than anyone else. I was fortunate in getting some smart people to work for me and we avoided mistakes that the others made. We learned from everyone else's book and added a few pages of our own.

Leadership

Our philosophy is that management's role is simply to get the right people in the right places to do a job and then to encourage them to use their own inventiveness to accomplish the task at hand.

Surprise Element

I like to keep everybody guessing. I don't want our competitors getting too comfortable with feeling like they can predict what we're going to do. And I don't want our own executives feeling that way either. It's part of my strong feeling for the necessity of constant change, for keeping people a little off balance.

Discussion

To me, the most important element in establishing a happy, prosperous atmosphere is the insistence upon open, free, and honest communication up and down the ranks of our management structure and with our associates.

The necessity for good communication in a big company like this is so vital it can't be overstated. What good is figuring out a better way to sell beach towels if you aren't going to tell everybody in your company about it?

Costs

[*Walton was vigilant in keeping overhead expenses down, no matter how prosperous the company became. In explaining his thinking on the subject, he made mention of his brother, Bud, who worked in the development of Wal-Mart from the beginning.*]

One way I've approached this is by sticking to the same formula I used back when we had about five stores. In those days, I tried to operate on a 2 percent general office expense structure. In other words, 2 percent of sales should have been enough to carry our buying office, our general office expense, my salary, Bud's salary—and after we started adding district managers or any other officers—their salaries, too. Believe it or not, we haven't changed that basic formula from five stores to two thousand stores.

Experience

I didn't start as a banker or as an investor or doing anything else than waiting on customers. And many people who run big companies never ring cash registers, nor do they wait on customers, and so I've always appreciated what it meant to be a salesclerk and how much a sales person can influence a customer in a business relationship.

If we don't have the customer satisfied at the cash registers, none of us have a job.

[*Walton established a company policy that corporate staff members spend a week each year working as salesclerks in a Wal-Mart store.*]

Computers

Truthfully, I never viewed computers as anything more than necessary overhead. A computer is not—and will never be—a substitute for getting out in your stores and learning what's going on. In other words, a computer can tell you down to the dime what you've sold. But it can never tell you how much you could have sold.

Education

We must all see to it that our people-training programs are the best in retailing. From the back door of the stockroom to the front office, we need to have our personnel prepared and trained to do a superior job at every level. They must be interested, enthused and involved. We should make this our No. 1 priority.

Expectations

[*In 1984, Walton told* The New York Times *how Wal-Mart had gained its foothold during the 1960s by opening stores in the Midwest, and why the chain's later emergence as the nation's leading retailer didn't surprise him.*]

The big discount entrepreneurs were in the East and hadn't come here yet. Even so, we were latecomers because there were already Woolco discount stores here, K Mart and Kuhn-Big K stores, along with small regional chains like ours. Later other discounters came. I had no vision of the scope of what I would start. But I always had confidence that as long as we did our work well and were good to our customers, there would be no limit to us.

Nonconformity

[*In the early days, Walton and his team went to great lengths to remain apprised of the competition. One executive described how they would make nighttime sorties to sift through the garbage of one rival store.*]

I guess we had very little capacity for embarrassment back in those days. We paid absolutely no attention whatsoever to the way things were supposed to be done, you know, the way the rules of retail said it had to be done.

Ideas

[*In March 1992, President George Bush presented the Medal of Freedom to Sam Walton. Suffering from cancer, Walton attended the ceremony in a wheelchair, but showed his charac-teristic optimism in accepting the honor. Making references to his wife, Helen, and the president of Wal-Mart, David Glass, Walton said of the award:]*

This is the labor of a partnership, of folks who have pulled together and enjoyed what they've done and have become partners in what we've accomplished. I've helped. Helen's helped. David's helped. We've had a lot of great leaders in this company, and the greatest thing is we've got ideas from all 380,000 associates. That's the best part—all of us working together. I hope we can keep it going. That's the key, and if we can, we'll lower the cost of living for everyone—not just in America. We'll show the world an opportunity to save and have a better lifestyle and a better life. We think we've just begun.

[Just three weeks later, on April 5, 1992, Sam Walton passed away. News of his death was delivered via satellite to all 1,735 stores, and relayed over the public address system in many of them.]

Flexibility

It's a trademark of ours. We are willing to change. I would just like us to continue to make changes as they need to be made, and everyday is a different situation in this retail business. That's one of the blessings that has made us what we are, what we believe in. We have been very flexible and have been look-ing every day for changes that need to be made and those ideas come from a lot of different sources. These people out here are smarter and more capable than many of us recognize, and they understand our business and certainly know what the customer wants. But change and the willingness to change, to try anything, try any one's idea, it might not work. But it won't break the company when it doesn't.

Attitude

The way management treats the associates is exactly how the associates will then treat the customers. And if the associates treat the customers well, the customers will return again and again, and that is where the real profit in this business lies, not in trying to drag customers into your stores for one-time purchases based on splashy sales or expensive advertising.

"From this day forward, every customer that comes within ten feet of me, I'm going to look him in the eye, I'm going to smile, I'm going to greet him with a 'Good morning,' or a 'Good afternoon,' or a 'What can I do for you?'—so help me Sam."

[*Walton created the preceding pledge on the spur of the moment at a store meeting. It was heartily embraced by many throughout the company.*]

Customers

Let's spoil those wonderful customers. Let's appreciate them every day on every visit and tell them so. The key to our success, though, must be that we all truly embrace the philosophy of being servant leaders, both with our customers and each other.

Mary Pickford makes a drive at the Riviera Golf Club in Los Angeles, as four men look on. Pickford was cast in little girl parts long into adulthood, though she could play grown women or even boys just as well—as she proved in Little Lord Fauntleroy, *in which she was double cast as both the little lord and his mother.*

Mary Pickford
1898–1979

Mary Pickford entered the movie business as a bit player and emerged as its first recognized star, yet it was her work behind the scenes that proved to be the most lasting of her career. She was one of the original movie moguls, a founder and longtime co-owner of United Artists in addition to operating her own production company. Like others vying for power in the early days of moving pictures, Pickford took advantage of the fact that there was not yet an establishment in mass entertainment. Most of her contemporaries among executives were foreign-born and uneducated; she happened to be both, and a woman, but as a pioneer in the picture industry she wielded power without meeting nearly the resistance to be found in other fields. As United Artists grew into a major force in Hollywood during its first thirty-five years, no person exerted more influence over it, especially in matters of finance and law, than Mary Pickford.

*I*n 1916, Mary Pickford was nearing the end of her first contract with Famous Players, the film studio that later became Paramount Pictures. Famous Players had turned Pickford into the nation's first movie star—and she had turned it into the industry's first major corporation. With that as the well-known formula of Famous Players' success, Pickford was besieged with offers from other production companies in the spring of 1916. After work one day, she stopped to meet with an executive from one of the other companies at his home. Just after arriving, she politely asked to see the new baby that the executive and his wife had recently brought home. "Oh," said the executive, "Let's get our business off our minds first."

"Then I'll never see it," Pickford replied.

Mary Pickford was the first celebrity born of mass communication, a movie star at a time when there were fewer than a half-dozen others even barely known to the public. Before Pickford seized her crown as the "Queen of the Movies" in 1913, the story line was the star. Actors on the screen were about as glamorous as the chairs and tables—receiving approximately the same respect and only slightly more pay. In the same dawning, the economics of sports were yet to multiply through radio and later television, and those of music had only barely begun to multiply through recordings. However, each industry would soon follow Hollywood's new invention, the movie star, into a new understanding of the real product of mass communication: people, a few certain people.

Where other early movie stars accepted weekly salaries in line with those of the stage, Pickford wiped away the concept of time. The time spent in performing a part didn't matter: What mattered was that she could, in name and appeal, match the worldwide range of the moving picture. Pickford recognized that she was the business itself. She was determined to be paid as such, however big that business became. Her viewpoint and the salaries she commanded as a result were shocking—and much emulated.

Inevitably, Pickford's constant negotiation for business power led her to require her own studio. By 1919, she had one, in the form of United Artists.

Mary Pickford was born in Toronto in 1893. She was four when her father died, and in the wake of the tragedy, she seriously considered herself the head of the family. After her mother took a minor acting job in Toronto, five-year-old Mary overheard in a conversation that the company needed a little girl to fill the part of "Bootle's baby." She approached the manager by herself and told him in typically few words that she could handle the part—easily. He gave her the role and she made enough of a success to continue acting as a full-time job.

Movie actors were anonymous commodities in 1909, when Mary Pickford began working in pictures for D.W. Griffith at the Biograph Studio in New York. Nevertheless, the nameless "little girl with the golden curls" developed a loyal following. She was not, however, a little girl; she was a teenager playing characters half her real age. Her hair was no longer golden. It was brown. And it was straight. But no one had to know any of that, and the "little girl with the golden curls" developed a following.

Pickford viewed her appeal as a tremendous asset for increasing business. Griffith, for one, considered her a pushy brat. One day she abruptly demanded a raise and he inquired whether that was supposed to imply that she was a better actress than she had been the day before. "No," she replied, "but two people on the subway recognized me." Griffith burst out laughing at her logic. Nonetheless, it would soon prevail. In 1910, most producers joined Griffith in fearing that name billing would give actors increased power in the industry: They were right, of course. It would, but that wouldn't be the only effect of name billing.

Pickford had to search hard for a studio interested in exploiting the true potential of the movies by giving her star billing—or any billing. After a couple of false starts, she signed with Adolph Zukor at Famous Players in 1913, and together they pioneered the star system in movie production. "She taught me a great deal," said Zukor later. "I was only an apprentice then; she was an expert workman."

Explaining that the worth of a stage actress was limited by her endurance, Zukor would point out that a movie actress, with no limit to her appearances, "becomes an article of manufacture and distribution." Mary Pickford was the first such article in which Famous Players invested. By 1918, Pickford was earning $10,000 per week, against 50 percent of the profits from her movies. As it turned out, she took home about $1 million per year. The only other performer earning as much was Charles Chaplin.

Samuel Goldwyn, who fought many a business battle with Mary Pickford, once asked D.W. Griffith if anything set Pickford apart in the days when her career was just starting under his aegis, when she was just another young actress. Griffith, for his part, had certainly fought his own share of artistic battles with Pickford—one of which ended with her biting him. However, he looked past all of that in his answer to Goldwyn's question. What set Pickford apart?

"Work," Griffith said. "I soon began to notice that instead

of running off as soon as her set was over, she'd stay to watch the others on theirs. She never stopped listening and looking. She was determined to learn everything she could about the business."

In making demands in contract talks, Pickford depended on even more meticulous research than she brought to her roles. Most people enter negotiations armed with a certain knowledge of their own needs. Instead, Pickford exercised a thorough knowledge of the company with which she was negotiating. She described the part she would fill for the company as a business asset, affecting not merely the obvious profit potential and prestige, but the company's actual credit rating and its leverage within the industry as well.

Studios did indeed leverage stars of the magnitude of Mary Pickford, by forcing theaters to book a half-dozen or more undistinguished movies for every Pickford feature. Pickford hated the practice more than anyone, feeling that it placed an unfair burden on her reputation. Through her contracts, Pickford began to address the situation, trying to shift her position further down the line, toward a balancing point between production and distribution in the movie industry. However, by the late teens, all of the studio heads had concluded that the real power in the industry lay in distribution (access to theaters and bookings), and they were working to consolidate a trust at that end of the business in order to control production — and greedy stars.

In 1919, Pickford helped to found a new distribution company, very accurately called United Artists, which would be owned and controlled by a partnership of moviemakers: D.W. Griffith and Charles Chaplin, in addition to Pickford and her fiancé, Douglas Fairbanks Sr.

Whether or not UA was Pickford's idea (several people claimed credit), it seemed a natural step in her own crusade for independence. The four founding partners were supposed to produce a steady stream of films, for which an executive office would find theaters and make bookings. Later, other filmmakers supplied movies to UA.

No individual exerted more influence over UA in its first thirty-five years than Mary Pickford. However, Charles Chaplin was her equal in voting power throughout their mutual association with the company. "I was astonished at the legal and business acumen of Mary," Chaplin later wrote in his *Autobiography*, "She knew all the nomenclature: the amortizations and the deferred stocks, etc. She understood all the articles of incorporation, the legal discrepancy on Page 7, Paragraph A, Article 27 and coolly referred to the overlap and contradiction in Paragraph D, Article 24."

"On these occasions," Chaplin added, "she saddened me more than amazed me, for this was an aspect of 'America's Sweetheart,' that I did not know."

Pickford and Chaplin were alike in many ways, having emerged against long odds to dominate the movie industry. However, they didn't like each other. After surviving a long, bitter struggle with Chaplin over the direction of United Artists, Pickford finally sold her shares in the company in 1956. She had also gained fifty-one percent of the Samuel Goldwyn Studio, shares she divested at about the same time. After that, she concentrated all of her attention on her private portfolio, heavily weighted with real estate, and left a fortune estimated at $50 million at the time of her death in 1979.

As an actress, Pickford made a fairly successful transition to talkies, but retired from performing in movies in 1932. Her marriage with Fairbanks had made her a celebrity of absurdly high standing in the 1920s. Even so, Pickford's private life was not enviable. Her mother and both her siblings became grave alcoholics: Her brother and sister died early as a direct result. By the early 1930s, Mary Pickford had also fallen victim to alcoholism—she would be mentally sharp in the mornings, but was reported to fade by the afternoon as a result of her drinking. In 1964, she returned from a trip to Europe, exhausted by everything, and took to her bed. By the end of the decade, she could no longer walk and didn't seem to want to.

For other silent stars, the advent of talkies was the shipwreck they couldn't survive. Mary Pickford continued to reign in Hollywood even after the end of her own acting career, but as a studio executive. The strength she showed in that regard was largely spent by the time she was forty, but she was not toppled by the industry, tough as it was. Her diminishment had nothing to do with the outside world.

In the words that follow, Mary Pickford exhibits the dispassionate view she took of Hollywood's business development, even as she shows the slightly warmer interest she took in filmmaking itself and the high quality she tried to achieve. Because one might be tempted to suspect that a star, even one who owned a studio, would manage by proxy, a letter from Pickford is included in which she describes a pending deal and analyzes it for her lawyer. Pickford gives several pieces of advice on scaling a profession, though in her case it wasn't necessarily much fun at the top—or so it appears in an exchange with her fellow mogul, Charles Chaplin, at a United Artists stockholders' meeting.

IN THE WORDS OF

Mary Pickford

True, there are occasional accidents of career, but the greatest successes are not accidental; they are designed.

Colleagues

I would say that the important thing, and I think it is at least 33⅓ per cent important, is to get with the right associates. I took a cut in salary to be back at the Biograph Studio, and I have always felt that it was a wise move. When you feel that you are with the right concern, you give a good deal of yourself in order to become valuable to your employers.

Self-worth

I never asked for a raise except when I felt sure that I would get it, and I always got it. Mr. Griffith has often said in talking about those days: "Mary was always the last one to leave the studio."

Shortcuts

In my career on the screen, I have seen so many people come into pictures with preconceived ideas that were calculated to revolutionize the industry, and they went out quicker than they came.

Handling Money

It is possible to save something, even if you have only fifteen dollars a week.

A great deal of the adverse criticism and unfavorable advertising that Hollywood and the motion-picture business have had has been in large measure due to the sudden acquisition of a great deal of money on the part of a few persons who never had it before. You cannot spend a large income wisely if you have not saved or handled a small one well.

Terminology

I hated that word, "movie," and had hated it from the first minute that I saw it in the advertising of the Majestic Company, a rival company to the Biograph with which I worked. "A movie a minute," was their slogan.

Principle

[*In 1914, the seventeen-year-old Pickford was appearing on Broadway in a play presented by impresario David Belasco. She already had a strong sense of principle about films, having been acting in them for five years.*]

While *A Good Little Devil* was running, a proposition was put up to the company to film the play with all the actors in the parts that they played in the theater. Everyone else accepted, but I refused. The proposition, which was between Belasco and this new company, The Famous Players, seemed to me unfair to the actors. We were to work in the theater, and on days when we were not playing matinees, we were to act in the studio. For this, we were to receive, in addition to our theater salaries, only one-ninth of our day's pay in the theater. I thought that it should be at least an eighth. This seemed cutting things pretty fine, but the argument was that we would be doing something for the women and children, who would especially like *A Good Little Devil*. And women and children were the great patrons of the five-cent shows. This difference would have amounted to about forty dollars, and it was nearly the means of my losing the wonderful opportunity that afterwards came through my playing that part with The Famous Players. It was not the fact of money alone, it was the principle of the thing that I did not like. Finally, I yielded . . .

Initiative

I was from the beginning interested in the technical side of the pictures. I was interested, too, in the cutting and editing of the film. At the Biograph I learned a great deal of all these things, and the knowledge has helped me ever since I came to make my own pictures. Actually, today, I'd rather confine myself to interpreting my own part before the camera, but I have found that just as soon as a person becomes efficient, another company bids for his services.

I am making only one picture a year. A company which makes many pictures a year can pay much bigger salaries than I can.

A technical director can easily look after eight or ten pictures at once. So I lose my directors, editors, and scenario writers. If I am to maintain the standard of my pictures, I must look out for these things myself.

Originality

If you ask me, modern Hollywood needs a little of the old-time craziness.

Independence

Not long after *Pollyanna* [1919], I saw one of my dearest dreams fulfilled—the formation of United Artists. Even with the autonomy offered me at First National (Studios), I still felt I could create a more efficient distributing service as an independent producer. Then the trade papers reported that the men ruling the industry were planning to clamp the lid down on the salaries of actors. And that was the moment that Douglas Fairbanks, Charlie Chaplin, D.W. Griffith and I decided to take our leave of the major companies and become our own bosses. When the news leaked out prematurely, someone made the flattering observation:

"The asylum is now in the hands of the maniacs."

Pickford at Work

[*In 1939, UA entered negotiations to secure films from Frank Capra (and his partner Robert Riskin). The company was then dependent on moviemakers Alexander Korda and David O. Selznick, even while defending a lawsuit from another UA producer, Samuel Goldwyn. The Goldwyn lawsuit precluded UA from offering Capra a full partnership, and so the partners— Pickford, Korda, Douglas Fairbanks, and Charles Chaplin— considered earmarking one-fifth of their own dividends for him, instead.*

Mary Pickford took the lead in trying to chart a legal means by which to bring Capra into UA. She described the situation for her lawyer, Dennis, "Cap" O'Brien, in the letter quoted below, making reference to two other lawyers—Murray and Schwartz—who were involved in the company. As can be seen in the letter, Pickford tried to bring the deal to fruition in the proper steps.]

. . . Korda and Douglas at Pickfair told Riskin and Capra they were all for giving them a unit [partnership]. I was apprehensive about this promise knowing full well it would take an unanimous vote. I did not want to make an issue of it before Capra and Riskin, but I told both Douglas and Korda after they left that I doubted if it could be done until Goldwyn was out of the picture. Murray was given authority by the four of us;

namely Douglas, Chaplin, Korda, and myself to negotiate with Capra. He returned after much negotiation two days later with an agreement . . . Chaplin was reluctant at first to agree but, after two hours, said he was willing to give Capra the unit by giving him one fifth of our dividends until we could give them a unit which would be just as soon as we were legally free to do so and to this we all agreed. Then Schwartz spoke to Murray on long distance the following day stating that he thought it a very poor deal and that in his opinion if we gave Capra one fifth of the dividends of the four of us we would legally complicate our suit with Goldwyn. It seems to me, Cap, it was a little late for Schwartz to give this advice and that it was inadmissible for him to upset the apple cart with Korda who, as you know, is a congenital barterer and trader. After Korda had talked to Schwartz, he immediately called Chaplin up and got him on the rampage too. It places Murray and United Artists in a very embarrassing position; in fact, I go on record in saying we are morally obligated to go through with our proposition with Capra providing it is legally possible . . .

[*UA never completed an arrangement with Capra.*]

Partnerships

[*One of the original UA partners, D.W. Griffith, sold out to his fellow partners early on. When Fairbanks died in 1939, Pickford and Chaplin assumed his shares.*]

Profoundly as I respect Charlie Chaplin's talents and much as I valued his early friendship, nothing in the world would induce me to live over the agonizing years I experienced with Charlie as a business partner. As a co-owner of

United Artists, I was convinced we could survive only by continually modernizing our setup. This Charlie would not permit. "Charlie," I would say, "We ought to streamline the company and keep with the general trend of the times."

But there was no moving him. I don't think Charlie knew himself what he wanted. I finally became convinced he just didn't want what I wanted, that, somehow, particularly after Douglas' death, I rubbed him the wrong way. It finally came to this: no matter what I proposed, or how I proposed it, Charlie would automatically, without giving the matter any consideration, flatly turn it down. As we were 50-50 partners, I was completely stymied.

[*Stockholders' meeting, October 1943*]

Chaplin: I think we have done very well in the past. I think your credit shows so.

Pickford: My credit is nothing to the United Artists. If my credit was run like that of the United Artists, I would be penniless today and that is just why I am going to get relief from the courts. If we can't sit down and discuss our business like any other modern organization, then it is too bad.

Chaplin: I don't think this was ever intended to be a modern corporation. We never intended it.

Pickford: It is not, if it was.

Accomplishment

Whenever I do something that seems pretty good, do you know what it is to me? It is a whip to beat myself with! That is what any achievement is to the sincere worker. It isn't something for him to sit down and look at and think how nice it is. It is something that lashes him on to a greater effort.

Opportunity

Looking back, there's nothing I would change in my life, except maybe I'd work harder.

Edwin Land snaps a picture with an SX-70 camera at a Polaroid shareholders' meeting in the mid-1970s. "I'm addicted to at least one good experiment a day," Land once confessed. In number of patents held, he was second only to Thomas Edison among American inventors.

Edwin Land

1909–1991

Edwin Land held over 500 U.S. patents, but the invention that interested him most was the high-tech company: equal parts research and business. Land founded Polaroid in 1937 as a reflection of his own balanced priorities, or twin conceits, in serious science and commercial success. His ultimate goal was that neither would be compromised, and for decades neither was. Polaroid profits, stoked by the popularity of the instant camera, made the company's stock a perennial darling of Wall Street. At the same time, the company's contributions in optical research inspired its unofficial designation as Cambridge, Massachusetts' "third university," after Harvard and M.I.T. Under the aegis of Edwin Land, Polaroid charted a course in which profitability and pure science overlapped, a band so narrow it might as well have been a tightrope. Edwin Land walked it once, though, and left it for other high-tech firms to follow.

$\mathcal{I}$n 1926, Edwin Land was a freshman at Harvard University, treating himself to a weekend in New York with a stroll up Broadway on Saturday night. At the time, the New York theater was rich with stars, including the Lunts, Eddie Cantor, Gertrude Lawrence, and the Barrymores, their names up in lights on one marquee after another. Gazing up at the lights of Broadway, Land was dumbstruck—the glare was awful.

"I grew up in a small town in Connecticut," Land recalled much later, "where there was one physics book, a copy of Ganot's *Physics*, and not much science, but I was a proud possessor, somehow, of the second edition of Wood's *Physical Optics*, and as a boy I would take that to bed with me and read it every night." Looking at the flood of conflicting light beams on Broadway, Land, who was at seventeen still not much more than a boy, started to solve one of the prevailing problems in physical optics.

It was chaos in the light patterns that caused the glare. Standing on Broadway, Land thought of a way to reduce the glare by polarization—combing out the many directions the light followed, so that it all struck the eye going in just one direction. Such polarization occurred in nature, through certain crystals, but Land thought that he could reproduce the effect by making a filter, using microscopic crystals to train the light. Instead of going back to his coursework at Harvard, he took a leave of absence and rented a small apartment in New York to use as a laboratory. As Land later said—and perhaps he could have been describing himself at eighteen—the type of person who makes discoveries is "some individual who has freed himself from a way of thinking that is held by friends and associates who may be more intelligent, better educated, better disciplined, but who have not mastered the art of the fresh, clean look at the old, old knowledge."

Three years later, Edwin Land returned to Harvard, not as a wayward son, but as a serious scientist. And within three more years, the university made a formal announcement that Edwin Land, by then a senior, had developed "polaroid," a film (like cellophane in appearance) that reduced glare and had implications in pure science, along with applications in industry. Land finally had the knowledge, which was all the diploma he needed, and so he quit school again. Not only did he quit, in fact, but one of his teachers did too, to help further the research and to market polaroid. They each invested money for space and equipment, Land's share coming from his parents, who owned a large scrap metal business in Bridgeport, Connecticut. Within a year or two, the American Optical Co. was using polaroid in sunglasses, and Eastman Kodak was using it in filters.

In 1937, Edwin Land was working out of his basement office in Boston when he heard that some fairly important financiers from Wall Street were interested in the prospects for polaroid. At first, he maintained a cool distance, but as it turned out, he was not the one who should have been intimidated.

In the agreement that led to the formation of the Polaroid Corporation, a select list of investors, including for example the Rothschilds, were invited to participate in the $750,000 capitalization. At 27, Land was not only president and director of research, but he was the chairman of a board that included W. Averell Harriman and James P. Warburg. In addition, for the first ten years, the internal policies at the company were to be decided by a panel of special trustees, the decisions of which would carry by majority. But only if Edwin Land was with the majority.

Soon thereafter, Harvard gave Land an honorary doctorate.

Having trained one disordered part of the universe—the light spectrum—Land was determined to train another . . . the business world. Its particular beams—new ideas—were sorely misdirected, in Land's opinion. At most companies, ideas emanated from the field and ended up in the lab. The job of the researcher was to fill in the blanks of the existing marketplace. Edwin Land's theory made science the master: Any idea produced by a sharp-witted lab was worth money to someone, somewhere. The less the researcher thought about the commercial potential in advance, however, the better the results were bound to be, the more unique and, ultimately, the more marketable. In fact, Land went even further in laying down a policy at Polaroid, claiming to be actively repelled by the thought of inventing anything for which a market already existed.

Polaroid may have been the first start-up company in history to get $750,000 out of Wall Street on the promise of inventing things for which there was no market.

"There is no telling what kind of money Polaroid will be making in the near future," *Fortune* magazine reported in 1938, when it published a detailed profile of the infant company. The answer by 1943 was: Not much. The company survived by accommodating its industrial customers for polaroid, while committing most of its resources to war work, such as developing specialized goggles for airmen and sailors during World War II.

In 1943, Land took a few weeks off for a vacation in New Mexico with his wife, Helen, and their two daughters. Not usually given to savoring personal anecdotes, Land was nonetheless fond of recalling the morning in Sante Fe when he took a picture of his three-year-old daughter, Jeffie, who then asked why she couldn't see the photo immediately. Being three, she had at least temporarily mastered the art of the fresh, clean look at the old, old knowledge. But so had her father, who wandered around experimenting in his mind with the possibility of instant photography.

"Within an hour," he later claimed, "the camera, the film and the physical chemistry became so clear to me." However, it would not be quite that simple to refine the invention for actual sale. If it were, then it might not have suited Land, anyway, because he preferred a greater challenge. He liked nothing better than to hurl himself into a question, a problem, a search, an experiment, or anything else that required everything he knew and then just a bit more. Long hours under pressure were experiences he craved, not ones that he resisted. In recruiting scientists for Polaroid, he regaled them with all the opportunities he would provide for all-nighters and cold pizza dinners, intense debates, a frenzied pace—and the fear that a solution might not be found, with the certainty that nothing else mattered until it was. Conditions weren't always like that at Polaroid, but when they were, Edwin Land was happiest.

In late 1944, with war contracts beginning to wane, Land turned seriously to the realization of instant photography, of a camera "with a built-in darkroom," as he called it. In February 1949, the Polaroid Land camera went on sale, producing finished prints in sixty seconds, and it was a sensation.

Polaroid sold a half-million Land cameras at the high price of about ninety dollars each in the first five years, and then launched a less expensive version, which vaulted to sales figures of over a million per year. Profit growth of thirty percent per year was not unusual for Polaroid in the 1950s and 1960s, and its stock shone among investors.

A pattern emerged in Polaroid's later product introductions, the color instant camera in 1963 and the high-quality SX-70 in 1972. In each of those cases, initial sales were surprisingly tepid. Confidence in Land—confidence in pristine science—wilted each time, until lower-priced editions of his marvels were introduced with surging success, proving that he was right, as ever. And so was pristine science.

Known as "Din" to his friends, Land was probably the subject of more instant pictures than anyone else ever, since he believed firmly in giving people demonstrations of new cameras rather than explanations of them. Solidly built, with straight features and jet hair, Land had an imposing presence and he spent a great deal of his time before audiences, delivering details of a new Polaroid invention or of one of his own breakthroughs in science. Land was intelligent enough to make complicated concepts simple, such that anyone in the audience could handle them. In that sense, he packaged his thoughts just as he marketed his concepts in photography.

At the head of Polaroid through four decades, Land didn't change his priorities as a scientist and he wouldn't let the corporation change, either, in terms of its profile as a research institution (if a profit-making one). The company was poised to enter many promising areas through the years, such as 35-mm photography, for example, but Land demurred. If the market existed, then entering it would bore him personally and moreover leave the company vulnerable to the kind of price competition that often chokes off advanced research. According to Land's model, Polaroid thrived by being all alone in each of its markets.

The model stumbled in the 1970s, though, when the company placed nearly everything it had in the way of research capacity into development of the Polavision instant movie system.

However, home video sprang into the market supposedly reserved for Polavision, which was discontinued after only three years.

Polaroid survived, but without Edwin Land. He was pressured to resign as chief executive officer in 1980, forty-three years after he'd taken the job. His most remarkable invention was the Polaroid Corporation itself. For all of the revolutions Land had started in optics and photography, the company was at the forefront of a much more influential tide as the model for a generation of high-technology companies to follow it, even in other fields. In establishing a base for serious science, the equal of any university, Land proved that an unfettered passion for research could lead to lavish business success—and, to his own way of thinking, other kinds of success as well.

In the words that follow, Dr. Edwin Land speaks with fervent interest about the subject most compelling to him: the beneficial, balanced mixture of science and business in a corporate setting. As a manager who was a confirmed individualist, Land tried hard to cultivate real creativity among his employees, but, as he relates, that can be a rather dangerous thing to do. And likewise, for a scientific company, it can be a dangerous thing not to do. Land, one of the century's ranking authorities on light, also explains black-and-white photography in a short passage that reveals to the century's uninitiated amateurs just how much there is to taking a picture or making a camera.

IN THE WORDS OF

Edwin Land

Every creative act is a sudden cessation of stupidity.

Competition

Work only on problems that are manifestly important and seem to be nearly impossible to solve. That way, you will have a natural market for your product and no competition.

The Workday

I don't regard it as normal for a human being to have an eight-hour day, with two long coffee breaks, with a martini at lunch, with a sleepy period in the afternoon and a rush home to the next martini. I don't think that can be dignified by calling it working and I don't think people should be paid for it.

Pressure

My whole life has been spent in trying to teach people that intense concentration for hour after hour can bring out resources in people that they didn't know they had.

❀

Frequently, problems can be best solved, perhaps solved *only* if the work is done in a relatively short time. In most of the worthwhile problems, so many variables are involved that the human mind cannot keep them in order in the presence of interruptions. It is simultaneous mastery of a hundred interacting variables that is the glory of the kind of scientist we are talking about for our scientific companies.

Principles

[*Edwin Land called these the "quasimoral maxims" he held forth for an ideal industrial company.*]
    Do not undertake the program unless the goal is manifestly important and its achievement nearly impossible;
    Do not do anything that anyone else can do readily;
    Industry should be the intersection of science and art;
    The second great product of industry should be the fully rewarding working life for every person;
    The most intelligent use of a science requires understanding that comes only from increasing the knowledge in that science;
    It is relatively easy to organize a company with a homogeneous set of good minds but the ultimate greatness of a

company depends on the variety of kinds of good minds within it.

Scientific Avenues

Any honest scientist will recognize that there are fads and trends in the pursuit of pure science and that many competent young men waste many years in activities in which they learn little and contribute little. Industry can provide a much larger field of inquiry for pure science and much greater human stimulus to many of the young scientists than are now provided by the university. In short, a continuum between pure science in the university and pure science in industry should stimulate and enrich our social system.

Individuality

There is something warm and appealing and cozy about the picture of the human race marching forward, locked arm in arm and mind to mind; and there are insecure ages in life and insecure people in life to whom this vision of progress by phalanx brings comfort and strength. But I, for one, think this is nonsense socially and nonsense scientifically. I think human beings in the mass are fun at square dances, exciting to be with in a theater audience, and thrilling to cheer with at the California-Stanford or Harvard-Yale games. At the same time, I think whether outside science or within science there is no such thing as *group* originality or *group* creativity or *group* perspicacity.

I do believe wholeheartedly in the individual capacity for greatness, in one way or another, in almost any healthy human being under the *right* circumstances; but being part of a group is, in my opinion, generally the *wrong* circumstance. Profundity and originality are attributes of single, if not singular, minds.

I find each new person whom I meet a complete restatement of what life and the world are all about. The individualization of people—the individualization of spirit, taste, emotion—this is what makes life ageless. For me, then, to search out people's faces, using photographs to retain some of what we see and feel when we are with them, is a very important application of photography.

Initiative

The specifications I now set for ideal scientific companies are no different from the ones I set for myself in 1927—pick problems that are important and nearly impossible to solve, pick problems that are the result of sensing deep and possibly unarticulated human needs, pick problems that will draw on the diversity of human knowledge for their solution, and where that knowledge is inadequate, fill the gaps with basic scientific exploration—involve all the members of the organization in the sense of adventure and accomplishment, so that a large part of life's rewards would come from this involvement.

Employee Potential

If IBM were to take its computers and use them for ballast for ships, or to drop out of their top windows to test Galileo's laws, you would think IBM was behaving strangely, but what we as a race do, what we as industry do, is strange. We let human minds walk in through the personnel door and we keep them separate by using our promotion systems and using all the lip service to democracy, which in this situation is a misleading and dangerous thing, because we substitute a political consideration, a warm and human consideration, a decent behavior situation, for something else. The "something else" should be the realization that these people coming in at random are carrying in them the greatest marvel of all times—the human mind that took hundreds of millions of years to make.

We as technologists in industry do not use these minds at all. Instead of regarding them as minds, we substitute other criteria for usefulness. Whom do we use? We use the people who competed with us in college. We use the people who went to the same clubs. We use the people who talk the same language. We try to find people brighter than the people our competitors have, naturally, to play them off against each other as if it were a hockey game—but that's not enough, and now I am not talking about compassion and now I am not talking of a movement towards democracy. I am pointing out that because of some curious habit of mind we have, it is our custom not to use these mental mechanisms as they come to us in our industrial society. I would like to urge that what we need is a new art and a new science, and that new art and that new science is the one which, without involving emotion, examines the question of "how do you use human minds?"

Thinking

[*Land started preparing for color instant photography as soon as the black-and-white system entered in production in 1949. The color version of the Land camera was introduced in 1963.*]

When I started on the actual program of making the black-and-white film for our camera I set down the broad principles that would also apply to color. I invited Howard Rogers who had worked with me for many years in the field of polarized light to sit opposite me in the black-and-white laboratory and think about color. For several years he simply sat, and saying very little, assimilated the techniques we were using in black-and-white. Then one day he stood up and said "I'm ready to start now." So we built the color laboratory next to the black-and-white laboratory. . . . My point is that we created an environment, in which a man was *expected* to sit and think for two years.

Land at Work:
Black and White

[*In a 1978 stockholders' report, Edwin Land wrote about the relationship between human perception and photography. It was a technically oriented piece that reflected something of Land's uncommon knowledge about something as commonplace as photography. In this excerpt, he explains the reason why black-and-white photography can be even more communicative than color.*]

The most extraordinary of man's artifacts in the reconstruction of reality is the black and white image comprising, of course, a series of greys. It can be shown that in seeing color, objects are separated out from each other by the preferential efficiency of the surface of one object or another for reflecting light of one wavelength or another and that this preferentiality remains intact irrespective of the variation in time and place of the illumination on the object from the world around it. Black and white photography generates, as it were, a substitute world: light of the same wavelength composition comes to the eye from any part of the scene. This preferentiality for reflecting at different wavelengths is absent and cannot be used to designate objects. Rather only the difference from object to object in the efficiency for reflecting a uniform mixture of wavelengths can be used. Here comes in the miracle.

The enormous variations in illumination of the objects by the world around them have led to enormous variations in the amount of light reaching one object or another in a random way, so that portions of the photograph delineating dark objects may send to the eye more light than portions of the photograph delineating white objects. In short, the photograph is two entirely different kinds of report transmitted to us by what appear to be mixed languages, the language for delineating objects and the language for displaying illumination.

There have not been many great photographers in history, but the great ones usually turn out to be masters of the vocabulary of these two utterly different languages in black and white photography.

Marketability

I believe it is pretty well established now that neither the intuition of the sales manager, nor even the first reaction of the public is a reliable measure of the value of a product to the consumer. Very often the best way to find out whether something is worth making is to make it, distribute it, and then to see, after the product has been around for a few years, whether it was worth the trouble.

Inherent Creativity

In our laboratories we have again and again deliberately taken people without scientific training, taken people from the production line, put them into research situations in association with competent research people, and just let them be apprentices. What we find is an amazing thing. (It is like taking the tulip bulbs which have been in the cellar all winter and putting them in the spring soil,—quite suddenly and amazingly they flower and they flourish.) In about two years we find that these people, unless they are sick or somehow unhealthy, have an almost Pygmalion problem; they have become creative.

If there is anything that is unpleasant to an unprepared administrator it is to find himself surrounded by creative people, and when the creative people are not trained it is even worse. They have two unpleasant characteristics: first, they want to do something by themselves and they have some pretty good ideas that do not fit in with policy; secondly, they have the most naive, uncharming and unbecoming direct insight into what is fallacious in what you are doing, and that, of course, is a blow to policy. I do not want to romanticize these people. I am simply reporting on what we seem to find is a fact; that is, that the incrustation will fall away and that the inhibition can be removed, and then you have them, like the rain in Spain, you have them, you are stuck with them, and you have to find out what to do with these awakened people.

Science

It bothers us at Polaroid to see a world that could be ever so much more tender and beautiful if the full potential of science were realized. We think photography is a field through which that potential can be achieved. That's the wonderful thing about photography—you can have an inner world of science and an outer world of aesthetics.

Power

The important thing about power is to make sure you don't have to use it.

Creativity

That creativity is tied to some youthful age is a myth that comes about, I believe, because for one reason or another men stop living this way, perhaps because they are encouraged to think that there is more dignity associated with tasks implying power over people than with tasks implying power over nature.

Invention

My view of business and the ordinary business world's view of business are quite antithetical. Our essential concept was—and mine still is—that the role of industry is to sense a deep human need, then bring science and technology to bear on filling that need. Any market already existing in inherently boring and dull.

William Paley enjoys a joke with Lucille Ball, a longtime star of CBS television, at a 1984 event. Under Paley, CBS diversified in the 1950s and 1960s, owning, among other things, Steinway Piano, the New York Yankees, and the rights to the Broadway musical, My Fair Lady.

William S. Paley

1901–1990

William S. Paley was among the very first to recognize the power of commercial broadcasting, entering the industry in 1928, shortly after its inception. He also came closer than anyone else ever has to fulfilling its potential. As the longtime head of CBS, the network he created, Paley demonstrated both a sharp eye for new talent and daunting ability as a negotiator. While recognizing as well as anyone the need to draw the largest audiences possible, Paley gave high-quality programming every chance to prove itself, rewarding integrity with patience unusual in the broadcasting industry. William Paley's standards helped to give television its golden age, and made the CBS News Division a force in journalism at a time when that field was the exclusive domain of newspapers. William Paley knew that he had good taste, but what is more, he believed that audiences did, too.

In August 1945, Col. William Paley returned home, exhausted and yet energized from his service in World War II. As a radio authority with the Allied staff in Europe, he had worked long, hard days. But in war, just as in life, William Paley couldn't allow hard work to affect his standard of living. His official Army bunk overseas had been an apartment at the George V, one of Paris's most luxurious hotels. The apartment was comfortable—far above the average serviceman's lot during the war. But still, it lacked a certain . . . *splendor* was the word Paley used. On his own, he arranged for the use of a friend's penthouse overlooking the Seine, much more suited to dinner parties.

In 1928, as the playboy scion of a wealthy family in the cigar business, Paley had risked his personal fortune to found the Columbia Broadcasting System. He was only twenty-seven at the time, and many people already in the industry dismissed him as nothing more than "a young man with lots of money to play with." He was that—and would be, in a sense, all through his long life. In part, William Paley was a snob, nothing more. In part, though, he was possessed by aspiration. When there was a real choice, a rare commodity amid the dictates of broadcasting, it was known that Paley had a preference for quality. "A passion for it," in his own words.

Paley dedicated relentless effort to both the business and creative aspects of radio. He demanded the same respect that he seemed ever to be claiming for himself for the fledgling CBS, and it quickly grew into a nationwide network. CBS pioneered educational and children's programming, even while introducing popular new talent, most notably Bing Crosby, a Paley discovery. In the reckless manner of broadcasting in the

1930s, though, Crosby's hit show soon leaped from CBS to the much more powerful National Broadcasting Company.

Loyalty did not exactly abound in radio, but cunning did and so did opportunity. Until Paley left to serve in the war, his career at CBS consisted of fifteen years of mounting excitement. That very past, however, for all of its excitement, loomed as a depressing portent of the future for Paley in 1945. The specter of another fifteen years as head of the nation's second-best network made him seriously consider a change of careers on his return from war service. The reason was that, according to the system under which broadcasting operated at the time, CBS could never pass NBC.

Programs and talent contracts were typically the property of the sponsors, those advertisers who leased airtime and then hired ad agencies to actually produce shows. A truly popular show was likely to end up on NBC, simply because it was the network with the most powerful stations and the greatest reach into the marketplace.

Without more stars, CBS was doomed to trail NBC forever, yet Paley couldn't get more stars unless he had more high-quality stations, and he couldn't get more stations unless he had more stars. That was the tiresome situation in late 1945, when William Paley finally returned to his office in New York. By the time he started work again, though, he had a plan. Instead of trying to improve the situation, he intended to replace it.

Under the new plan, CBS stepped up to create, write, and produce shows for sponsorship, replacing ad agencies in that regard. Insinuating itself into the production process, the network would offer sponsors programming, not merely the air underneath it. No longer could a CBS hit jump to NBC. At first, the reaction was tepid, and through 1946–1947, CBS was forced to air expensive entertainment programs without sponsors. By the second season of the experiment, however, sponsors had no choice but to address Paley's new system if they wanted to associate themselves with the rising popularity of shows such as *Arthur Godfrey's Talent Scouts.* Arthur Godfrey was a very popular personality, but he wasn't a perennial favorite, a living legend, a master of audiences, a superstar. He wasn't Jack Benny.

In 1948, the Jack Benny Show was the top-rated radio show in the nation, a pillar of Sunday nights and of NBC. Normally, it would have been impossible to dislodge it, but Benny's agents had recently discovered that there were tax advantages to be had by selling a performer's whole production company to a network, rather than selling the performer's services on salary to a sponsor. The new method suited Paley perfectly. Offered the chance to purchase Benny's company in September 1948, he leaped to agree, but the offer was withdrawn when NBC suddenly stepped in.

For weeks, Paley walked around feeling betrayed by Benny's agents. The feeling didn't go away. Finally, Paley decided to call Jack Benny personally in California, initiating a new set of circumstances and a new round in the fight.

Benny told Paley that he would be willing to meet him in California.

Meanwhile, Benny kept working on the NBC deal, and seemed so close to affirming it that the network sent three lawyers from New York to review the contract. According to a Benny gagwriter named Milt Josefsberg, Benny met with them the next morning. He soon returned in a rare fury.

Inexplicably, one of the lawyers that NBC sent was a former government prosecutor who had mercilessly investigated Benny on smuggling charges years before — charges that turned out to be unfounded. Benny resented the very sight of the man. "I went to the meeting with an open mind," he fumed, "but the moment I walked into the office I knew that even if they doubled the other offer, I'd turn them down."

Later the same day, Paley arrived, suave and confident. Presented by Benny's agents with the contract just as it had been written for NBC, he signed it without delay and then returned to New York, having purchased, for $2.6 million . . . practically nothing.

CBS owned Benny's production company, but the American Tobacco Company owned the right to choose which network would air the Benny show. The cigarette maker was ill-disposed toward CBS, the second-leading network. Through one tense meeting after another, company officers insisted that the show would lose part of its audience if it moved to CBS. Paley argued, but so did they. He insisted, but so did they. He had facts and experience on his side, but so did they. Suddenly, though, Paley knew what to do. After giving it, as he said, a second or two of thought, he offered to return $3,000 to American Tobacco for every ratings point the Benny show lost each week after its switch to CBS. A guarantee for a show's ratings had never been tendered before, but after one more second or two, Paley had a deal.

On the first CBS broadcast of the show, January 2, 1949, Phil Harris introduced Jack Benny by saying, "Well, if it isn't Paley's Comic." From the first, the show drew even higher ratings than it had on NBC.

William Paley used the same smooth and tenacious style to lure Amos 'n Andy, Red Skelton, Bing Crosby, Frank Sinatra, and Edgar Bergen to CBS. NBC, having lost Jack Benny in January, 1949, spent a whopping $100,000 to publicize his replacement, bandleader Horace Heidt.

In July, Paley signed Heidt.

The "Paley Raids" worked: In 1949, CBS easily held the lead in the ratings race, carrying nine of the top ten shows. In retrospect, it might seem a Pyrrhic victory, since radio programming was just about to collapse in the face of competition from television. However, William Paley had keenly anticipated television's arrival as a force in broadcasting. As television swept the nation in 1948 and 1949, Paley made sure that CBS was veritably flush with stars. Stations, he knew perfectly well, would come. And they would be powerful stations. That constituted the real purpose of the Paley Raids.

CBS grew into a far greater role than ever before during the first decade of television. Many of its stars did make the transition from radio; the most successful of them all was undoubtedly Lucille Ball, with *I Love Lucy*. CBS's news division, expanded during World War II, was burgeoning with ambitious journalists when network television became a reality. They were poised for the larger opportunities of television, and through their efforts the news division reflected CBS at its best through the next decade.

Starting in the 1960s, Paley tried on numerous occasions to divest himself of the ultimate leadership of CBS. Each time he left, though, he returned with or without cause, dismissing his replacements to take back his place at the epicenter of CBS. Robust well into his eighties, Paley finally lost control of CBS in 1987. Pushing himself as hard as ever, he remained active in company matters, despite a precipitous decline in his health. Paley died in 1990, at the age of eighty-nine. After that, CBS continued apace, but in a different way: It lacked . . . *splendor* might be the word.

In the words that follow, William Paley describes the power that he discovered to be inherent in commercial broadcasting, a field that was only a year or two old when he entered it. He speaks about the hard choices facing a business expected to place its priority on excellence and quality, despite the demands of competition: not an uncommon tug-of-war, but one demonstrated very publicly in television, and especially at CBS under Paley. He also tells an anecdote he used early on in order to ameliorate CBS's status as the second-ranking company within its industry: an anecdote, however, that he was happy to leave behind as soon as CBS ranked first.

William S. Paley

Noncaptive Audiences

The sovereign right of every listener in America to snap the switch and shut off his radio or to shift his dial from one station to another has been the greatest single factor in broadcasting's onward march.

Government

It is noteworthy that the United States is the one important nation in which broadcasting has not been made a government monopoly. Here, radio has been from the beginning not an instrument made by the government, but rather an instrument for the making of government.

Partisanship

[*In 1938, Paley went on the air over the CBS network to explain his attitude toward radio ethics.*]

Broadcasting as an instrument of American democracy must forever be wholly, honestly and militantly non-partisan. This is true not only in politics, but in the whole realm of arguable social ideas.

We must never have an editorial page, we must never seek to maintain views of our own on any public question except broadcasting itself. Moreover, we must never try to further either side of any debatable question, regardless of our own private and personal sympathies. I state this principle of nonpartisanship first and I state it as emphatically as I can because it is the cornerstone of democratic broadcasting.

[*The issue of strict objectivity loomed as one of the most difficult facing Paley as the CBS News Division exerted its muscle in the 1950s. At times, correspondents breached the line and were applauded; at other times, they were dismissed. Paley was often placed in the position of arbiter over the conflicting passions of journalism—the desire to report situations and the desire to improve them.*]

Debate

I don't give orders. I am a kibitzer. I like to encourage debate, to play the devil's advocate, even if it means taking a position I don't really believe in, just to get the positions out in the open.

Details

I've always been interested in details. I'll call up one of our program guys and ask why someone is wearing a hat on a particular show. They'll tell me, "Well, he likes to wear a hat." I'll say, "Tell him to wear a hat when he goes out and not on the show."

Quality and Commercialism

Experience has taught us that one of the quickest ways to bore the American audience is to deal with art for art's sake, or to deify culture and education merely because they are worthy gods. Interest of the general American audience in the arts, the sciences, the humanities in general, goes only hand in hand with a passionate interest in the direct application of all these to living what has been called the full and more abundant life.

❦

Each broadcast must have a vital creative spark. It must appeal to either the emotions or the self-interest of the auditor, and not merely to his intellect, if it is to hold his attention. Listener interest is radio's life-blood. We cannot, assuredly, calmly broadcast programs we think people ought to listen to if they know what is good for them and then go on happily unconcerned as to whether people listen or not.

Quality and Competition

I don't think people always understand that television is a mass medium. I care about quality, but I also care about the bottom line . . . You want quality, but you have to know where to make the cutoff. If one network gets too far out ahead, the others would take a beating. It's a competitive situation. We do have some shows that combine quality and popularity. I think M*A*S*H is one, for the writing, and *The White Shadow* is another, because it always has an important social message. There are usually one or two a week.

[*CBS was the number one rated network for twenty-two years in a row, from 1954–1955 to 1976–1977.*]

The Underdog

[*In his memoir,* As It Happened, *Paley recalled the frustration at CBS during the 1930s, when the network perennially ranked second to NBC. A large part of Paley's job as president was selling CBS to potential program sponsors. One day, he realized how he could turn the common perception of CBS as an underdog into a chance to emphasize its strongest asset.*]

In those early days NBC was the more prestigious network and it had the larger, better-equipped studios, fancier offices, more people working for it and greater financial resources behind it. But I thought CBS made up for all of that with our youthful zest and drive and our better ideas for new and popular programs. And yet it caused me considerable anguish until one day my whole attitude of being the perpetual underdog changed.

I was walking down Broadway and on one side of the Great White Way was the Capitol Theater, the largest and most beautiful movie house of its day, showing a rather mediocre movie, and on the other side was a very ordinary, rather run-down theater showing a movie that I had heard was very good. And there were far more people lined up to see the good movie in the ordinary theater than there were in front of the resplendent Capitol. The analogy struck me so forcibly that I never forgot it. "You know," I said to myself, "for radio, it's what goes into a person's house that counts. The radio listener doesn't know what kind of office I have, what kind of studios I have, he only knows what he hears. And I can forget about all these advantages my competition has . . . I just have to put things on the air that the people like more. And that's my job. I've got to find things that will be popular . . ."

I began to tell advertisers that story about the Capitol Theater versus the good movie in the smaller movie house, asking them which they would choose. Invariably they would choose the good film over the more spectacular house and that story became a very strong point in my being able to persuade advertisers to sponsor programs on CBS.

That insight affected me too, for I became extra careful about spending money on anything in the company that did not affect the product, the program itself.

Professionalism

It is my belief that if we know what we are doing in the world of news and public affairs, we are secure; if we do not know, we are in danger — in danger of encroachments from government, in danger of criticism, destructive and deserved from other powerful organs of opinion, in danger of criticism from the thinking and leading citizens of our Republic.

Documentaries

To radio's democratic audience, history must be made to seem not a recitation of facts and dates but rather a spyglass into the past where characters live again. Science must be discussed not as a series of abstract phenomena but as an answer to the daily needs of man in his struggle with his environment. Classic literature must become a living expression of today's thought. Geography can be no mere description, but rather an actual experience of the world. Every listener, in short, must be made so aware of the direct application of this material to his own life that he listens as avidly as to sheer entertainment.

Diligence

It is quite amazing to me now when I look back and see just how small CBS used to be [in the 1930s] and how seriously we took our problems then and how hard I worked, as though everything were a matter of life and death. Now, those same things would take none of my time at all — they would be considered too unimportant for the chairman of the board.

Nevertheless, it was precisely those small things, that slow building-up process during those early years, which enabled CBS to go on and to grow and to do bigger and better things.

Standards

I suggest that we have reached a point where it is incumbent upon the whole industry to be concerned with the good name of the whole industry, and if that means pointing directly to certain units in the industry, then let's not be afraid to do so. Too long now we have tolerated, with too much good nature, the cynical and irresponsible ones among us.

Dimensionality

My decision to separate my business life at CBS during the day from my social life at night came rather naturally. I could see the dangers of socializing with my office associates, or with the advertising agency men, or corporate officers who were so important to me in the development of CBS. I just did not want to mix the two. I feared the one-dimensional kind of existence it might lead to and the risk of encumbering my business affairs with my social ones. This separation was more or less understood and accepted at CBS and became a long-standing way of life for me.

The Information Stream

[*In 1980, Paley delivered a speech before the Associated Press Broadcasters Convention. In it, he anticipated the importance of the dawning information age, and forecast the blurring of the media through what we now know as the Internet.*]

What we've done is to create a vast complex of information machines, which are being fed by a storehouse of knowledge and entertainment of every conceivable kind. This endless mass of material is fed from diverse sources into the process, and it comes out the other end in a variety of ways. . . . With the aid of new computerized equipment, people will be able to select a remarkable range of what they want to see and hear, and have it brought to them aurally and visually, whether by pictures or printout. It is already technically possible to bring newspapers and magazines into the home, both in the television screen and by printout. Before long all this will be delivered as easily as the television pictures which now come to you. And all of this refers to technology which already exists. Just think of the next wave of revolutionary communications technology which is in planning or will soon be off the drawing boards. The possibilities border on the incredible.

This new era of information plenty, with its convergence of delivery mechanisms for news and information, raises anew some critical First Amendment questions about our freedom which merit comprehensive rethinking. Once the print media comes into the home through the television set, or an attachment, with an impact and basic content similar to that which the broadcasters now deliver, then the question of government regulation becomes paramount for print as well.

[*Paley was a longtime enemy of government regulations that dictated strict "equal time" rules for broadcasters but not for newspapers. His speech was a warning that print media utilizing Internet-type technology "may be drawn into the regulatory web" already constricting broadcasters.*]

Speaking for one of the agencies that have made a business of floating a ceaseless stream of intelligence into the ears of the world, I can testify that we are awed by the power that has been placed in our hands.

PART III

The Thoughts That Count:
SELF-MADE SUCCESSES

A business mind-set can be created through apprenticeship or education, but some people are launched without any such luxuries. What they have as working material is themselves, and not much else, and so they cultivate their acumen out of nothing at all. Except, perhaps, desperation or pride, possibly anger or fear, stubbornness and jealousy—or any of the other many emotions that find form in sheer ambition. A self-made success makes sense out of that swirl of emotions and turns it into a business mind-set, with all that that implies in terms of a process for decision-making.

John D. Rockefeller started as an assistant bookkeeper, the Bank of America's A.P. Giannini was a produce clerk, and Madame C.J. Walker, the first self-made African-American woman millionaire, was a laundress. Henry Ford II practically inherited command of Ford Motor in 1945: Even so, he'd received less preparation than the average clerk. He would go on to prove, though, that to be self-made is much more than a question of merely starting out poor and ending up rich.

John D. Rockefeller, left, rides in an open car with a fellow businessman in Cleveland. Even after moving Standard Oil's head offices to a long-famous address, 26 Broadway in New York, Rockefeller spent much of his time in Cleveland.

John D. Rockefeller
1837–1936

John D. Rockefeller was a billionaire at a time when there was only one billionaire. Recognized as the richest man in the world, he was commonly reviled during his lifetime for dishonesty and even for cruelty in the way he amassed his fortune. Ironically, he maintained that the single most important factor in his success was his reputation for fair dealing. As president of Standard Oil, Rockefeller organized one of the first trusts, uniting his company with other refiners. Both the trust and the dominant Standard itself were eventually broken up under pressure from the federal government. Rockefeller, who emerged unscathed from his legal battles and certainly from his financial ones, was widely regarded by the public as a sort of monster of capitalism. That was partly due to the transition over which he presided: The nation, not yet used to corporations on the scale of Standard Oil, persisted in thinking that a person or a small group of people necessarily owned a company. One part of Rockefeller's genius, though, was in how much he controlled that he did not own. That feat marked the birth of the modern corporation.

If one word could describe the Standard Oil Company under John D. Rockefeller, that word would be . . . Amelia.

Amelia was the secret code word used in telegrams sent by the trust's most senior executives. The official translation was, "All is lovely and the goose hangs high." A top manager receiving some mundane message about Aunt Amelia's train or Cousin Amelia's health would know that a colleague was reporting very good news. That the goose was hanging high.

John Rockefeller was the head of Standard Oil for just over twenty-five years, every one of them Amelia years by any financial measure. Yet the very use of secret terms among the top executives also recalls the stealth with which the Standard operated. For a company that raised a great industry where only adventure had existed before, the Standard was practically invisible. Even those within the oil industry saw only as much of the company as necessary. Businessmen as formidable as H. Clay Frick and William Vanderbilt openly admitted that they stood in awe of "the Standard crowd," the men who controlled the trust in unusual concert.

John D. Rockefeller would dominate the oil refining business, as he would dominate the whole of American industry: He still dominates its horizons. First, though, he gathered about a dozen of the keenest and most hotly ambitious business minds in the country and induced them to work together—domination of a higher kind.

The secret of Rockefeller's power over others did not lie in guile—that would be superfluous—but in the conviction that to be right in each matter faced was to be supreme. He didn't raise his voice, and he never cursed or made cutting remarks. To anyone who ever met him in person, Rockefeller was the most kindly mannered person in the world. He spoke with a quaint formality and evinced an ingenuous interest in others. Rockefeller may have been reticent in demeanor, but no one mistook that for weakness.

Uniquely, and almost unnaturally, John Rockefeller was prepared for anything. He must surely have changed over the course of his ascendancy from a $10-a-week clerk to one of the richest men in the world. In several respects, though, he owed his success to his utter imperviousness to change. Many $10-a-week clerks gain a promotion by finding errors of a penny; then they advertise their newly mounting importance by hunting only for errors of a dollar (or a thousand of them) thereafter. John Rockefeller never outgrew his interest in saving pennies on the company's behalf. His interest in them, on a scale of millions, had nothing to do with humility, however. He was not still thinking of himself as a diligent clerk when he was the titan of Standard Oil. Rockefeller didn't change his basic values over the course of his career, for the reason that when he was a diligent clerk, he already considered himself a titan. "An hour was a year to him, and a year was an hour, it didn't matter, as long as he won out in the end," said a man who dealt with Rockefeller directly.

John Rockefeller, born in 1839, was from the Finger Lakes region of upstate New York. His mother came from an established farm family, and she ran a very efficient home. If the mother was self-contained, the father, William Rockefeller, was an exaggerated character of a man; an unruly sort of businessman who sold patent medicines from town to town. He seems to have been most useful as a detailed description of everything that the son would never be, if he could possibly help it. John could barely abide the man.

After quitting high school for a short course at a commercial college in Cleveland, John Rockefeller was hired as an assistant bookkeeper at a wholesale produce company. Rockefeller was tall, like his father. He had delicate features: thin lips and a small nose, dull blue eyes, and high-boned, rosy cheeks.

In his own recollection, he was hotheaded as a youngster, given to angry fits at people whom he considered second-rate. Such shows didn't become a habit. Rockefeller began to discipline his temper through his peculiar characteristic: knowing patience. It became the bedrock of his style. A year after joining the produce company, he resigned over a pay dispute and went into the produce business for himself. His partner was an Englishman named Maurice Clark, who was older and more experienced in business. One of the clearest images of Rockefeller's controlled temper is betrayed by his own recollection of Clark: "He tried, almost from the beginning of our partnership, to dominate and over-ride me. A question he asked several times in our discussions of business matters was, 'What in the world would you have come without *me?*' I bore it in silence. It does no good to dispute with such a man."

Rockefeller counted "infinite patience and courage" as the secrets of success. In jest, he put it this way, "You can abuse me, you can strike me, so long as you let me have my own way." He worked hard at perfecting many of his own thought processes. For example, he walked away from conversations mentally repeating the points that had been made by others. His natural tendency, not an uncommon one, was to savor what he himself had said, soon forgetting anything that could have been learned. The habit of repeating important points not only made all of his conversations more productive, they taught him to become a superb interviewer—and listener.

Another of Rockefeller's habits, which even he made fun of, was to talk out loud to his pillow before he went to sleep. He liked to review the events of the day, putting them in perspective, of course, while voicing his fears. He also analyzed his own performance, berating himself constantly not to become overconfident.

In 1859, while Rockefeller was still establishing his reputation in Cleveland in the produce business, a huge reserve of oil was discovered in Western Pennsylvania. Long regarded as a nuisance, oil had became a vital commodity in the short span of about ten years in the middle of the nineteenth century, after a frustrated businessman in Pittsburgh introduced refined oil as an illuminant. Other derivatives, from axle grease to petroleum jelly, created even more demand.

John D. Rockefeller was among the many who rushed into the refining business. In 1863, he and his partner Maurice Clark joined with a chemist named George Andrews to start the partnership that would lead into the Standard Oil Co. Rockefeller, a successful produce dealer, did not seem suited to the lowbrow refining business, with its disordered ways and strange characters. In all, it was antithetical to his personality. Although that could have repelled him, it had the opposite effect. He intended to impose his personality on the refining industry, not the other way around.

Other refineries were little more than shacks, reflecting as little capital investment as possible. From the first, the Rockefeller refineries were built to last. However the company was organized at first, though, it was a system that Rockefeller and his managers never stopped perfecting in large ways or small ones. Stories of Rockefeller's attention to detail were legendary. As president of the new concern, every single penny was of interest to him. It was a question of business practice. A penny was the stuff of his life, the stuff of business: It could not be inconsequential. Once he asked a workman soldering the tops on metal barrels how many dots of solder were used. Forty, he was told. "Have you tried thirty-eight?" Rockefeller asked. As it turned out, thirty-eight dots of solder made a seal that leaked. However, thirty-nine worked. In other cases, Rockefeller sent memos to low-ranking clerks pointing out minute errors he'd detected in his own perusal of company records. But no detail was minute.

Hushed and careful as a manager, Rockefeller was, by deed, the boldest of expansionists. It was not so much a dual personality as a balancing act—which he conducted at a very high altitude. "I never knew anyone like him for borrowing money," Maurice Clark once exclaimed. Another early partner said of Rockefeller that he "went to bed at night wondering how he could pay the loan he had negotiated and awoke in the morning wondering how he could increase it."

Rockefeller was determined that his company grow even faster than the oil business itself. He "wore out the knees of his pants," as he once said, in begging bankers or investors for money. It wasn't easy, in light of the sloppy reputation of the refining business in general. It didn't even seem prudent, in light of the harsh competition of the thinly spread industry. Maurice Clark was first on a long list of early partners and potential investors who simply didn't have the stomach to risk so much on the unstable industry. Having left Clark and several other partnerships behind, Rockefeller decided in 1869 that incorporation would provide some relief from dependence on loans.

As a corporation, the Standard Oil Co. expanded both

through its own building program and through absorption of competing firms. The company couched its offers in terms of a choice between Standard Oil stock and cash. Many refiners who chose to accept the stock became nervous about it later: Rockefeller seemed to be risking too much and borrowing too much, and the company seemed to be growing too much. For his part, Rockefeller made it a practice to buy any block of stock a jittery shareholder might want to sell.

At the age of ninety-two, he was still at it, picking up millions of shares of Standard Oil companies in the weeks after the stock market crash of 1929.

For a man with a humble demeanor, John Rockefeller had, of course, an unmatched ego. He recognized with a certain sly delight that many people who are in business delude themselves, and so defeat themselves. However, when Rockefeller came up against people who were as astute as he, and who possessed the same dedication and vision, he worked at drawing them into the Standard. "It was very interesting and to us a gratifying thing," he once said, "that the men who had been our most bitter opponents, when they came to understand from us and not from rumors which filled the air about our purposes and plans, were among the most loyal and enthusiastic supporters of the cause."

In many cases, Standard Oil vice presidents had been presidents of companies nearly as large. In 1882, Rockefeller was instrumental in formally organizing the nation's first important trust, a cooperative league of eight major refiners, the largest of which was the Standard. The organization was generally known as the Standard Oil Trust and it made Rockefeller effectively the president of seven other presidents.

John Rockefeller maintained formal friendships with most

of his associates in business, but did not presume to adopt a first-name basis with any of them. Despite the image that conjures, he was not a rigid man: After work, he preferred the company of his family, making up games for his five children and spoiling them—not business associates—with his time and friendship. John Rockefeller Jr. vividly recalled how his father, ever anxious to go skating on the lake near the family's house, would walk out on the ice to test it. In case he broke through, he held two long boards under his arms: characteristic Rockefeller contingency. He might fall, but he wouldn't drown, and his son thought he was fearless. For all of the time he devoted to relaxation, however, John Rockefeller was eventually worn down by the intensity of his business. He suffered digestive problems and all of his hair fell out during what was considered a nervous breakdown in the early 1890s. "I'd give a million dollars for a new stomach," he once said.

The Standard Oil Co. was the most aggressive force in a rough business. Shipping huge quantities of oil by train, it took advantage of its inordinate power over the railroads, engaging in the "rebate" system of the late nineteenth century. Rebates (a percentage kicked back to the shipper) were individually and very privately negotiated. Under the cloak of secrecy, shippers, including and especially Standard Oil, not only named their own rates, but insisted on setting the rates that competing refiners would pay for shipping. Such dictates inspired the first government investigations of the Standard Oil Co.

John Rockefeller had succeeded in accomplishing the unimaginable: His company controlled one of America's most vital industries. Standard Oil advanced the industrial age by perhaps thirty years, making oil and its derivative lubricants and fuels available at a reasonable cost practically anywhere in the world. Rockefeller maintained that a trust was necessary to accomplish such an expansive goal; his attitude ran counter to the accepted wisdom that competition is necessary to progress. Constant jousting with other companies, he felt, would waste money and effort, both of which could be better spent in building a great system — one matched to more daunting competition from overseas (he was especially mindful of the threat from imperial Russia). John Rockefeller happened to trust himself and his lieutenants to control that system. The public did not. Ultimately, of course, neither did the government. First the trust itself was dissolved, more or less voluntarily, in 1892, replaced by an even more effective monopoly organized under a Standard Oil holding company. In 1911, under stern pressure, Standard Oil was finally broken into competitive companies.

Rockefeller had retired from the Standard Oil Co. by 1896, when he was not yet sixty years old. In a sense, he left because his goal had indeed been accomplished. His company, at its peak in that decade, refined more than ninety percent of the oil pumped in the United States, shipping it efficiently all over the world. For about a dozen years following his corporate retirement, Rockefeller was an active private investor.

Rockefeller spent most of his time in his later years at his home near Tarrytown, New York. After the children were grown, Mrs. Rockefeller became an invalid and was confined to her bed most of the time. John Rockefeller sought the company of lighthearted people in place of the companionship he had formally found in being surrounded daily by his family. If he had a dinner party for his new friends, though, he would often excuse himself from the table to run upstairs to treat his wife, Laura, to any little witticism uttered at the table. He liked to tell jokes himself, and one of his young friends, H.M. Briggs, later said, "He had a natural gift for acting. I have seen him play the small boy and the old man's parts, and both to perfection." Each role accompanied the long life of John D. Rockefeller.

In the words that follow, John Rockefeller reveals something of the discipline of his mind and his ability to balance within it an unlimited number of concerns. Rockefeller prided himself on being an utter realist about business conditions, and many of the points he makes are admonishments not to depend on hope and to resist delusions of any sort. A number of his points are backed up by deeds in actual circumstance, as reflected in letters concerning his business affairs.

John D. Rockefeller

Ambition

The man who starts out simply with the idea of getting rich won't succeed; you must have a larger ambition.

Leadership

It takes infinite patience and courage to compel men to have confidence in you. I believe I have both of these qualities, and I also believe that they are the secrets of my success. I learned to cultivate both of them when I was sixteen years of age. My first real test was when I was making out bills of lading for canal and lake boats here in Cleveland. There was much to try the patience there, and the first opportunity in my life to take the wrong course—to repel rather than compel confidence from my associates . . . I insisted upon what I thought was right, but had patience with all who opposed me.

Flexibility

You can't hold up conditions artificially, and you can't change the underlying laws of trade. If you try, you must inevitably fail. This may be trite and obvious, but it is remarkable how many men overlook what should be the obvious. These are facts we can't get away from — a business man must adapt himself to the natural conditions as they exist from month to month and year to year. Sometimes I feel that we Americans think we can find a short road to success, and it may appear that often this feat is accomplished; but the real efficiency in work comes from knowing your facts and building upon that sure foundation.

Expectation

Don't even think of temporary or sharp advantages. Don't waste your effort on a thing which ends in a petty triumph unless you are satisfied with a life of petty success.

Strict Economy

The practice of strict economy is an everyday matter.

※

[*Rockefeller addressed a class of young people interested in going into business, bringing along the ledger he had kept as a boy. In showing it to the class, he joked that he dare not let them read it, "because my children, who have read it, say that I did not spell tooth-brush correctly."*]

Now let me leave this little word of counsel for you. Keep a little ledger, as I did. Write down in it what you receive and do not be ashamed to write down what you pay away. See that you pay it away in such a manner that your father or mother may look over your book and see just what you did with your money. It will help you to save money, and that you ought to do.

Detail

As I began my business life as a bookkeeper, I learned to have great respect for figures and facts, no matter how small they were. When there was a matter of accounting to be done in connection with any plan with which I was associated in the earlier years, I usually found that I was selected to take it. I had a passion for detail which afterward I was forced to strive to modify.

Responsibility

[*Rockefeller's recollection of his early days as an assistant book-keeper:*]

One day, I remember, I was in a neighbor's office, when the local plumber presented himself with a bill about a yard long. This neighbor was one of those very busy men. He was connected with what seemed to me an unlimited number of enterprises. He merely glanced at this tiresome bill, turned to the bookkeeper, and said:

"Please pay this bill."

As I was studying the same plumber's bills in great detail, checking every item, if only for a few cents, and finding it to be greatly to the firm's interest to do so, this casual way of conducting affairs did not appeal to me. I had trained myself to the point of view doubtless held by many young men in business to-day, that my check on a bill was the executive act which released my employer's money from the till and was attended with more responsibility than the spending of my own funds. I made up my mind that such business methods could not succeed.

I could not have done for myself better than I did for my employer. How I wish all young men could know that the way to hold a position is to do just that thing!

Principles

How hard it is sometimes to live up to what one knows is the right business principle.

Not long after our concern [Rockefeller's early partnership in the wholesale produce business] was started our best customer—that is, the man who made the largest consignments—asked that we should allow him to draw in advance on current shipments before the produce or a bill of lading was actually in hand. We, of course, wished to oblige this important man, but I, as the financial member of the firm, objected, though I feared we should lose his business.

The situation seemed very serious; my partner was impatient with me for refusing to yield, and in this dilemma I decided to go personally to see if I could not induce our customer to relent. I had been unusually fortunate when I came face to face with men in winning their friendship, and my partner's displeasure put me on my mettle. I felt that when I got in touch with this gentleman I could convince him that what he proposed would result in bad precedent. My reasoning (in my own mind) was logical and convincing. I went to see him, and put forth all the arguments that I had so carefully thought out. But he stormed about, and in the end I had the further humiliation of confessing to my partner that I had failed. I had been able to accomplish absolutely nothing.

Naturally, he was very much disturbed at the possibility of losing our most valued connection, but I insisted and we stuck to our principles and refused to give the shipper the accommodation he had asked. What was our surprise and gratification to find that he continued his relations with us as though nothing had happened, and did not again refer to the matter. I learned afterward that an old country banker, named John Gardner of Norwalk, Ohio, who had much to do with our consignor, was watching this little matter intently, and I have ever since believed that he originated the suggestion to tempt us to do what we stated we did not do, as a test, and his story about our firm standing for what we regarded as sound business principles did us great good.

Fair Dealing

There is no mystery in business success. The great industrial leaders have told again and again the plain and obvious fact that there can be no permanent success without fair dealing that leads to widespread confidence in the man himself, and that is the real capital we all prize and work for. If you do each day's task successfully, and stay faithfully within these natural operations of commercial laws which I talk so much about, and keep your head clear, you will come out all right, and will then, perhaps, forgive me for moralizing in this old-fashioned way. It is hardly necessary to caution a young man who reads so sober a book as this not to lose his head over a little success, or to grow impatient or discouraged by a little failure.

[*Rockefeller's philosophy of fair dealing was not altruistic, but a self-serving business practice, as he explained in the third person, correcting something someone had just quoted to him in conversation.*]

It was apparent to Mr. Rockefeller always in connection with his relation to the oil business and all other business undertakings that the wisest and best way to conduct business, irrespective of any moral governing principle, was to be fair to all parties concerned, and this law was so manifest that it resulted in a cohesive power in the Standard Oil Company interests which had commanded the admiration and confidence of the whole world, including those many people who were in the outset led to believe something else than the truth, and consequently worked against the Standard Oil Company until, with personal contact with Mr. Rockefeller and others and careful observation of their methods and the particular way in which they carried out every covenant and the fairness with which they dealt not only with each other, but with all with whom they had to do, brought an astonishing change in attitude . . .

[*The sentence was only half-finished at that point, as Rockefeller went on to note the stabilizing effects of his reputation on local and world markets. That he could unravel such a long sentence within the bounds of syntax may also reflect something of the capacity of his mind, or of his anger in defense of his ethics.*]

Bankruptcy

It has been our experience never to allow a company in which we had an interest to be thrown into the bankruptcy court if we could prevent it. . . . Our plan has been to stay with the institution, nurse it, lend it money when necessary, improve facilities, cheapen production, and avail ourselves of the opportunities which time and patience are likely to bring to make it self-sustaining and successful . . .

My excuse for dwelling on the subject at this late day is to point out the fact to some businessmen who get discouraged that much can be done by careful and patient attention, even when the business is apparently in very deep water. It requires two things: some added capital, put in by one's self or secured from others, and a strict adherence to the sound and natural laws of business.

❋

[*Rockefeller's commitment to nursing businesses back to strength is borne out in a letter he wrote to Frederick Gates, an executive who helped to manage the Rockefeller fortune.*]

May 13, 1905
Dear Mr. Gates:
    Referring to yours of the 12th, with reference to the fortunate termination of the transactions in connection with our old smelter, the result has been most gratifying indeed, and I think it teaches us one thing—that in this progressive age and in our progressive country, if we can wait, and if we have nerve to <u>put some money in</u> enterprises, it very often is better than to close out interests precipitately . . .

Persistence

What if the president of a bank refused to make me a loan? That was nothing. He might even lecture me on the folly of taking a loan for the purpose for which I was seeking it. That made no difference to me: simply meant that I must look elsewhere until I got what I wanted.

Competition

It is to be remembered that oft-times, the most difficult competition comes, not from the strong, the intelligent, the conservative competitor, but from the man who is holding on by the eyelids and is ignorant of his costs, and anyway, he's got to "keep running or bust."

❀

[*Rockefeller believed that desperate competitors caused disruptions in the market, being heedless of anything but the short-term effect.*]

In my early days men acted just as they do now, no doubt. When there was anything to be done for the general trade betterment, almost every man had some good reason for believing that his case was a special one different from all the rest. For every foolish thing he did, or wanted to do, for every unbusiness-like plan he had, he always pleaded that it was necessary in his case. He was the one man who had to sell at less than cost, to disrupt all the business plans of others in his trade, because his individual position was so absolutely different from all the rest. It was often a heart-breaking undertaking to convince those men that the perfect occasion which would lead to the perfect opportunity would never come, even if they waited until the crack o' doom.

Then, again, we had the type of man who really never knew all the facts about his own affairs. Many of the brightest kept their books in such a way that they did not actually know when they were making money on a certain operation and when they were losing. This unintelligent competition was a hard matter to contend with. Good old-fashioned common sense has always been a mighty rare commodity. When a man's affairs are not going well, he hates to study the books and face the truth. From the first, the men who managed the Standard Oil Company kept their books intelligently as well as correctly.

We knew how much we made and where we gained or lost. At least, we tried not to deceive ourselves.

Opportunism

None of us ever dreamed of the magnitude of what proved to be the later expansion. We did our day's work as we met it, looking forward to what we could see in the distance and keeping well up to our opportunities, but laying our foundations firmly.

Fortune Building

[*Rockefeller built his stake in Standard Oil through consistent purchases of stock, in up times and down. Many of his early partners and others were known to deride his unshakable faith in the stock.*]

If I may be pardoned for making a personal reference, the writer of these notes was regarded as being extremely sanguine and was often opposed in his movements for forward movement and large expenditure, and was always ready to give cash for stock. This he continued to do, day by day, week by week, month by month, year by year. And not a few there were who expected that sooner or later he might swamp himself, and he is very grateful to state that it turned out better than he dreamed of.

It is but fair here to state that in making these purchases, he did not "go it blind." He carefully used his lead pencil, carefully surveyed his earnings and the depreciation, did not forget the liability of the burning of the works, taking into account of the losses, not forgetting the increase in working capital, and setting aside reasonable amounts to provide finally for the costs of many of the worthless old plants which more and more with the years were being less and less of value.

Opportunism

[*In 1921, a writer interviewing Rockefeller quoted a passage from Ida Tarbell's* History of Standard Oil. *The quote related to the increased rates (or "discriminations") that a large shipper such as Standard Oil could insist that railroads impose on other refiners. Tarbell's book, first published in 1904, portrayed John Rockefeller as vicious opportunist. Rockefeller, who respected Tarbell's knowledge, if not her conclusions, never responded to the book in public, assuring himself that time would judge him more kindly. In his response to the reporter's question, posed during a private conversation, he revealed his view of his opportunism.*]

Reporter [quoting]: "He (Mr. Rockefeller) was willing to array himself against the combined better sentiment of a whole industry, to oppose a popular movement aimed at righting an injustice, so revolting to one's sense of fair play as that of railroad discriminations—"

JDR [interrupting]: "A whole industry! What does she mean? In other words, she would say: 'He was willing to make the best freight arrangement he could, although the others did not want him to make a specially good freight arrangement for himself?' Under the conditions, what would Miss Tarbell have done?"

Realistic Thinking

Study diligently your capital requirements, and fortify yourself fully to cover possible set-backs, because you can absolutely count on meeting set-backs. Be sure that you are not deceiving yourself at any time about actual conditions.

Focus

We devoted ourselves exclusively to the oil business and its products. The company never went into outside ventures, but kept to the enormous task of perfecting its own organization. We educated our own men; we trained many of them from boyhood; we strove to keep them loyal by providing them full scope for their ability; they were given opportunities to buy stock, and the company itself helped them to finance their purchases. Not only here in America, but all over the world, our young men were given chances to advance themselves, and the sons of the old partners were welcomed to the councils and responsibilities of the administration. I may say that the company has been in all its history, and I am sure it is at present, a most happy association of busy people.

[*"Outside ventures" weren't the only distractions for Rockefeller. Once he became symbolic of big business in America, he was frequently the subject of damning articles and editorials. He seems to have been impervious, as he maintained in recalling a conversation with Henry Flagler.*]

Mr. Flagler used to say to me, "John, you have a hide like

a rhinoceros!" But that wasn't it. In the first place, a man cannot concentrate his faculties at the same time on two opposite things: and I was concentrated upon extending and developing and perfecting our business, rather than to stop by the wayside and squabble with slanderers.

※

[*In this excerpt from a letter to his associate, Frederick Gates, April 3, 1905, Rockefeller discusses his views regarding a man threatening to make a public accusation against Standard Oil.*]

While I would not desire to offend him, I would not have us deviate from our course of doing just what we think is wisest and best, and what is true in this case will be true in every case, regardless of all that may be said in the newspapers.

We shall survive and live and prosper when these wicked men shall have seen the error of their ways. I think good will come out of all this agitation, and I do not at all shrink back from it, but in any and every view of the question, my great desire is that we keep the brakes on, and do not go off half-cocked.

Humility

As our successes began to come, I seldom put my head upon the pillow at night without speaking a few words to myself in this wise:

"Now a little success, soon you will fall down, soon you will be overthrown. Because you have got a start, you think you are quite a merchant; look out, or you will lose your head—go steady." These intimate conversations with myself, I am sure, had a great influence on my life. I was afraid I could not stand my prosperity, and tried to teach myself not to get puffed up with any foolish notions.

Reputation

The Standard has not now, and never did have a royal road to supremacy, nor is its success due to any one man, but to the multitude of able men who are working together. If the present managers of the company were to relax efforts, allow the quality of their product to degenerate, or treat their customers badly, how long would their business last? About as long as any other neglected business. To read some of the accounts of the affairs of the company, one would think that it had such a hold on the oil trade that the directors did little but come together and declare dividends.

Do you think this trade has been accomplished by anything but hard work?

Cooperation

It is not always the easiest of tasks to induce strong, forceful men to agree. It has always been our policy to hear patiently and discuss frankly until the last shred of evidence is on the table, before trying to reach a conclusion and to decide finally upon a course of action.

Debate

It's a pity to get a man into a place in an argument where he is defending a position instead of considering the evidence. His calm judgement is apt to leave him, and his mind is for the time being closed and only obstinacy remains.

Discretion

[*Standard Oil was an innovative business, constantly on the lookout for ways to improve operations and increase profits. Rockefeller worried that the company's competitors would copy its methods . . . if they knew about them.*]

We knew that we had not a patent on our many methods of saving, eliminating waste, in every department of our business. And we were not beating a gong to call those bankers or anyone else into this field; we were not calling to them: "Come on, gentlemen! Here is the gold mine waiting for you! The way to make money is thus and so!"

Here is an example of one of the ways in which we achieved certain economies and gained real advantage. Fires are always to be reckoned with in oil refining and storage, as we learned by dear experience, but in having our plants distributed all over the country the unit of risk and possible loss was minimized. No one fire could ruin us, and we were able thus to establish a system of insuring ourselves. Our reserve fund which provided for this insurance could not be wiped out all at once, as might be the case with a concern having all its plants together or near each other. Then we studied and perfected our organization to prevent fires, improving our appliances and plans year after year until the profit on this insurance became a very considerable item in the Standard earnings.

It can easily be seen that this saving in insurance, and minimizing the loss by fire affected the profits, not only in refining, but touched many other associated enterprises: the manufacture of by-products, the tanks and steamers, the pumping stations, etc.

John Rockefeller at Work: Secrecy

[*Even in private business affairs, Rockefeller was careful and furtive. Here is a memo from Rockefeller's secretary to Frederick Gates, a ranking executive in the management of the Rockefeller investments.*]

Sept. 21, 1904
Dear Mr. Gates:

Mr. Rockefeller has requested me to send you five or six code words which will mean "Buy", and five or six others to mean "Sell". These are to be known to you exclusively. The reason he wants so many different code words for the same word is that there may be greater variety in the messages to and from you. The code words are as follows:

BUY:- Adverse. Beneath. Flippant. Grape. Rome. Tincture.

SELL:- Oriental. Destroy. Hedged. Master. Soda. Wisdom.

Whenever an open message is sent to you, "Sell" will mean <u>buy,</u> and vice versa.

Philanthropy

[*In addition to making donations totaling over $510 million to educational, medical, and religious charities, Rockefeller took a personal interest in helping any of his old neighbors from upstate New York or Cleveland who fell on hard times. In offering the benefit of his thinking, he was probably even more generous than in simply handing over a check. This letter was written to a social worker who contacted Rockefeller.*]

Sept. 19, 1904

Dear Mr. Lang,

I have yours of Sept. 16th in reference to the affairs of Mrs. Rowena Sawyer Haskins, and I am pleased that you went into the case so thoroughly. I have not known much about her for many years, but I went to school with her when I was ten years of age in a little country school house in the state of New York. There are others of those school days whom I look after and I do not know just what is best in her case. Those sons ought to take care of her, and I am glad that you are looking after the unemployed one.

If you think best, we might pay the taxes ($57.75) and interest ($21.32), $79.07 in all. I assume the title is in her name. If it is not, would it not be well to have it placed in her name, so that if this boy goes wrong he cannot squander his share? She is evidently boarding him, without charge, now. If the other boy is worthy, it would eventually be of some help to him.

Since writing the above, I am wondering if it would be well for us to make a condition in paying the above taxes and interest, that the boy remaining at home should pay his board.

Planning

Be sure that before you go into an enterprise you see your way clear to stay through to a successful end. Look ahead. It is surprising how many bright business men go into important undertakings with little or no study of the controlling conditions they risk their all upon.

Self-appraisal

My ideas of business are no doubt old-fashioned, but the fundamental principles do not change from generation to generation, and sometimes I think that our quick-witted American business men, whose spirit and energy are so splendid, do not always sufficiently study the real underlying foundations of business management. I have spoken of the necessity of being frank and honest with oneself about one's own affairs: many people assume that they can get away from the truth by avoiding thinking about it, but the natural law is inevitable, and the sooner it is recognized, the better.

M o n e y

I believe it is a religious duty to get all the money you can, fairly and honestly; to keep all you can, and to give away all you can.

Henry Ford II, age twenty-nine, with his grandparents Henry and Clara Ford in 1946. Henry and Clara are sitting in the very first Ford car, a handmade 1896 model.

Henry Ford II
1919–1987

Henry Ford II was responsible for the rebirth of the Ford Motor Co. after World War II, a feat as brilliant in its sheer urgency as his grandfather's founding of the company had been in its own faultless timing forty years before. While much of Ford Motor was sadly antiquated by 1945, its management was downright medieval, ruling in shrouded, often violent ways. The company was losing money and expected to collapse when Henry II took command at the age of twenty-six. Stepping in all alone at first, Henry II hired the kind of managers who could turn Ford into one of the nation's most advanced corporations. Under the young boss, they did so, in a matter of only a half-dozen years. Later, Henry II turned his attentions to industry overall, leading it to acknowledge deeper responsibilities within society. A forthright man, Henry Ford II helped define new attitudes in business by building a modern corporation out of the bricks and grit of the past.

In July of 1940, Henry Ford announced that once he retooled his company for defense work, he would produce airplanes at the rate of one thousand a day. It was an astounding prediction, but no one doubted that Ford just might be able to do it. In the mid-1920s, he had turned out cars at the rate of 7,000 a day. The Ford Motor Company had set standards in production that had jolted world industry, although Henry Ford himself cared less about that than the fact that production had always been the profit center of his company. On his factory floors, shrill efficiency combined with hard demands on labor to pour forth cars as though from a tap.

In fact, there was not much more to the $1 billion Ford Motor Company than production and Mr. Henry Ford. In the accepted sense, there was no management staff. There was no accounting, no planning, and only a negligible sales office.

Engineering, research, and styling were also inconsequential. Henry Ford took care of all of those things as needed—or as he cared to. With no outside stockholders, he and his immediate family owned the company outright, and he was the one to speak for the family: his wife, Clara; their only child, Edsel; Edsel's wife, Eleanor, and their children, Henry II, Benson, Josephine, and William.

No one knew where the company lost money—or lost the opportunity to save money. The simple arithmetic that revealed the company's annual earnings only showed that it was barely breaking even by 1940, with a profit of less than one percent of sales. Ford, once the leading automaker in the country, was by then a fading third. Wartime contracts might have given the company a chance to solve its problems, except that in the midst of the war years, two things failed at Ford Motor Co.: production and Mr. Henry Ford.

In 1942–1943, Ford fell woefully behind in its wartime quotas, especially those for its ambitious B-24 bomber program, causing genuine concern in Washington. Meanwhile, Henry Ford, who was seventy-eight when the war began in 1941, suffered a series of strokes that marked the decline of his mental powers. General Motors and Chrysler surveyed his ghastly old empire and could hardly wait for the war to be over so that they could put the Ford Motor Co. out of its misery in their own carnivorous way. The War Department, however, appraised the situation at Ford and insisted on action. In 1943, the secretary of the navy sent a letter to twenty-six-year-old Lt. Henry Ford II and told him to go home: His country needed him. It needed him far more in Dearborn, Michigan than in the navy.

Had the secretary of the navy looked at resumes rather than bloodlines in searching for someone to bolster the future of Ford Motor, Henry Ford II might not have survived the first cut. To all appearances, he had never been anything more than a rather fleshy rich kid from Detroit. He had been over to Europe and off to college without evincing much of an interest in anything in either place. In fact, he had flunked out just before graduating from Yale University with his class in 1940. The same year, he married Anne McDonnell and the ceremony was covered in the pages of *Life* magazine, a social event of national interest—Henry II's greatest distinction as a youth was his wedding.

As a young man, Henry II was a charmer: That's all anyone expected of him at the time. Respectful of his elders, easygoing with his pals, he was well liked. In the measured way that would draw him to great heights later, he was also obedient—not to others, but to the expectations of others. "There is nothing I ache to do," he said soon after his return from the navy, "for I learned long ago you are too easily disappointed by some change in plans." Those who took to calling him "Prince Henry" at the time were not so far off in describing someone in whom inner ambition had been chased away by duty a long time before.

Upon arriving in Dearborn in the autumn of 1943, Henry II didn't know much more than anyone else about the Ford Motor Co. His grandfather was at least as secretive around the family as he was with most others. In fact, the profound failing of Henry Ford's career—and perhaps his life, too—was his ruination of his own son, Edsel (Henry II's father), a competent executive who was isolated, spied upon, and belittled until the time of his death in 1943.

The man old Henry Ford did trust was his former bodyguard, Harry Bennett, who ran the company as though it were the setting of a Damon Runyon short story in which thugs and ex-wrestlers undertake to manage an industrial empire. Anyone—with one frail exception—could see that Harry Bennett couldn't run a major corporation.

When Henry II showed up in Dearborn, he was nothing more than his father's replacement, in everything that implied. He wasn't even given a desk, let alone responsibilities, during his first year. As he later recalled, however, without a desk, he was forced to tour the facilities endlessly, meeting people and seeing for himself how things were done. It was a habit he kept all through his career, and he never visited a Ford facility of any sort without scheduling time to walk the work spaces, looking and talking, just as he had at his start. In 1943, as the uncertain heir apparent, Henry II considered that his first job was to rid the company of Harry Bennett. Harry Bennett seems to have felt the same way about Henry II—and Bennett had strength on his side, both within the factory and in Henry Ford's loyalty.

In the course of his chats and wanderings, Henry II identified a handful of men he could trust. As far as possible, he engendered the respect of his ailing grandfather. He maneuvered slowly on those two fronts, proving that he was not going to be a weakling. That done and that proved, he turned to his mother.

As Edsel's widow, Eleanor commanded the sympathy of Edsel's mother, Clara. With Henry growing more senile and even more paranoid every day, Clara finally convinced him to turn the company over to his grandson. On September 23, 1945, Henry signed a company order naming Henry II president of the Ford Motor Co. Within a week Harry Bennett was banished.

The company over which Henry II presided, at twenty-eight, employed 130,000 people at 14 assembly plants around the country, including the largest manufacturing facility in the world, the River Rouge factory in Dearborn. The company also counted major facilities on every continent except Antarctica. It had large cash reserves, having ultimately fulfilled $4 billion in war contracts, and it would surprise the industry by being the first company in production with a postwar car (though manufactured to a pre-war design). Nonetheless, in 1945–1946, the company was losing $9 million a month, or $300 for each of those cars to exit the factory.

At the start, Henry II fired thousands of employees left over from Ford's dark ages, and he did so personally in many cases, without hiding his actions behind anyone else's shoulders. When he heard that one executive kept a rogue's lair for himself in the River Rouge factory, he found it and broke down the door with a club: The executive was soon fired. In fact, Henry II broke through locks and let in light throughout the whole company. In the new atmosphere, so different from the old, reporters were invited to ask questions and executives were told to answer freely.

Husky and tall, standing six feet, Henry Ford II had a square face with intense blue eyes. He smiled readily—a beaming, toothy smile—but never without cause, as an admiring reporter pointed out. If someone cornered him too closely, he was likely to respond with a question—a natural tactic, because it seemed that asking questions always interested him far more than his own answers did.

Henry II's management style was not painted of broad strokes on big issues, as might be expected of a man dropped onto the top of a huge company after a life of isolation in the upper class. Instead, he took responsibility for important issues by attending on his account to all kinds of the smallest ones. His minute interest in the company's every activity was not appreciated by everyone. Late in his career he said, "My problem is, I'm told, that I get into too many details, and therefore I'm mucking up everybody else's water."

In 1945, as the newly appointed president at Ford, Henry II was well aware of one significant fact: He didn't know much about business. All that he brought with him was a great respect for what he didn't know, an attribute even more valuable than knowledge itself to a manager in the purest sense.

In constructing a complete, multileveled executive staff

from scratch, Henry II's most important selection was Ernest Breech as executive vice president. Breech was a former General Motors executive who was suited to the simultaneous challenges of jump-starting Ford's own automaking engine and of instituting a corporate structure to replicate the one at GM. In fact, even while Henry II was telling anyone who asked that his corporate goal was simply, "to beat Chevrolet," he kept a copy of GM's organizational chart on his desk. To that end, Breech and Ford hired other GM transfers, and they instituted controls and processes intended to reduce risk while (according to the master plan) enhancing incentive.

The new team constructed seven divisions out of the ether that had been the previous corporate organization: Within two years, the finance department alone employed 4,000 people.

As Henry II built Ford into a corporation with productive layers of management, the company proved that it could still build cars: Its homegrown 1949 Custom was a runaway success. It also started the momentum that resulted four years later with Ford's passing Chevrolet in sales.

With the company's prosperity, Henry II's own increased self-confidence became apparent in his treatment of Ford Motor Co.'s leading executives. Ernie Breech's dismissal in 1961 was only the first of several controversies that made Henry II seem less the organization man of modern times than a revived version of his grandfather.

Henry II, however, was not a version of anybody's grandfather in the mid-1960s, when he was openly described in the press as a "swinger." After living quietly and conventionally with his family during his first decades as Ford's president, he began to have a good time with an international circuit of friends, including a new wife and then, after that, another one.

He let himself go, according to many who disapproved, including his mother. At fifty and then at sixty, Henry II was not becoming more staid, but less so. However, he had had an unusual life. Saving a business (that employed 130,000) is not the same as building one; the pressure bears down hardest at the start and then eases up, instead of the other way around. Perhaps that is one explanation, if one is needed. Another might be that, just like his grandfather, Henry II was a free spirit who didn't always care what other people thought.

In 1979, though, Henry Ford II did something that his grandfather could not have done. He retired, leaving the company to the organization he had built.

In the quotes that follow, Henry Ford II discusses some of the problems facing the head of a big company—he was never anything else—with his perspectives on productivity and morale. He was committed to practical and appropriate ways by which corporations could contribute solutions to some of society's problems, and he comments on the role business ought to take in controversial issues. Henry Ford II looked at many national problems with a mixture of impatience and hopefulness—a practical businessman, but a liberal-minded one.

Henry Ford II

Progress

Progress comes from discontent, not from complacency. It would be a stagnant world if all young people knew as well as their elders do what can't be changed and shouldn't be changed.

Productivity

"Management productivity" is a more appropriate term than "labor productivity."

I am always puzzled to find union leaders speaking of "increased worker productivity," as though workers must sweat harder in order to produce more. Improved productivity means less human sweat, not more. Industrial productivity generally is increased through investment in better, more-efficient plants, better machinery, better methods and processes, better scheduling, and so on.

Profit Theory

Those of us who are in business management face the challenge of proving—not in words, but in deeds—that profit is good and more profit is better.

The idea that profit is good is difficult for many people to accept. The idea that higher profits are even better is still harder to accept. What the critics of profit see on the surface is that business aims, not at helping people, but at making profits through people. Their instincts tell them that one man's profit is another man's loss, and so they conclude that profit means exploitation. But experience is a better guide than instinct, and experience tells us that in a competitive economy businesses profit most from those ventures that best serve the general economic welfare.

Preparation

[*Ford's advice to people considering a career with a large corporation:*]

Never forget that specialized training alone is not enough. It may get you that first job; but if it is all you have to offer any employer, it may also bury you in that first job.

The greatest help of all to a young employee, as he seeks control of the variables that confront him, is his own flexibility of mind which allows him to accommodate to rapid social and

economic shifts that affect his company. It is important, therefore, that his mind be stored with knowledge acquired not just
during the formal educational period but afterward, too,
through experience and independent reading. Language and
marketing, literature and capital, philosophy and taxation, psy-
chology and manufacturing—the more the young man knows
of these and other branches of human knowledge, the more
effective his work will be and the faster he will grow.

Authority

[*On assuming the presidency at Ford, Henry II paid new respect
to mid-level managers.*]
   The man you work for day after day and year after year,
whether he's a foreman or superintendent or whatever, is the
one who represents the Company to you. He is the Company
to you. And if the man you work for gets pushed around by
his boss, gets orders issued to him with "never mind why,"
there's an awful good chance you are going to get pushed
around too.

Communication

Informed employees are more productive than uninformed
employees.

❀

Information about company objectives and accomplishments
should be made available to all. People want to know what the

other people they work with are doing and thinking. They want to know what "the score" is.

It is fairly easy for everybody to "know the score" when there are only fifty employees in a plant. But when thousands of employees work at assembly lines in a single plant they create a problem of communication which has not yet been effectively solved.

In an age in which the world prides itself on speed and efficiency in human communication it is absurd that we should not have been more successful in this field.

Social Conscience

[*In college at Yale, Henry Ford II switched from the engineering major selected for him by his family to studies in sociology. As head of Ford Motor, he would use that perspective to question the place of both a major corporation in society and the individual within a major corporation. In a 1969 speech, Ford termed the newly emerging corporate initiative in the area of social responsibility "the hidden revolution." In the 1960s, he was recognized as the leader of the new movement.*]

In seeking to serve social needs because it makes good business sense to do so, a corporation is doing what it knows how to do best.

It is clearly in the self-interest of business both to enlarge its markets and improve its work force by helping disadvantaged people to develop and employ their economic potential. Similarly, it is in the self-interest of business to help reduce dependency, frustration, crime, and conflict in the community. The costs of occasional civil disorder are impossible to overlook, but they are far smaller than the continuing costs of welfare, crime, preventable disease and ignorance. These costs are borne by business as well as by the rest of the community.

This then, is one aspect of the hidden revolution—the growing understanding that the profit motive is not an antisocial force acting against the community interest, but a very practical reason why business should help solve the social as well as the economic problems that beset our nation.

The idea that conscience and profit may actually be pulling in the same direction is difficult for some people to accept.

Business cannot solve the race problem, but each business can make sure that it does not discriminate.

Business cannot eliminate unemployment, but each business can do its competitive best to expand its own sales and employment. Business cannot stop inflation, but every business can strive for greater efficiency and lower costs.

Educational Investment

Technological progress, in short, is the key to the opportunity to earn a better life. To fulfill the promise of American life, we need, in addition, to make that opportunity an equal one. It will not be equal, and we will not be true to our dreams, as long as we fail to teach so many of our young people what they need to know to take their place in our advancing technology.

Unemployment

Providing a larger total number of jobs is only one of the things we need to do to solve the unemployment problem. Unemployment is too high, not only because we do not have enough jobs, but also because many of the unemployed are poorly qualified by skill and education to fill the jobs that are available.

Hiring

It is difficult to do good without being condescending and paternalistic on the one hand, and without perpetuating dependence and resentment on the other hand. To hire a man because he needs a job rather than because the job needs him, for example, is to assure him that he is useless.

Conversely, to help a man because it is in your own interest to help him, to hire him because you need his labor, is to treat him as an equal. In such a relationship, the message comes through loud and clear—the employer has confidence in the ability of the man he hires to earn his pay and stand on his own feet.

※

[An excerpt from a letter to all Ford supervisors, initiating a new equal opportunity priority at Ford Motor in 1967:]

The company's Detroit inner-city hiring program is one example of the new approach I am calling for. Its aim is not only to offer employment opportunities, but actively to invite the interest of people who would not normally come to us — not to screen *out* doubtful applicants but to screen *in* if possible — and not merely to hire, but to help them make the grade after they are hired.

Human Relations

If we can solve the problem of human relations in industrial production, I believe we can make as much progress toward lower costs during the next ten years as we made during the past quarter-century through the development of the machinery of mass-production.

Progress

When you think of the enormous progress of science over the last two generations, it's astonishing to realize that there is very little about the basic principles of today's automobiles that would seem strange and unfamiliar to the pioneers of our industry.

We in the United States have a problem, or, if you will, an opportunity — an opportunity to break away from technological traditions and to find really new and better ways of making really new and better products for the markets of the world. The slow and patient work of refining and improving on existing technology will always be important. But what we need even more than the refinement of old ideas is the ability to develop new ideas and put them to work.

※

[*Ford mentioned one example of a technological problem/opportunity in an interview in 1963, in which he was asked if the car had yet evolved to its fullest potential.*]

There are an awful lot of things that could be done, but you'd have to change the whole habit system of the driver. These are things you can't do in an evolutionary manner. For example, you don't have to have a steering wheel to drive a car, surprisingly enough. You can do it with buttons, just one finger, maybe by mechanical control—lots of possibilities.

[*"Where would you put your hands?" Ford was asked.*]

Well, that's the point. These are habits people have.

Energy

We're still living in a fool's paradise in this country. We have always thought that we could have an endless supply of cheap energy and we can't. We've got a major energy problem, but the American people don't believe it. We waste so much. We waste everything in this country.

Planning

America has many problems. But the time has come to curb our habit of turning problems into crises that require crash solutions.

Government Regulation

With the labyrinth of regulations, many in Washington and elsewhere find themselves possessed of a power greater in some respects than that of the Congress or state legislatures.

What the regulators evidently do not recognize is that they are forcing some fundamental changes in the structure of our economy. To the extent that some companies are unable to sustain the level of spending required by government regulation, they could find it necessary to cut back operations, reduce product lines or—at the extreme—simply go out of business. One automobile company has already dropped out of the heavy-truck business because, by its own account, it "could not keep pace with the growing list of government standards." Despite efforts by government throughout the years to prevent concentration in industry, the regulators are in fact bringing us to the point where only the largest companies can survive.

I don't know anybody or any group of people smart enough to mastermind and manipulate artificially our economy without doing much more harm than good.

Unions

Unions tend to [view social awareness as their private domain and to] resent sharply any poaching by business on that domain. The hapless businessman who publicly explores a novel economic idea risks having it hurled back at him across the bargaining table, doubled in spades and scarcely recognizable. If he then demurs, he stands publicly revealed as a welsher who won't put his money where his mouth is.

It's awfully hard to be farsighted with that big-union thumb in your eye.

Business Image

[In 1959, Ford concluded a speech at Yale University with an admonishment typical of his double-edged sword.]

Now let me admit that up to this point I have not said much that the boys down at the Union League Club would not applaud. Clamp down on the unions? Resist direct government interference in business? By all means, they would say. They might take issue with me, of course, for not having proposed a reduction of Federal Government activities and the federal budget to the levels of the Harding Administration.

But, if business can't come up with anything better than merely negative proposals, if it can't come up with a positive and workable program for a stronger and more dynamic economy, then it will certainly lose out in the political race with those who paint a more brilliant picture of the future, who offer action now—however ill-conceived it might be—and who appeal directly not only to the desire for more, but to commonly held, deep-seated American ideals.

Cooperation

A company needs to be constantly rejuvenated by the infusion of young blood. It needs smart young men with the imagination and the guts to turn everything upside down if they can. It also needs old fogies to keep them from turning upside down those things that ought to be right side up. Above all, it needs young rebels and old conservatives who can work together, challenge each other's views, yield or hold fast with equal grace, and continue after each hard-fought battle to respect each other as men and colleagues.

*Madame C.J. Walker taking her niece and two employees
for a ride in Indianapolis in 1912.
Madame Walker also took long automobile tours throughout
the country, leaving the driving to a chauffeur. In 1917, she
revisited the Louisiana plantation on which she'd grown up,
and saw the one-room shack she'd once called home.*

Madame C.J. Walker

1867–1919

Madame C.J. Walker was earning a few dollars a week as a washerwoman when she decided to go into another business, one with far greater opportunity. Within a dozen years, she was a millionaire, the first African-American woman to earn a fortune that size. Originating a line of high-quality hair products, along with the techniques to use them in professional haircare, Madame Walker created a system that made success stories of thousands of new entrepreneurs. Remarkably, the former washerwoman had had no previous training in business methods. She could not even read and write when she started the Madame C.J. Walker Manufacturing Co. in 1904. Yet Madame Walker made sure she learned everything she needed to know about standard business methods. Adding lessons from her own experience, she passed along what she knew to a generation of new business owners. In doing so, Madame Walker taught anyone who came in contact with her that ambition alone is indeed enough to start on.

$\mathcal{A}$s a little girl of eight or nine, Sarah Breedlove liked to sit in the evening by the waters of the Mississippi River, indulged by the fragrance of the trees that grew there: sassafras trees and sweet plums. Breedlove was an orphan, working with her older brother and sister on the Grand View plantation in northern Louisiana. Their parents had lived there under slavery through the Civil War and as sharecroppers afterward, working daily in the cotton fields, sleeping in a shack on the plantation. Freedom had barely changed their lot, yet few people in any part of history would leave as sweeping a definition of freedom as their youngest daughter, Sarah—Madame C.J. Walker.

Fevers periodically swept the delta region, and by the time Sarah Breedlove was seven, in 1874, both her parents were dead. Three years later, in the midst of a yellow fever outbreak, Sarah and her sister took refuge in Vicksburg, across the river in Mississippi, where they found household work. Even at ten, Sarah Breedlove was a good laundress. At fourteen, she married a laborer named Moses McWilliams, in part to escape the violence of the man her sister had married. Her life lit up with the birth of her daughter, A'Lelia, in 1885, and stayed lit: She was still calling A'Lelia "my darling baby" in the last letter she ever wrote. When A'Lelia was only two years old, Moses died and Sarah took her daughter to St. Louis for a new start, and more work as a laundress.

Sarah McWilliams handled her small earnings well enough that eventually she could afford to send A'Lelia through Knoxville College. At thirty-seven, she had created a gratifying story for herself out of a fairly dismal beginning. One might think she would declare herself a success, and wait for A'Lelia to take over the lead—or at least to pay for both their meals—ever afterward. But Sarah's sense of obligation didn't diminish.

"I was at my tubs one morning," Sarah later recalled, "with a heavy wash before me. As I bent over the washboard, and looked at my arms buried in soapsuds, I said to myself, 'What are you going to do when you grow old and your back gets stiff? Who is going to take care of your little girl?' This set me to thinking, but with all my thinking I couldn't see how I, a poor washerwoman, was going to better my condition."

Since the prospects of becoming rich enough to support A'Lelia seemed bleak, Sarah put them aside and worried instead about her hair—of which there was not very much, because large patches of it had fallen out.

Under the mantle of slavery, African-Americans had had no choice but to wear their hair in its most natural way, which was in most cases nappy, growing straight out into a rounded shape. For several generations afterward, that style continued to be associated with slavery, and many black Americans looked for other ways to wear their hair. Whether they wanted to straighten it—the source of bitter debate through the years—or simply style it, most of the pomades then on the market were harsh enough to be detrimental. As a result, baldness was common among black women in the late 1800s, though poor diet may have contributed as well.

Sarah McWilliams was one of those afflicted, and she didn't like it any more than the rest. One night in 1905, she had a dream in which "a big black man appeared and told me what to mix up for my hair." She followed his advice, in general terms, and started to regrow her hair. By then, other companies had begun to market creditable hair products to the black community, but Sarah was convinced that she was on the verge of creating a superior product. With her daughter, A'Lelia, in her final year of college, Sarah moved to Denver, where her late brother's family lived. By the time she arrived, she only had $1.50 with which to start her new business.

After taking a job as a cook, Sarah started the experiments that led to her first product: "Wonderful Hair Grower." Bottling it herself, she walked through black neighborhoods, making sales door-to-door.

Although Denver wasn't heavily populated with African-Americans, Sarah managed to spark steady interest in Wonderful Hair Grower. Whenever she accumulated profits from door-to-door sales, she invested them in newspaper advertising to build a mail-order trade, adding other products all the while. Her advisor on advertising was a newspaper sales representative named Charles J. Walker, whom she married in 1906. Adding a continental form of address for a bit of flair, Sarah McWilliams became known as Madame C.J. Walker.

To Mr. C.J. Walker's annoyance, Sarah would not consider his best business advice, which was to slow down and be contented with the mail-order trade. After only one year, that side of the business was already generating a good middle-class income. By then, however, Madame Walker had a different idea entirely. She had found one degree of success by identifying a commercial market for high-quality hair products aimed at black Americans. Next, she spotted an opportunity at least as significant: In fact, she spotted many thousands of them.

With only a few exceptions, black women at the time were relegated to two jobs—fieldhands or domestics. Sarah had done both, and knew it was honest work but poorly paid. Many black women were as desperate to better themselves as she had once been. Madame Walker taught them the hairdressing and business skills they would need to start beauty salons.

Through booklets, conventions, and personal appearances, Madame Walker taught her sales agents the basic elements of business, including salesmanship, bookkeeping, and promotion. She had learned those skills on her own, and continued to educate herself on a range of topics; she was particularly interested in history.

Madame C.J. Walker exuded quiet self-confidence, a quality she sold into the climate of her times, just as she sold her beauty products. Her great-great-granddaughter, A'Lelia Bundles, author of *My Mother's Mothers: The Legacy of Madame C.J. Walker,* has written, "She taught her agents to create an atmosphere in which their customers would feel pampered and valued. . . . For black women, who rarely found themselves valued in American society, the psychological lift was enormous."

Within twelve years of starting her own company—within twelve-and-a-half of scrubbing laundry at her washtubs—Madame C.J. Walker had a national reputation for integrity, an income of a quarter-million dollars a year, and a mansion overlooking the Hudson River. All of that impressed her, however, only when it led others to follow her example by finding in business a place where no one can be stopped.

In the words that follow, Madame C.J. Walker can almost be heard speaking as she advised others to do, pleasantly, calmly, and with a measured responsiveness. Though she also advised against boasting, she described her own success in business frankly in hopes of inspiring other people, especially disenfranchised people, to start their own businesses. A number of Madame Walker's "commandments" are included, with succinct advice for the business owner.

Madame C.J. Walker

Confidence

If I have accomplished anything in life, it is because I have been willing to work hard. I never yet started anything doubtingly.

Self-sufficiency

[*In 1917, a reporter for* The New York Times *visited Madame Walker at her newly completed mansion overlooking the Hudson River in New York State, and asked her about her background.*]

   When, a little more than twelve years ago, I was a washerwoman, I was considered a good washerwoman and laundress. I am proud of that fact. At times I also did cooking, but work as I would, I seldom could make more than $1.50 a day. I got my start by giving myself a start. It is often the best way.

Push

I believe in push, and we must push ourselves.

Opportunity

I am not merely satisfied in making money for myself, for I am endeavoring to provide employment for hundreds of the women of my race. I had little or no opportunity when I started out in life, having been left an orphan . . . I had to make my own living and my own opportunity! But I made it!

Getting Started

I began, of course, in a most modest way. I made house-to-house canvasses among people of my race, and after awhile I got going pretty well, though I naturally encountered many obstacles and discouragements before I finally met with real success.

Stock Market Trading

I do not believe in taking chances, and I have never played the stock market.

Commandments

[*Madame Walker's* "*Commandments*" *were printed in* The Madame C.J. Walker Schools Text Book of Beauty Culture *several years after her death.*]

- Love your business. This will lighten your labor, make you forget the clock, bring improvement to your patrons and bring compensation to you.
- Do not be boastful but be sure of your ability.
- Go about your work silently, accurately and with confidence.
- Do not cut prices or hold enmity against your competitor. Remember every knock is a boost.
- Do not neglect to advertise. If you do not your competitor will.

Philanthropy

I am not a millionaire, but I hope to be some day, not because of the money, but because I could do so much then to help my race.

My object in life is not simply to make money for myself or to spend it on myself in dressing or running around in an automobile, but I love to use a part of what I make in trying to help others.

[Madame C.J. Walker was worth over a million dollars by 1919, and made major contributions to African-American colleges, in addition to her support of progressive political causes and charities.]

Wringing Success Out of Opportunity

I found, by experience, that it pays to be honest and straight-forward in all your dealings.

In the second place, the girls and women of our race must not be afraid to take hold of business endeavor and, by patient industry, close economy, determined effort and close application to business, wring success out of a number of business opportunities that lie at their doors.

Building an Organization

I started in business eight years ago with one-dollar-and-a-half cash capital. I put that into business, since which time, in addition to putting on the road to success and giving employment to more than 1,000 women who are now making all the way from $5, $10, and even as high as $15 a day, my income has increased from that time until it now amounts to $34,000 a year.

Self-image

I am not ashamed of my past; I am not ashamed of my humble beginning. Don't think because you have to go down in the wash-tub that you are any less a lady!

Reputation

I attribute my success to honesty of purpose, determined effort, the real merit of my preparations and the fact that I am not and never have been "close-fisted," for all who know me will tell you that I am a liberal hearted woman.

Promotions

[*In 1912, Madame Walker attended the convention of the National Negro Business League in Chicago, where she wanted to speak about the success of her business. The head of the organization, the eminent Booker T. Washington, was skeptical about the role of women as business leaders and he discouraged her efforts. On the last day of the proceedings, Madame Walker simply appeared on the podium and confronted Washington by saying, "Surely you are not going to shut the door in my face." He had no choice but to step aside and let her continue. A reporter made meticulous notes on her impromptu speech.*]

I feel that I am in a business that is a credit to the womanhood of our race. I am a woman who started in business seven years ago with only $1.50. I went into a business that is despised, that is criticised and talked about by everybody—the business of growing hair. They did not believe such a thing could be done, but I have proven beyond the question of a doubt that I do grow hair! . . .

I have been trying to get before you business people and tell you what I am doing. I am a woman that came from the cotton fields of the South; I was promoted from there to the wash-tub (laughter); then I was promoted to the cook kitchen, and from there I promoted myself into the business of manufacturing hair goods and preparations. Everybody told me I was making a mistake by going into this business, but I know how to grow hair as well as I know how to grow cotton.

And I will state in addition that during the last seven years I have bought a piece of property valued at Ten Thousand Dollars. (Prolonged applause.) I have built my own factory on my own ground, 38 × 208 feet; I employ in that factory seven people, including a bookkeeper, a stenographer, a cook and a house girl. (Prolonged applause mingled with laughter.) I own my own automobile and runabout. (Prolonged applause.) Please don't applaud—just let me talk! (Laughter.)

Worry

The most hideous monster in the pathway of beauty and success is worry. Worry produces anger and mental turmoil . . .

Let us banish worry.

Initiative

Don't sit down and wait for the opportunities to come. You have to get up and make them for yourselves.

A.P. Giannini, founder of the Bank of America, in about 1940. Refusing to become a millionaire, he would give away large sums whenever his fortune approached the $1 million mark. Giannini's favored charities were predominantly educational and medical. He also supported orphanages operated by various religious denominations.

A.P. Giannini
1870–1949

A.P. Giannini was the founder of two vast financial institutions, the Bank of America and Transamerica Corporation, yet he spent the first part of his career as a San Francisco vegetable broker. Entering the field of finance in 1904 with a single storefront bank in San Francisco, Giannini was to become a leading proponent of branch banking, a concept barely even known at the time. Perhaps because of his unlikely start, his thinking clashed with that of other bankers. But it coincided spectacularly with the needs of customers. Giannini devoted much of his career to battling other banks and regulators in order to establish his belief that branch banking would add to—not decrease—financial stability. Before he was finished with his career, the Bank of America was the largest bank in the world. Catering especially to small-time customers, Giannini changed the image of banking in America, doing more than anyone else to turn the perception of banks from fortresses of the rich to financial engines to be used by all.

*I*n February of 1931, Amadeo Peter Giannini checked into a clinic in Bad-Gastein, Austria, racked with pain from a condition called polyneuritis. He was sixty years old but looked much older, lying in bed and unable to so much as hold a pen. For months, Giannini confined himself to his room, surrounded by members of his family, as waves of specialists arrived and left, trying in vain to help the old man.

Without any experience in finance, Giannini had founded the Bank of America in San Francisco twenty-five years before, forging it into the largest bank on the Pacific coast. A revolutionary in his field, Giannini insisted that banks should not be granite storehouses, concentrating power in big cities, but that they should be hubs within a far-reaching system. A system of *branches:* The very word was anathema to bankers and regulators used to banking as it had always been. Undaunted, Giannini insisted that branches were "the only way a small town can get the resources, brain power and equipment of a billion-dollar bank." Catering to the small-time customer, Giannini became a folk hero: the nation's first populist banker, and probably its only one.

In order to expand into other regions and into other areas of finance, Giannini formed Transamerica Corporation as a holding company in 1928. He had initiated his revolution in branch banking on the West Coast, but he intended to spread that revolution from coast to coast through Transamerica.

The stock market crash of 1929 stalled the most grandiose of Giannini's plans for Transamerica, but even afterward, he felt it was on track in his push for nationwide banking. He also felt exhausted, and was already suffering from periodic bouts of polyneuritis. In 1930, he turned his companies over to a cadre of handpicked executives.

The rise of Giannini's empire in California may have been steep, but the concentration of power in American banking remained in New York. And in New York, the power was concentrated in "the corner," as J.P. Morgan & Co. was known. (The bank was headed at the time by J.P. Morgan Jr.) As an unwritten rule, but an accepted reality, all important banking activity had to be approved by the corner—an institution that happened to represent everything A.P. Giannini detested about big banking. His bank—his very career—had been built in contradiction to entrenched privilege and closed-door dealings, and especially to disdain for outsiders. Nonetheless, A.P. acquiesced to the corner's preferences in nearly all matters. He considered that he had been particularly adroit in choosing a Wall Street banker named Elisha Walker as his successor at Transamerica.

The plan went drastically awry. Manipulated by speculators, the price of Transamerica stock plummeted in 1930. Walker did little to protect the company, a fact that made Giannini immediately suspicious of his loyalties. Yet A.P. no longer had either the position or the strength to exert influence. Dejected and sick, he left with his wife for Bad-Gastein—an Alpine town located a world away from San Francisco's Montgomery Street banking community.

In June, Elisha Walker announced that he was breaking up Transamerica, selling off its assets, in order to save it from ruin. At best, he was in the throes of panic, taking action before the situation deteriorated even further. At worst, he was in league with the Morgan corner and others who coveted

Transamerica's undervalued assets. A.P. suspected the latter and called the plan a "betrayal."

He helplessly absorbed each wave of bad news at the Austrian clinic. While he tried to regain his strength, reports in the New York press praised the Walker initiative, dismissing Giannini as the exiled architect of a house of cards. By fall, Walker and the other executives were confidently making preparations to sell Transamerica's properties. Then something shocking happened.

A.P. Giannini was spotted in California.

Traveling under an assumed name, Giannini had returned home by way of Canada, giving his opposition no advance warning. One of the most humane people ever to enter business—where his customers and shareholders were concerned—he was also one of the most pugnacious men ever to enter any field. "I thrive on obstacles," he once said. Wall Street and the corner were arrayed against his return; so was the banking establishment, and so were the managers of his own company. Turning to the shareholders, Giannini initiated a proxy fight like no other before or since. Folk hero that he was, he drew thousands—sometimes even tens of thousands— of people to rallies staged throughout the West Coast. For those who attended, it was not merely a matter of Giannini versus Walker, but of the old East versus *their* new West, of faceless big business versus their own neighborly bank.

For over three months, the two sides campaigned hard for the 15 million available proxy votes, a fight covered in the daily press as though it were a political contest.

On February 15, 1932, the votes were counted. A.P. Giannini, having started from a standstill five months before, was named on sixty-three percent of the proxies. In his mind, he had resoundingly settled the question of who owned his company. The shareholders did.

A.P. Giannini was born in San Jose, California in 1870, the son of Italian immigrants. Because he was long associated with Northern California's Italian-American community, strangers frequently assumed that he spoke with an accent. He did—but it certainly wasn't broken English. He spoke with a long Western drawl, picked up during his childhood in the farmlands. Joining relatives in the produce business after leaving school at thirteen, A.P. worked in the single-minded way that would become his trademark, and retired comfortably at the age of thirty-one. A few years later, he and his wife, Clorinda, inherited a share in a small bank. Appalled by its methods, Giannini stormed out in 1904 and scraped together just enough money from friends and relatives to start the Bank of Italy (to be known as the Bank of America after 1930). Perhaps because of his unlikely background, Giannini's thinking would constantly clash with that of other bankers. With the needs of customers, however, it coincided spectacularly.

Giannini was a large man, standing six-foot-four with a broad, fleshy frame. He always wore a mustache, though his small, sharp blue eyes were the aspect of his face that most people remembered. They also remembered the volume of his voice. "Nobody knew why he wanted to go to the expense of a telephone. You could hear his voice from the ferry building to Twin Peaks," said a fellow banker, referring to two California landmarks. In person, Giannini was uninhibited, frank, and more than a bit volatile.

"I'm a fellow when I have an idea I never wait, but always act on it at once," he said, in a typical spill of words. He was right.

Even after the Bank of America took its rank as the world's largest bank in the 1940s, Giannini's desk remained out in the open on the bank floor. He maintained standing orders that anyone — anyone at all — could come to see him, from a shareholder with a question, to a fisherman looking for a loan, to all of those with more standard business for a bank president. It was his preference not to shield himself from the actual business of his business.

Giannini undoubtedly loved power, yet he had no use of his own for a large fortune. In fact, he set a personal goal of *never* becoming a millionaire, and insisted on drawing a salary of just one dollar per year after 1924.

A financier, a booster, a bruising adversary, Giannini changed the image of banking in America. At a time when commercial banks were widely despised as the domain of the most privileged citizens of a town, a state, or the nation, the Bank of America was something different. Each branch was specifically charged with providing careful service to the very smallest of customers. And the bank's executives had to be mindful that they answered to thousands of small shareholders; the founder-chairman, who certainly did not answer to anyone else, was quick to remind them of it.

At the time of Giannini's death in 1949, the combined assets of the Bank of America and Transamerica exceeded $7 billion; the two were then the world's largest bank and the nation's largest holding company, respectively. A.P. Giannini, whose bank and its stock had made millionaires out of so many working-class Californians, left a surprisingly modest estate of $480,000. A few years earlier, when he realized that his fortune was drawing precariously close to the $1 million mark due to the accrual of company bonuses, he donated $500,000 to charity, just in the nick of time.

In the words that follow, A.P. Giannini displays his unique personality—at any rate, unique and unexpected in a master financier. Where others in his field might cultivate a bland exterior, Giannini is plain-spoken and sometimes gruff. Where they might be, perchance, selfish inside, he is truly a man of the people. Giannini's personality makes a point all by itself, but in his remarks he cuts much that is superfluous out of the business day and also discusses adversity, from which he always drew the greatest of strength.

A.P. *Giannini*

Energy

Work does not wear me out. It buoys me up.

Focus

It's no trick to run any business if a man has the intelligence and industry to concentrate on the job. The great trouble with most men is that they scatter too much. A few men can go into many things and succeed, but they are few.

Concentration

I have always gone in for concentration.

I have interested myself only in things of interest to me in my business. I have avoided loading my mind and my memory with stuff of no earthly use to me. I don't try to keep track of baseball records or golf championship doings or of the latest developments in any line wholly foreign to banking. When I arrange to put up a building, I don't try to become an expert judge of stones or other building materials. I don't, therefore, waste a great deal of time going over details. I know just what kind of a building I want and what facilities must be provided. The execution of the plans I leave to others whose business it is to be posted on such matters.

Expediency

[*A.P. learned his business on the front lines of finance, touring farms in Northern California and negotiating produce contracts.*]
Too many people waste time in useless ways. My sole object on these rounds was to induce growers and other "prospects" to give us business. I always came to the point just as quickly as I decently could. I wasn't a bit interested in any of the local gossip or scandal or in anything whatsoever not connected with my business. I had a clearcut object in view. And I went after that object as straight as I knew how. I have never believed in beating about the bush.

Office Efficiency

At the age of 56 and after 44 years in harness, I have yet to have anyone answer the telephone for me. I have had very little use for a private office. I have hardly had an assistant who might, in the accepted sense of the term, be called a private secretary.

I have found it quite possible to dispense with most of the trappings which many executives find necessary. Perhaps I do not impress people as much as I might. But of this I am convinced—I can accomplish more work without the trappings.

❧

[*Giannini was well known for shouting and for interrupting, habits that were motivated largely by expediency. During the course of a typical business morning, he could see as many as a hundred different people.*]

As president of the Bank of Italy I had my desk on an unpartitioned floor which is entirely given over to the major executives and their assistants. One advantage was that I could see those who were waiting to interview me. Frequently, if I was engaged in a long interview and knew someone waiting would only require a moment, I would beckon to him, taking the necessary time to attend to him from the longer interview.

Worry

We don't want on our staff anybody who worries. If a man gets into debt, we don't want him.

[*For the same reason, Giannini also made it a policy to fire anyone known to be having an extramarital affair.*]

Aggressiveness

[*Giannini was criticized for the gusto with which he solicited business for his bank, both personally and through advertising, long a taboo within the industry.*]

They used to say I was undignified. Old fogies!

❀

It was no secret that we wanted to make money and make the bank grow. And I cannot, for the life of me, see how going after business, as any mercantile firm would do, is undignified.

Fighting Pessimism

[*The Bank of Italy, which Giannini launched in a San Francisco storefront in 1904, was the nation's fourteenth-largest bank in 1930, the year it was renamed the Bank of America. One of those responsible for the fulfillment of the bank's potential was Attilio Giannini, A.P.'s brother. A practicing physician, Attilio was enlisted to oversee two lagging branches, one in the Gianninis' early hometown of San Jose and one on Market Street in San Francisco.*]

The Bank of Italy was launched and has had its remarkable record of growth on a policy of conservative yet energetic and enthusiastic optimism. The institution has never known and should never know the word, "failure," in any matter, large or small; nor will "cold feet" ever bring it enduring or any sort of success. Our flourishing San Jose and Market Street branches are pertinent illustrations of what "boosting" and constant optimistic demeanor accomplished for us in the face of trying and at times disheartening odds.

Age Discrimination

[*Late in his career, Giannini rejected a candidate for an execu-tive position at a branch on the basis of age. He immediately changed his mind.*]

That proves that I should retire. For a minute, I forgot that I was a good executive myself at 22.

Hiring

The gathering together of brainy executives I have always regarded as one of the most important parts of my job. I have always kept my eyes wide open for sprouting talent. For exam-ple, one youth caught my eye; I watched him as he developed into a lawyer; and then, when I figured he was ripe, I got him to become one of us. You can't afford to sit back and wait for talent to come to you. You have to be constantly on the look-out for it and then go out and lasso it.

Integrity

The main thing is to run your business absolutely straight. When you have a good, clean bank, absolutely unentangled in any speculative exploits, nothing can happen to you. When-ever banks fail, you find it is because of outside ventures or crookedness by someone inside the institution. No man, no bank, no business, should put itself into the grip of any one else. Failure usually comes from doing things that shouldn't have been done—often things of questionable ethics.

Service

Be ready to help people when they need it most. Get ready to yank them out of a hole. The glad hand is alright in sunshine, but it's the helping hand on a dark day that folks remember to the end of time.

Powerful People

Some men come to grow away from the people who helped make 'em. When they climb higher, they forget the old friends and reach out for new ones who, they think, will give them something different they haven't got. The big fellow doesn't give you a thing. You'll find a lot of the big guns will pay attention when they want something; they will use you when you get big enough for their purposes—and a lot of people fall for that stuff. The fellows at the top of the ladder will leave you alone till you get there on top. Then they become interested only for what they can get out of you, not for what they can give you. Some exceptions, yes. Not many though.

Bank Expansion

It was easy to merge banks. People don't understand that as soon as you have bought a bank, you have assets and cash, and as soon as you take over, you get your money back.

Branch Banking

[*Giannini did not invent branch banking, though he was with-out doubt its most effective champion in this country. Branches had long been standard practice in other countries. In 1929, when the United States counted 24,600 separate banks, Great Britain had 16 and Canada 10. In his crusade for branch bank-ing, Giannini emphasized the stabilizing influence of a system widely braced both geographically and industrially.*]

Under nationwide branch banking, an enterprise located in either the big city or the small village would have equal potential reservoirs of credit—perhaps running into hundreds of millions. Big business could do business anywhere. More: this borrowing power would be absolutely independent of local conditions. . . .

Under a nation-wide system a section distressed through crop failures, floods, unemployment, or for any other reason, would experience no diminution in its local financial support for any legitimate purpose. A new factory, for instance, would be financed as well in a distressed section as in a prosperous one. The amount of distress would be lessened and business recovery greatly speeded up.

Money

My hardest job has been to keep from being a millionaire. Per-sonally, I have never been able to understand the passion for storing up a great fortune. Wealth is a hard master, imposing many burdens, worries, fears, and distractions. They say it's for their children. That's bunk. The worst thing that can happen to a boy is to be barred from the right to work and struggle and make his own way.

Problem-solving

In working out any plan or idea, I use what you might call the intermittent method. I hit the problem hard, then leave it for awhile, and later come back. This method permits me to bring to the particular problem many ideas that come from mature reflection.

Failure

[*In 1924, just before retiring for the second of five times during the course of his career, Giannini made an address to the board of directors and retaliated against remarks regarding the Bank of Italy's first Los Angeles branch.*]

The foregoing remarks have been prompted by certain criticism . . . to the effect that the establishment of a branch of the Bank of Italy in Los Angeles was now considered a mistake; that it was not paying, and that it was about to be closed down. On January 1st 1914, the deposits of said branch amounted to $2,400,000 which deposits have since suffered a shrinkage of about $500,000. Said branch is at present, nevertheless, earning from $3,500 to $4,000 per month, net, of which about $1,500 is to be attributed to profits on moneys furnished it by the head office, and about $2,000 per month net is being realized by it on its present deposits.

The criticisms and rumors to which I have hereinabove

referred, have operated and will necessarily continue to operate as a serious detriment, and the situation should, without delay, be cleared up by either closing down or obtaining new quarters, which are absolutely essential for the bank's future growth.

In the event that this Board should decide to discontinue said branch . . . I hereby guarantee within 60 days to organize a syndicate, in which I shall have no interest whatever, to take over said branch and pay the bank of Italy therefor every dollar it has paid out . . .

[*The Board voted to keep the branch.*]

Retirement

[*In 1945, on the occasion of the last of Giannini's five retirements, he had the following exchange, retold by Matthew Josephson in an article for the* Saturday Evening Post. *On his seventy-fifth birthday, Giannini called in newspapermen and said:*]

"I'm ten years past the retirement age by our rules. I'm quitting for good."

"It seems to me we've heard that before," said one reporter.

"And I meant it that time, too," A. P. shot back.

Philanthropy

I believe in using money to help worthy causes while one is still living, and thus get some fun out of it. Of course, it is every man's duty to strive to give his children the best possible equipment for life. But to leave millions to young sons is dangerous. Each of us is better for having to make our own way in the world. God meant us to work. Those who don't work never amount to anything. To take from anyone the incentive to work is a questionable service.

[*At the time of his death on June 3, 1949, A. P. Giannini left an estate valued at $480,000. He left no bequests to his two surviving children, to whom he was extremely close: They had not expected to receive anything. Dividing $9,000 in small amounts for other relatives, he left $471,000 to charities.*]

Motivation

If my opponents hadn't forced me time after time, there would have been no driving, sustained effort to top the field.

I thrive on obstacles, particularly obstacles placed in my way by narrow-gauged competitors and their political friends. If it hadn't been that I encountered so much antagonism while I was trying to give the State of California a series of strong, well-managed branch banks, the Bank of Italy today might have been perhaps the three-hundredth in point of size in the United States instead of fourteenth.

Inspiration

There is no fun in working merely for money.

I like to do things, to be a builder. The upbuilding of the

Bank of Italy and its various associated institutions has been tremendously fascinating.

Distractions

I long since mastered the knack of thinking on whatever subject was in my mind whenever any one started and kept on talking about something of no interest to me. I can let such a conversation go in at one ear and out at the other without ever interfering with my own mental machinery.

[*Giannini did work constantly, or as he once said, from morning until he fell asleep. However, he had a few diversions. He played piano and liked to sing operatic selections to his own accompaniment. He also liked to bake himself in the sun of Florida on long vacations. In both cases, though, his mind might well have continued to work on banking.*]

Timing

The time to go ahead in business is when the other fellows aren't doing much.

Mission

[*In 1945, after turning over many responsibilities, Giannini told his successors:*]

If I ever hear that any of you are trying to play the big man's game and forgetting the small man, I'll be back in here fighting.

PART IV

The Buck Stops: BOSSES

Everyone in this section worked for someone else—but not for long. Starting companies or acquiring them, or taking the more arduous route through promotion, each gained control of a company somehow. After that, each had to keep control, that is, to try and gain the confidence of employees—and also of colleagues at related companies, of clients and of government officials: A boss is a boss over strangers, too.

Both David Packard of Hewlett-Packard and Alfred P. Sloan, longtime head of General Motors, started their careers as model employees. So did J. Paul Getty, who acquitted himself honorably on a work crew in an oil field.

The impetus to be a boss, and to be a good one, may well emanate from the experience of being a good employee first, and the need to multiply that sense of accomplishment by thousands or even hundreds of thousands.

Harvey Firestone felt strongly that a company should have one boss: clear-sighted, unencumbered, and quick to act. But then, at the time he formed that opinion, that's just exactly what Harvey Firestone was.

Harvey Firestone builds a tire at one of his plants in Akron, Ohio. Firestone was an authority on tire construction. He also became an expert on the subject of rubber and even wrote a technical book on the subject, Rubber: Its History and Development.

Harvey Firestone
1868–1938

In 1900, Harvey Firestone started one of the first companies to manufacture automobile tires—one of the first, but at the time, just another small entry in a treacherous industry. Under Firestone, the company kept itself under taut control and assumed an increasing share of the market, surviving to become one of the country's four dominating tire companies. A pleasant but opinionated man, Firestone firmly believed that one company should have one boss. In contrast to the newly styled "organization men" who came to the fore with his generation, he scoffed at management by committee and pitied stockholders who were burdened with the payroll of a complex organizational chart. Through nearly forty years of what might be called keenly active conservatism, Firestone placed his faith in common sense, unadorned and oblivious to business fashion. Any decision that was right for Firestone Tire & Rubber, even if for no other company—perhaps especially if for no other company—received Harvey Firestone's support as though there were no other course. But then, for a man of common sense, there never is any other course.

The commercialization of the automobile in the late 1890s was rooted less in the glamorized invention itself than in the availability of commodities to keep the contraptions running. Before the automobile age could get started, for example, there had to be fuel. John Rockefeller and his new refining industry took care of that—about a dozen years in advance of the auto boom, not coincidentally.

Second, but not by far, there had to be a ready supply of tires, which wore out quickly in those days. Bicycle and carriage shops existed throughout most countries, and they could supply the very earliest automobilists with spares made of rubber from the Amazon jungle. As the new century began, though, more and more people were buying cars—and therefore lots and lots of tires. Even with everyone in a newfound hurry, the only source for rubber remained the inner reaches of the Amazon, where wild *hevea brasiliensis* trees were tapped—and soon tapped out in the effort to supply the auto-crazed world with tires.

Hell-bent pioneers in America, France, Germany, and Italy dashed into the auto boom and grabbed at fortunes by building cars—rather an obvious thing to do. The English paused for a moment, and then started planting rubber trees as far as the eye could see in the Far East. In the very first days of the century, English capitalists quietly staked out almost complete control over one of the two vital commodities of the automobile era. From Malaya to Ceylon, England's *hevea* trees were growing.

Harvey Firestone would have been happy to hear it. As a tiremaker, he'd been drawn into what he considered to be an exciting industry and it behooved him to welcome any source of new supply. Twenty years later, seeming more a swashbuckler than a tiremaker, he would lash back at the English control over rubber—and over him—in a colonial sort of a war that took his company all the way to Africa.

Firestone's father, a farmer in Ohio, raised him to be sure of himself. The father considered himself unmatched as a livestock trader, but he turned all of his horse dealings over to his oldest boy. Constantly encouraged by his mother as well, Harvey was brash—pleasant, but unyieldingly confident. In 1888, at the age of twenty, he graduated from business college near his home in northeast Ohio.

Within a few years, Firestone became the Detroit representative for a company in the carriage business. Henry Ford himself could later describe the very moment in 1895 when Firestone, an avowed horseman, entered the automobile business. Ford was then an unknown factory mechanic. "At that time," he said in 1938, "I was building my first automobile. It was about complete, and I was using bicycle tires. The car weighted 500 pounds, which was too much for the light tires. I went to the buggy works to see about obtaining some solid rubber tires as a substitute. Mr. Firestone told me he had just received some new tires, that were a great deal softer, on a buggy being unpacked in the rear. They were pneumatic tires and I had him order me a set. That was in 1895. They are still on the car and still serviceable." The sale was one of Harvey's more worthwhile ones: the Ford Motor Co. has been a Firestone customer ever since. The car that Ford built, and the tires that Firestone supplied, can be seen in the photograph accompanying the chapter on Henry Ford II.

As a speed demon, even one in a sulky, Harvey Firestone recognized that no vehicle is faster than its tires, and he soon combined his dual interests in motion and business by starting a tire company in Chicago, where he was typically among the workmen cutting and attaching the tires. Selling that business, he used the proceeds to start the Firestone Tire and Rubber Co. in 1900 in Akron, on his home turf in Ohio.

Supervising all areas of his rapidly growing company, Firestone proved himself to be a versatile man. In the early days, he was the financier, reaching investors through any connections he could muster. As chief salesman for the fledgling company, he called on his old friend Henry Ford in Detroit in 1906 and came home with the contract to supply tires for a new vehicle, the Model T. When faster, heavier cars kept slipping on turns, Harvey Firestone decided to design a nonskid tire for 1909.

Proving that function also follows form, he took out a piece of paper and wrote *Firestone Non Skid* in diagonal repetition down the page, telling his production engineers to mold tires with that phrase in raised relief. It may not have been the most adhesive tread ever designed, but it was undoubtedly interesting to look at. It also worked surprisingly well and became the most popular tire in the lineup.

The company's chief financier, salesman, and production supervisor, Firestone was also in charge of procurement. As volume rose from the company's start in manufacturing in 1903 to almost 400,000 tires in 1912 to 4,250,000 in 1919, Firestone tried to take control of his supplies. Early on, he had had to worry that the Amazon supply would simply give out. After the English trees began producing rubber in volume, around 1906, Firestone was even more vexed, as prices vacillated over 100 percent in a typical year, due in some measure to the manipulations of traders in London, where the primary rubber market was located. Buying rubber at a bad price was ruinous: So was missing it at a good price.

In 1922, the English rubber suppliers agreed that the market was too uncertain. Their response was to stabilize rubber at the steep and malevolent price of over $1 a pound. As an American, as a tiremaker, and as a stubborn man used to being in charge, Harvey Firestone was outraged.

Firestone made speeches about the English rubber cartel, wrote booklets, and testified before the Senate. When he finally accepted the fact that no one in America could do anything about the English, he enlarged the fight. He took out a map, drew a line through all the land within a few degrees of the equator (where rubber trees would grow), crossed off the possessions of other countries, looked again, and leased 1 million acres in Liberia, Africa.

In the mid-1920s, several other American tire companies joined Firestone in developing American sources for rubber in the tropics, but they concentrated on smaller plantations located mainly in the Far East.

In Liberia, Harvey Firestone was charting virgin territory. Nothing of any use could be purchased in the country: every single item required had to be shipped in. The company sent rubber trees and bathtubs, generators, ice machines, botanists, and barges on which to ship the raw rubber until the company got around to sending roads. Firestone even sent radios, and went to a lot of trouble using them to connect Akron, Ohio, to Liberia's jungles.

In December 1928, Harvey Firestone made a short speech at the beginning of a musical concert over the National Broadcasting Company network, in which he said as a special note,

"I hope that our American and native staff, as they are gathered around our radio station at one o'clock in the morning, surrounded by the African jungle, will hear every word that I say and enjoy the complete program." And so the company brought Harvey Firestone and American music to Liberia.

The Liberian operation was expensive and complex, but it served its two main purposes. The first, and not the least important, was to mollify Harvey Firestone's outrage and to satisfy him that regarding the English cartel, he was where he liked to be—on the offensive. The second was to destroy that cartel. The Liberian plantations didn't do so, but they helped. The Dutch, with fair-sized holdings in the Far East, rode quietly along with the cartel's high prices for a few years, but by the mid-1920s were undercutting them. Because of that, and perhaps because of the specter of new supply from other regions including Liberia, the cartel fell apart in 1928. Firestone then closed his Liberian plantations. Ninety-five percent of rubber came from English—and Dutch—growers in the Far East, but that didn't matter. It was no longer a point of patriotic rage. Rubber was only 16 cents a pound.

Harvey Firestone was a slight man in build, standing about five foot five. His face had a European look, with a high forehead, deep-set eyes, and a substantial nose. Natty in dress, he had a wry sense of humor and a great knack for friendship. He made the news in 1932 when he played a round of golf with John Rockefeller—for whom a round was always eight holes. At the time, Firestone was fifty-eight and Rockefeller was ninety-one. The score was a tie, which may say something about Rockefeller's vim or Firestone's decorum.

A sanguine borrower early on, Harvey Firestone reduced his company's long-term debt to a scant minimum during the prosperous days of the late 1920s. As a result, Firestone Tire & Rubber weathered the Great Depression without even having to consider reducing its dividend. Harvey Firestone died in his sleep at his Palm Beach home in 1938, after a pleasant day that included a habitual Sunday drive.

In the quotes that follow, Harvey Firestone offers the lessons he learned firsthand in letting his company swell during a boom time and downsizing it thereafter. He describes in detail what parts of the company needed to be thrown out and what merely needed to be invigorated. He also lists the two questions that turned every employee at Firestone into a permanent member of his downsizing committee. Firestone, who was an ace networker, relates methods that work in making sure to meet the right people—along with the methods that only annoy them.

Harvey Firestone

That is the trouble with prosperity—it hides the defects of a business.

Detail

Success is the sum of detail. It might perhaps be pleasing to imagine one's self beyond detail and engaged only in great things. But, as I have often observed, if one attends only to great things and lets the little things pass, the great things become little—that is, the business shrinks.

Decision-making

The only firm rule I have is to take up one thing at a time and to take up nothing else until my mind is free. I do not believe in quick decisions unless in an emergency. I would rather take my time about making up my mind, and I nearly always manage to do so. Indeed, anything that can be decided in an instant is something that ought not come to me.

Thinking

Almost every man tries to dodge thought or to find a substitute for it. We try to buy thoughts ready made and guaranteed to fit, in the shape of systems installed by experts. We try to substitute discussion for thought by organizing committees; a committee may function very well indeed as a clearing house for thoughts, but more commonly a committee organization is just an elaborate means of fooling one's self into believing that a spell spent in talking is the same as a spell spent in thinking.

Competition

Competition rarely puts any one out of business—a man usually puts himself out of business either by not making a good article or by wrong methods in sales or finance.

Deal-making

[*Firestone credited his father, a farmer in Columbiana, Ohio, as the finest businessman he ever knew. The elder Firestone was active in the local livestock markets.*]

It was a whole course in trading to watch him at work. First he saw the whole market and heard what everyone had to offer or say—saying almost nothing himself. He often told me:

"Never rush in on a deal. Let it come to you."

That is the course he followed, and by the time he was

ready to trade, he knew the whole market. If his survey convinced him that the market was not a good one either to buy or to sell in, he simply went home again.

Management

Power has to be transmitted before a wheel will turn. We give various names to the thought which has the power to turn the wheels. Sometimes we call it management. But there is another kind of management which is not based on thought and which is not management at all; for instance, there is the kind of management which operates solely on records. Records will guide thought, but they will not substitute for thought. Good management—that is, management with real thought behind it—does not bother trying to make its way by trickery, for it knows that fundamental honesty is the keystone of the arch of business. It knows that you will fail if you think more of matching competitors than of giving service; that you will fail if you put money or profits ahead of work, and that there is no reason why you should succeed if what you do does not benefit others.

This is not idealistic philosophy; it is the hardest kind of common sense. If you ask yourself why you are in business and can find no answer other than, "I want to make money," you will save money by getting out of business and going to work for someone, for you are in business without sufficient reason.

Appraisal

[*From a letter Harvey Firestone wrote to his sales staff:*]
    I am continually advising the organization not to compare present-day business with our past records—although it is a

natural thing to do. We are doing much better business than we did last year. But to do a better business than we did last year really is not much of a credit to us. We must compare what we are doing today with our opportunities of today.

Advancement

Hard work and faithful work isn't everything.

If you find that you are going around in a little routine circle, your head down, just plugging, the only thing for you to do is look around you, pick out a definite goal which you want to reach, and begin traveling toward it. It may not be some remote and difficult peak. . . . When you have gained that one, you can pick out the next higher one, and begin climbing toward that. But a man must have *some* goal to work for, or he is not likely to do much traveling.

Work

The man or the woman who doesn't accomplish anything doesn't get much out of life. I believe most men will make good if they find the work they are happy in doing.

Hiring

I have never found that pay alone would either bring together or hold good men.

❈

[*In 1908, when Firestone decided to hire a chemist, the company's first, he interviewed a man named John W. Thomas.*]

He was getting, so he told me, ninety dollars a month.

"Will you come with me and lay out a laboratory and take charge of it?" I asked. "And how much would you want?"

"I'd like to think it over," he answered. "But it seems to me I'd like to do it. However, I ought to have one hundred dollars a month."

"No," I answered, "we might as well decide it all right now, and I can't afford to pay you over ninety a month."

"If I have to decide, then I'll decide to come out, and I'll start at ninety dollars. I think there is a chance to do something."

"If that's the case," I continued, "then we'll make it one hundred dollars and call it a bargain!"

I will never bid a man away from a job. It is not fair to the man and it is not fair to his employer. If a man comes to you for the single reason that you offer him more money than he has been getting, he is not worth having, for then he is thinking too much of the money and too little of the job. Very often a man is underpaid in his job and perhaps treated unfairly in a number of ways. He may be in the kind of an organization in which there is no future; there may be a good many reasons why a man feels he ought to change his job. If such be the case, he ought to change his job and he would be a fool if he made the change simply because the second job offered less money, but he would be almost as much of a fool if he changed simply because the second job offered more money. The money part cannot be put aside; everyone has to live, and there are unfortunately times when a man has to look solely to the pay, but from the employer's standpoint the really valuable man is the one who is willing to take the chance of eventually making himself worth a large salary.

[*In 1932, Firestone named John W. Thomas his successor as president of Firestone Tire & Rubber Co.*]

Overhead

[*For a half-dozen years leading up 1920, Firestone's company became burdened with bureaucracy. Firestone looked back on that era with a shudder.*]

I let the business get away from me in the easiest of all fashions—by thinking of an organization as something of itself instead of as a means of getting work done quickly and well.

Gradually, I contracted the chart fever. The first step was to departmentalize the business, which is always a fine, satisfying thing to do.

And, naturally, when one gets the business into departments with department heads, those heads begin to departmentalize their own departments. And just as naturally, the head of a big department has to be a vice president and imitate the president in doing nothing but direct. Gradually we got an organization—a real organization, second to none in its division of duties. It seems—now that it is all over—that we never faced a duty without dividing it; I did not attempt to follow the divisions and subdivisions, for that was the duty of the vice presidents, and, under the rules of the game, I was not to interfere with them. And then, inevitably, the men began to write letters to one another. I know of no better way of fooling oneself than writing interoffice communications and asking for reports. A man can keep himself busy that way all day long and completely satisfy his conscience that he is doing something worth while. We wrote so many notes that the vice presidents and their assistants and their assistants often used to get a day or two behind in the reading of them, and we had to devise a bright red inter-office telegram for really urgent business!

Expenses

[*During the overexpansion, Firestone offered dealers a range of advertising products, including a glossy magazine called* Milestones, *to be distributed to potential customers.*]

I began to see salesman's reports like this:

Fifty *Milestones*

One thousand blotters

Five hundred buttons

Ten tires.

Looking through the accounting department, I noticed a new division of clerks that I had never seen before. I asked what they were doing.

"Billing advertising," came the reply.

That set me to thinking. I began to ask myself:

"Are we in the business of selling tires or are we publishers and sellers of advertising?"

[*Firestone answered his own question by telling his sales staff to "sell tires and nothing else."*]

Every addition to the indirect or overhead expense should be studied vigilantly. This is especially true in these days when luxuries so rapidly become necessities. An executive is the better off for having a comfortable desk and chair and a convenient place to work, and there is no reason why surroundings should not be good looking rather than ugly, but an office is essentially a place in which to work. It is not a club and it ought not to be fitted up as a club — else it may turn into a club.

Judging Expenditures

We have cut our manufacturing turnover from sixty to fifteen days. We have cut our seconds to a negligible fraction, and we have so simplified processes that, whereas a few years ago we were in pressing need of space in which to build more tires, we are now, with a far larger output than then, using less than all the space we have at our command. All of this due to: "Is it necessary?" and "Can it be simplified?"

Mapping the Future

Unless one can see and plan for a year or two ahead, one's business will not grow evenly and naturally. It will pass through a series of emergencies, and one of those emergencies will wreck it. Emergencies will come about in any business, but they will be few and not hard to meet if the future has been mapped. This is so self-evident that I wonder why it is so much neglected. The only danger in mapping the future lies in making the plans inflexible.

Vision

[*Firestone had a careful definition of the process called* "vision."]
    Much of the thinking in business has to be along the lines of comparing values. If we make a change in manufac-

turing or selling methods, will the added return pay the cost? This appraising operation in business is continuous. For instance, in 1920, when we began to compare expenditures and results in our office, we promptly discovered that instead of 1,500 office employees we actually needed only 300—or, in other words, we had 1,200 men performing operations of no value to us. We found an even worse situation in selling; in a period when no selling was necessary since people rushed in to buy, we had built up, because we had lost our sense of values, a most intricate organization that could not possibly pay its way. It was being paid for by rising prices and not by work . . .

Many of the values are intangible and cannot be put down on paper in terms of dollars and cents—but this is the point—if you can make a picture of a situation in your own mind, then you can make comparisons and relate values, even if you cannot express them. Some people call this vision, and we hear a great deal about the necessity for vision. But vision, as I see it, is not dreaming forward. It is a thinking through with the values ever in mind. For instance, I should not be exercising vision if I looked forward to a day when I should supply all the tires in the world. That would be just idle, profitless dreaming. In quite another class is thinking out ways and means to get a certain percentage of all the tires used and relating prices and manufacturing schedules and so on to that end. It is perfectly possible to make an exact mental picture of what would be required to do a decided percentage of business—and if that picture be kept in mind, the decisions to carry them out can come quickly.

Sales Climate

[*Firestone was continually fascinated, and disgusted, by the way his company bloated during the boom years around America's entry into World War I.*]

Every change we made in sales methods brought results — and proved the new method. We did not know that we would have shown as startling an increase had we abolished our whole sales force, closed all our branches and dealers, and just sent out our tires in freight cars to be thrown off on sidings and taken away by clamoring buyers.

No end of sales reputations are established by salesmen taking the credit for the public resolutely refusing to be deterred from buying.

Salesmanship

We do not care for sales contests or high pressure selling. We have tried most of the approved devices for stimulating sales. For several years we set up quotas. If the end of the month were near and a salesman were below his quota, it was natural for him to go to a dealer that he knew well and say:

"Help me out with an order to make my quota."

That is not selling — that is asking for alms. A dealer with a charitable bent of mind will order to help the agent, which is no reason at all for ordering. We have had sales contests with prizes and bonuses, and these, too, were successful, in that they produced results, but the results were not permanent. When a sales contest closed, the salesman took things easy for a week or two, and we would have a sharp drop in sales. We did not gain any permanent advantage by the contests.

Sales Management

[*Telegram from Harvey Firestone, vacationing in England, to his home office in Akron, 1920:*]

Glad sales improving. Regret your policy of giving prize money for increased sales. It exhibits a weakness in management and impresses your branches that you do not have confidence that they are making their best effort in these strenuous times. My judgment is that all your branch organization wants is helpful suggestions, confidence and inspiration from the home office.

Losing Money

[*In its first years in business, Firestone Tire & Rubber ordered tires made to its specifications from other tiremakers. The suppliers made money, but Firestone couldn't resell the tires at a high enough price to include a profit for itself.*]

There was nothing at all complicated about the business or its finance, excepting that we did not have money enough to swing our volume of operations—and not having enough money is always complicated!

Our margin of profit was very narrow at the best, and at the worst we lost money. For three years we lost money operations as a whole, but this did not bother me as to the eventual success of the enterprise, because I knew how and why we lost our money. Losing money is not pleasant, but every business must at times lose money. Losing money is really serious if you do not know why you are losing, or if you do know why and cannot help yourself.

Networking

[In the first years after the founding of Firestone Tire & Rubber in 1900, Harvey Firestone was, as he recalled, "on the hunt day and night for men to buy our stock." He particularly targeted an Ohio banker named Will Christy.]

The trouble was I could not get to him. He had a big office and secretaries and all the usual safeguards of a busy man, and I could not get past those guards. The fact that he was a brother of James Christy, who was already in the company, did not help at all. Of course, I might have tried him at his house in the evening, but that would have been poor policy. A man of affairs does not want to be bothered in the evening. A great many salesmen make the mistake of thinking that pestering a man is the same as selling him, and they get their prospects into such a state of exasperation that they would not buy a gold dollar from them at 50 percent off. Just getting to a man is not enough — it is when and how you get to him. There are more wrong times to sell a man than there are right times, and if I ever should write a book on salesmanship I should give about one third of the book to the topic, "Common Sense." I have been buttonholed thousands of times by salesmen who, if they had just exercised a grain of common sense, would have known that, while the moment might be a very good one in which to make my acquaintance, it was no time at all to persuade me to buy anything. A good salesman will never intrude. In the first place, he will know that intruders do not make sales, and in the second place, he will have brains enough to arrange for the right kind of meeting with his prospect—no man likes to be panhandled and some selling comes close to panhandling.

[*Firestone carefully arranged to bump into Christy in a Chicago hotel, where they had breakfast, and naturally the topic of the tire business arose. Christy subscribed for $10,000 worth of stock in Firestone's new company.*]

Cash

A man with a surplus can control circumstances, but a man without a surplus is controlled by them and often he has no opportunity to exercise judgment.

Start-ups

It is unusual, and indeed abnormal, for a concern to make money during the first several years of its existence. The initial product and the initial organization are never right . . .

The new company will think that it has taken every precaution. It will think that it has made every sort of an investigation, but really the most searching trials that a new company can make are of small moment, first, because the promoters can never get themselves into the cold, detached frame of mind in which the public approaches anything new, and, second, because the knowledge of what really is a test will be lacking.

[*Firestone recommended that a business plan or prospectus be written without embellishment or even optimism.*]

A statement of condition can be a prospectus—in fact, it is the best possible kind of a prospectus—but it ought not to be prepared in enthusiasm. It ought to be absolutely frank and entirely conservative; then an explanation will show that actual conditions are a little better and not a little worse than represented.

It is more than unsafe—it is just a waste of time—to start into business with money that has not been embarked for better or for worse.

It may be possible in exceptional cases to pay the interest on borrowed capital, but unless one strikes a bonanza, any undertaking quickly to pay back borrowed capital is bound to result in failure.

Dimensions

I notice that when all a man's information is confined to the field in which he is working, the work is never as good as it ought to be.

This thing of sleeping and eating with your business can easily be overdone; it is all well enough—usually necessary—in times of trouble, but as a steady diet it does not make for good business; a man ought now and then to get far enough away to have a look at himself and his affairs. Otherwise, he gets lost in the details and forgets what he is really doing. One often sees that in foremen.

Promotions

Strange as it may sound, it is sometimes an actual injustice to a man to advance him. If he is promoted too rapidly, or is put into a position for which he is not fitted, he may fail to make good; and that failure may be a setback from which he will never recover.

Problem-solving

I think the best way to settle trouble is face to face.

Materialism

Why is it that a man, just as soon as he gets enough money, builds a house much bigger than he needs? I built a house at Akron many times larger than I have the least use for; I have another house at Miami Beach, which is also much larger than I need. I suppose that before I die I shall buy or build other houses which also will be larger than I need. I do not know why I do it—the houses are only a burden. . . . In most cases, and especially with men who have earned their own money, the house is just built, and when it is done, no one knows why it was ever started.

Transformations

[*Firestone looked back on the days when he and his wife, Idabelle, were just starting out in a modest mode of living:*]

Sometimes it seems that it might be better to go back to those simpler days, that one might get more out of a less complex life. But it cannot be done. One changes with prosperity. We all think we should like to lead the simple life, and then we find that we have picked up a thousand little habits which we are quite unconscious of because they are a part of our very being—and these habits are not in the simple life. There is no going back—except as a broken man.

Diligence

If you know absolutely that what you are doing is right, then you are bound to accomplish it in due season.

I say this not because I read it somewhere in a book, but because I have lived it. For if there is any phase of adversity which our business has not met and beaten I should like to know it.

Leadership

I hold that, if anything in the business is wrong, the fault is squarely with management. If the tires are not made right, if the workmen are unhappy, if the sales are not what they ought to be, the fault is not with the man who is actually doing the job, but with the men above him and the men above them, so that, finally, the fault is mine. That is my conception of business.

J. Paul Getty, age seventy, dances the twist at a party for children at his home in England in March 1963. Getty had been asked by a newspaper to host a party for the children, residents of a local group home.

J. Paul Getty
1892–1976

In 1958, J. Paul Getty was judged to be the richest private citizen in the world, which was fitting since he had devoted most of the previous decade to the creation of a pioneering global corporation, Getty Oil. Paul Getty had built his initial fortune in the oil industry through tautly operated drilling ventures in the United States, as well as through marauding stock transactions. After World War II, he staked his future on Mideast oil exploration and reaped the fullest benefit of strikes there by integrating his interests into the world market. With headquarters that might be anyplace where there was a telephone—though usually working out of Paris and London—Getty created a complex of overlapping companies that was ingenious, if impenetrable. "I'm a bad boss," he once said wryly. "A good boss develops successors. There is nobody to step into my shoes." Getty was a socialite in his private life, but a loner in business—a man who managed without friendship, and without favor.

T here are not many places on earth so worthless that no one will even bother to fight over them. Saudi Arabia and Kuwait designated one when they concluded their 1922 diplomatic accord with a pronounced shrug, calling a 1,500-square-mile tract situated between them a "Neutral Zone." Neither side cared much who owned it: They couldn't even muster the interest to map it.

With or without diplomatic accords, the Neutral Zone was the real thing: a no-man's-land, too hot and dry even for the hardy Bedouins. Scorpions, snakes, and occasionally a canopy of locusts tried to live there, but no humans. Even the shore along the Persian Gulf was unfriendly, with sharks, sea cobras, jellyfish, and barracudas. A no-man's-water, to boot.

In March of 1954, J. Paul Getty arrived in the Neutral Zone, zooming around in a Cadillac and cooling off from 125-degree temperatures with a daily swim in the ocean. The barracudas left him alone.

If ever there were a man to thrive in a no-man's-land, it was J. Paul Getty. He had risked a vast amount of money on the hope that the Neutral Zone would justify the business complex he'd developed over the previous thirty-five years. Getty was tough, physically and certainly mentally; but moreover, he was oblivious to most of the things that affect other people. A no-man's-land held no horrors for him, not if it had money or oil.

Before World War II, Getty had built a fair-sized petroleum business, mostly in drilling. Even he didn't seem to know quite what to call his business, relying on the suitably amorphous term, "the Getty interests," because it was such a complicated array of companies. Getty came by the tendency to intertwine companies naturally. His father, George Getty, had been a corporate attorney in Minnesota in the years before 1903, when he went to Oklahoma on business and bought an oil lease just as a lark. It yielded a gusher.

A wildcatter can make a lot of money, and George Getty did—the family moved to the Los Angeles area in 1906, living in true Beverly Hills style even before the city of Beverly Hills grew up around them. However, a wildcatter is just a supplier of crude, and *crude* is an apt word. An ambitious wildcatter longs for the vertical integration of a full-scale oil company, with pipelines, refineries, tank trucks, and retail distribution. It is a hard transition to make, though, both because the risks are constant and the outlay is staggering.

J. Paul Getty had two qualities that allowed him to build an integrated oil company out of a bunch of wells. Those two qualities were not, as some implied, first, his father's money and second, his mother's money. Wilshire Boulevard was crowded with young sports in fancy cars who had those two kinds of qualities. Paul Getty was different.

Raised as an only child, Paul was adored and enjoyed by both his parents. Even while making stops in his college education at the University of California at Berkeley and England's Oxford, he worked as a roustabout in an Oklahoma oil field owned by his father.

A rich young man with an eye for fun-loving women, Paul Getty then went home to Hollywood . . . and was divorced or separated three times before he was in his mid-thirties. That disgusted his father. When George Getty died in 1930, he left just about all of his money, $15 million, to his widow, Sarah. He loved Paul, but couldn't countenance his son's moral judgment where women were concerned; few people ever would. As for Sarah Getty, she loved Paul, too, but was just as exasperated by him, especially by his insistence during the very depths of the Depression that she sell her boring old government bonds in order to speculate in stocks.

No one was more delighted with the stock market situation in the 1930s than Paul Getty, largely because the first of the qualities that brought him his big oil company was hard-tempered courage. Into downbeaten stocks, he poured all of his cash and as much of his mother's as he could pry loose — and as much of E.F. Hutton & Co.'s money as he could borrow, too. Whenever the stocks sank even further in price, Mrs. Getty groaned and Paul bought more. Mother and son remained devoted to each other nonetheless, and spent many of their afternoons together on simple outings such as feeding the sea lions at the Santa Monica pier. Mrs. Getty died in 1941. And after that, Paul Getty was on his own, whoever happened to be around him.

One of Getty's favorite stocks was Tide Water Associated, a medium-sized petroleum company with refining facilities in New Jersey. Tide Water was much larger than the "Getty interests." However, for eighteen years, starting in 1932, Paul Getty accumulated Tide Water stock, having gained a fantastic boost through his early purchases at bargain prices. Meanwhile, he ignored the overt antipathy of the company's board. The second quality that Paul Getty possessed to a frightening degree was patience, the patience of a piranha. In 1948, he moved closer to control of Tide Water with an important purchase, and in 1951 he finally acquired enough stock to take over the company, which offered retail distribution through a chain of gas stations controlled by a subsidiary.

Getty's problems seesawed, as in any business that is growing fast. Instead of having plenty of oil and nowhere to refine or sell it himself, Getty was finding himself in need of a far greater supply than his own fields in Oklahoma and California could supply.

In 1948, just when Getty foresaw the extent of his need for oil, the rights to drill in the Neutral Zone came up for bid. It was the last great parcel to be had on the Arabian peninsula.

All oil derived from the Neutral Zone was controlled equally between Kuwait and Saudi Arabia. Kuwait quickly sold its rights to a coalition of American companies called Aminoil, leaving Getty just one last chance to bid for the last great parcel: the half-interest controlled by Saudi Arabia. Getty gave simple orders to his representative in the bidding for it—don't lose. The Getty interests paid $10.5 million, along with a hefty royalty, far more in both respects than Aminoil had paid Kuwait for the other half of the Neutral Zone oil concession. If there even was any oil: Oilmen around the world said that Getty would be ruined by paying such a high price for an unknown quantity.

As Getty's share of the expenditures mounted, totaling $30 million in the first five years, he and Aminoil had nothing to show for all their drilling but five empty holes. The joke was that with four more, the Neutral Zone would have a golf course.

Getty tried to remain patient, though he resented the fact that Aminoil continually ignored his advice on the exploration project. He went to Europe in 1949, permanently as it turned out, to develop the international side of his business.

In building the Getty interests in Europe, Paul Getty worked for himself and by himself. He didn't even have a home of his own until 1960, but lived in suites at hotels such as the Georges V in Paris and the Ritz in London. Company reports and unmade beds, telegrams and unfinished meals all blended carelessly but comfortably in his suites, the way his work and his life blended throughout his career. Nothing separated Getty from his business. Nonetheless, he was anything but a recluse, as a convivial figure in the Swinging Set of the 1950s and 1960s.

In late March of 1953, the Neutral Zone finally yielded a gusher. Within a year, Getty had authorized construction of a new refinery in Delaware, at a cost of $200 million. He was busy solidifying plans in all directions, on the basis of a flow of oil from the Neutral Zone, but by early 1954, he had yet to see much progress in starting that flow. In March, Getty arrived in the desert to change the outlook somewhat.

The problems in shipping oil from the zone were almost as daunting as finding it in the first place, but shipments began in 1955. Listening to the men and letting the supervisors listen to him, Getty began to see progress, and shipments grew past 60,000 barrels a day within 5 years. Afterward, he would make visits to the fields every year to check on progress. He must have loved the place, despite the poor comparison it made to Paris or London; it had made him the richest person in the world, not including royalty.

In the words that follow, J. Paul Getty discusses the various types of people who worked for him, analyzing good traits and bad from his perspective as a notoriously unsentimental boss. He cites many specific examples, including a means by which he tested the priorities of three executives who worked for him. (Two passed and one flunked out.) At times delighted with his rank as "the richest man in the world," and at times burdened by it, Getty also speaks about money, wealth, and luxury, which are not as closely related as one might think.

J. Paul Getty

Capital

Just as a bad workman invariably complains that he has bad tools, so the bad businessman always wails that he does not have enough capital.

It is entirely possible, even in this day and age, and will remain so in the marvel-filled future, to start small and grow big. There are always individuals and legitimate lending institutions willing to provide capital for a promising business at reasonable rates of interest or in exchange for reasonable quantities of stock.

Overhead

Years ago, businessmen automatically kept administrative overhead to an absolute minimum. The present-day trend is in exactly the opposite direction. The modern business mania is to build greater and ever greater paper-shuffling empires. Many business firms employ battalions of superspecialized executives, reinforce them with regiments of office-working drones, give them all grandiloquent titles—and then mire them down in bottomless quagmires of forms, reports, memoranda, "studies," and "surveys."

Thus, it is hardly surprising that so many young men start their business careers with the idea that "administration" is not only the tail that wags the whole business dog, but that it is, in itself, the whole animal. These young men will spend half their time trying to find out what they're doing through studies and surveys, then spend the other half informing each other about what—if anything—they've learned through the media of committee meetings and interoffice memoranda.

I'm still a wildcatter at heart, I suppose. I don't hold with the ultra-organization and superadministration theories at all. I still believe that the less overhead there is in business, the better.

Details

My fear of getting bogged down in administrative detail and paper work being all but phobic, I stayed in the field as much as possible.

Leadership

[*Getty listed the primary points of leadership in his book,* How To Be Rich.]

1. Example is the best means to instruct or inspire others.
2. A good executive accepts full responsibility for the actions of the people under him.
3. The best leader never asks anyone under him to do anything he is unable—or unwilling—to do himself.
4. The man in charge must be fair but firm with his subordinates, showing concern for their needs and doing all he can to meet their reasonable requests. . . . On the other hand, he does not pamper them, and always bears in mind that familiarity breeds contempt.
5. There is one seemingly small—but actually very important—point that all executives should remember. Praise should always be given in public, criticism should always be delivered in private.

Character Traits

There is a quality that some prefer to call resiliency—the ability to accept setbacks and criticism manfully, without going into a brooding blue funk. The outstanding man will accept the setbacks, take the criticism and, learning his lessons from both, will energetically strive to do better the next time. Also, the promotable man will certainly be an executive who does not hesitate to accept responsibility for any of his actions. As far as I am concerned, nothing eliminates an individual from consideration for promotion faster than the knowledge that he is a buck passer.

Expectations

There are far too many men who hold—or would like to hold—management positions in business whose outlooks are virtually identical with those of the average postal clerk. They don't really care whether the company that employs them makes a profit or shows a loss as long as their own paychecks arrive on time.

Dimensions

Assuming other considerations to be equal, the executive who most thoroughly familiarizes himself with the diverse factors that could involve or affect the company for which he works is the executive most likely to achieve success in his business career . . .

It is by no means enough for the executive to know his own job thoroughly. If that is all he knows, the job he holds is the only one for which he is at all suited. And, even then, unless the position is one that requires no imagination or enterprise, he will not be able to perform the job well. A man with narrowly limited perspectives cannot move beyond those limits, and the course of his career is charted for him—to a dead end.

Self-evaluation

One extremely successful businessman I know tells me that he has been rating himself every six months for the past 20 years. His method is simple: He uses a standard personnel evaluation sheet—and grades himself in the same manner as he would a subordinate employee. He claims this private system of self-evaluation has enabled him to recognize and thus try to correct his deficiencies. He declares the system has worked wonders and has contributed in no small degree to his success.

Flattery

Like any individual who has achieved any degree of authority in the business world, I have encountered my share of toadies who sought to gain attention through flattery. However, while their numbers are considerable and the energy they expend is great, their successes in achieving their goals are few. It has been my observation that such individuals are predestined to fail because they almost invariably make several major mistakes.

First of all, they are too eager for quick results. Hence, they employ what they consider the most potent, quickest-acting stratagems, which 99 times out 100, are so unsubtle and maladroit that they are completely transparent.

Second, the devoted apple polisher is so intent on his truckling and favor currying that he neglects his official duties . . .

Third . . . were he to devote as much time and effort to productive work as he does to playing the slavering spaniel, he would advance much faster.

Fourth, most seasoned businessmen have long since learned the hard way that there is more than a grain of truth in George Herbert's acid adage: "Many kiss the hand they wish cut off."

Priorities

[*Getty conducted an experiment in priorities with three executives at one of his companies.*]

Their monthly salaries ran into four figures. One month, shortly before payday, I instructed the accounting department to "short" each of their paychecks by five dollars—and, if they complained, to send them directly to me.

As I more or less expected, all three of the executives concerned presented themselves at my office within an hour after their checks were delivered on payday. To each, in turn, I delivered a little speech that was hardly calculated to brighten his day.

"I've been going over the company's books," I announced sourly, "I've found several examples of what I consider unnecessary expenditures which have cost this company's stockholders many tens of thousands of dollars in the last year. Apparently, you paid little or no attention to them. Certainly, I've seen no evidence that you tried to reduce the expenses or correct the situations which caused them to rise as high as they did. Yet, when your own paycheck is involved, you instantly notice a five-dollar underpayment and take immediate steps to have the mistake rectified." Two of the executives got the point, took it to heart and quickly mended their ways. The third did none of these things—and was soon looking elsewhere for work.

Loyalty

Loyalty—another important quality in executives—can only be recognized and judged after it has been demonstrated. The executive's loyalty should not be to any individual—but to the stockholders, employees, his associates, superiors and the company as a whole.

Responsibility

The executive's attitude toward the company's money is all-important. He must be acutely profit conscious, unequivocally dedicated to the principle that every task, if humanly possible, should be translated into a profit. The executive who is promotable is the man who views the company's money as something that he is obliged to administer wisely and well, to see it spent with maximum care to achieve maximum results. How he handles company money is all the more significant because, after all, the higher he goes, the more money he will control.

I took over active management of the Spartan Aircraft Corporation during World War II at the request of Secretary of the Navy Frank Knox. It was a time of considerable stress in all industries and good personnel were scarce. There was one executive in the company who, according to his immediate superiors, deserved promotion. I was about to approve a boost in both salary and responsibility for him when I happened to learn, purely by accident, that he made a habit of bringing his personal letters to the office and having his secretary run them through a company postage meter.

I immediately discarded all idea of promoting the man and, indeed, let him know diplomatically that his resignation would be most welcome, the sooner the better. I explained my reasons to his superiors who had plumped so hard for him.

True, the total amount involved was small—ten dollars, perhaps fifteen dollars over many months. But the amount isn't what counted.

[*A few years later, Getty read in the newspaper that the man had been arrested for embezzling over $200,000 from the next company for which he worked.*]

L a b o r

Interviews conducted recently with young executives and business students show that the majority declares itself to be against unions. At the same time, some 75 percent of them cite security as the principal reason why they work—or want to work—for large corporations:

"There's very little chance of getting fired or laid off . . ."
"Regular salary increases . . ."
"Retirement and medical benefits . . ."
"Yearly vacations with pay . . ."

Now, I would begrudge no executive what so many of them have evidently come to regard as their due—be it job tenure or an annual holiday. But I see no logic or consistency in the admittedly security-seeking organization man's opposition to organized labor's search for a similar degree of security.

G o v e r n m e n t   D e b t

Any attempt to compare the Federal balance sheet to the balance sheet of a private individual or corporation is akin to trying to compare an apple to an elephant.

The Federal budget and the national debt are, in a manner of speaking, purely accounting fictions. The former is purely a *cash* budget, while the latter is a cumulative cash debt. No balance sheet or report concerning either ever reflects the immense assets—tangible and intangible—that the nation possesses to offset its deficits and debts.

Press Relations

[*After being named the world's richest private citizen in a 1957 survey made by* Fortune *magazine, Getty became an instant celebrity. He enjoyed his fame, but learned how hard it is to control the media, as the following humorous anecdote shows.*]

I once told a prominent writer—not a journalist, an author with the highest of credentials—the following:

"One of the troubles with books, motion pictures, television and advertising today is that everything is sex. I'll be the first to admit that sex is important, but it is being overemphasized, overdone. I think sex, to a certain extent, should be fugitive."

That is what I said.

But the author extracted three words—three only—from my statement. When I read his book, I found myself being quoted as flatly declaring that: "Everything is sex."

Extravagance

I enjoy (and love) comfort and luxury. But—and let these be my last words on the score—I do not need to overspend or be wildly extravagant in order to bolster my ego to prove anything to the world. I would far rather spend $17 million on a public museum than a like sum on the finest yacht afloat. A new, fully-equipped Cadillac would cost close to $10,000. Allowing for trade-in values, I most certainly would have spent $100,000 over the last fifteen years, buying two new cars annually. That $100,000 can be put to far better use. It is the same sum as is represented by the two $50,000 prizes I have made available to the World Wildlife Fund.

[*Getty was known for his frugal ways. He did buy a sixteenth-century English manor house in 1960, an ostentatious residence to be sure, although he turned much of it over to office and meeting space. By far, most of his personal spending was directed into his collection of art and fine antiques, which formed the basis of the Getty Museum in Los Angeles.*]

Possibilities

I've made many mistakes and miscalculations—more of them than I'd care to remember on days when I'm wearing a tight collar. There aren't any .1000 batters. If there were, baseball wouldn't be much of a game—and if businessmen always made the right decisions, business wouldn't be business.

The point I'm driving at is that the successful businessman is the one who makes the right choice between the possible and the impossible more often than not. The seasoned businessman does not arrive at such decisions by haphazard guesswork. Nor does he decide one way or another because he has a hunch or a clairvoyant premonition. A great deal of careful thought and consideration goes into resolving the problem of the possible versus the impossible.

Individual Thinking

To be truly successful, the businessman must first discard—or at the very least, greatly discount—most traditional concepts of success.

Success

There is no such thing as success that is inherently lasting, that will not fade unless it is nurtured.

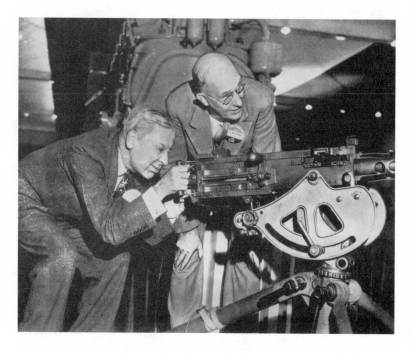

*Alfred Sloan looks through a machine gun sight in the com-
pany of research chief Charles Kettering in 1945, when General
Motors factories were turned over to production of war matériel.*

Alfred P. Sloan Jr.
1875–1966

Alfred Sloan Jr. was educated as an engineer and worked in the automobile industry all of his life, but the machine he engineered wasn't a vehicle. It was the corporation itself. Sloan was either president or chairman of General Motors from 1923 to 1956, during which time it grew to be the world's largest industrial company. Sloan's blueprinted structure for management was copied throughout American business, where office workers were abstracted into flow charts intended to replace personality in the executive suite with a more predictable framework for progress. In the overall advancement of American business, Henry Ford's brilliant industrial vision was matched (and perhaps even overmatched) by Alfred Sloan's insistent new standards in corporate management: The blue-collar genius and the white-collar one met in the same industry, leaving a legacy that pulled nearly every other American company forward. Sloan prevailed in those years with a bracing but unsentimental attitude. "He's a tough sonofabitch, but he's our sonofabitch," said a GM executive once, watching Sloan, then eighty, enter a room.

In the summer of 1920, Alfred Sloan requested a long vacation from General Motors, where he was a vice president. He'd glumly reached the conclusion that the company was hopeless, a conglomerate that was weaker, not stronger, than the sum of its parts. Whenever he'd reached the same conclusion during the previous year-and-a-half, he'd reacted with a certain schoolboy impetuosity: He'd written a report. In college at the Massachusetts Institute of Technology, Sloan had been something of a prodigy, graduating in only three years. As a forty-five-year-old executive, he was still the overachiever, meticulously researching his analyses of such subjects as GM's interdivisional billing, its appropriations, and its overall organization.

In most cases, no one had asked in advance for Sloan's reports, but then, in most cases, no one read them anyway. GM was burgeoning with activities more appealing than the in-depth study of GM. Production men were busy turning out cars — Buicks, Cadillacs, Oldsmobiles, Oaklands, and Chevrolets, in addition to smaller names such as Sheridan and Scripps-Booth — while other independent divisions made parts for GM and other cars. In the corporate offices, executives concentrated on the acquisitions that made GM even bigger with each passing year. The third activity at GM more alluring than the reading of reports was the juggling of stock and capital loans to provide the money to buy more and more companies.

The adventure of finding money by way of Wall Street belonged to William C. Durant, the president of General Motors. Ardently optimistic about the automobile industry, Durant had had the brilliant idea of creating General Motors in 1907. Oddly enough, though, he didn't quite understand why it was a brilliant idea. Sloan did.

Alfred Sloan Jr. was born in 1875 and grew up in a large, prosperous family in Brooklyn. As a boy, his favorite hobbies seemed to be studying and trying to get ahead: the same could still be said of him after he grew up, when he had all the money he could want and still didn't care for sports, collecting, or the other usual diversions. Entering MIT at seventeen, Sloan graduated early and then, for all of his ambition and education, found a job just next door to working in a dump. The Hyatt Roller Bearing Co. was a fading business located adjacent to the dump in Harrison, New Jersey. However, Sloan eventually purchased the company with help from his father and nurtured it into a success by finding uses for roller bearings in the automobile business.

Having sought training as an engineer, Sloan was nonetheless committed to a career in business management. His perspective would always remain that of an engineer: making a machine composed of minds work smoothly. The pride of auto production in the early part of the century was the concept of interchangeable parts, wherein parts were not custom fit to each other, but produced to specific tolerances, so that any piston, say, would fit within any valve for the same engine type. Sloan's mind worked toward the same concept, in which managers could indeed be replaced, and a company was not dependent on matching any certain people.

In cars, interchangeable parts became a reality through exacting conformity. As an engineering challenge, though, Sloan's management structure would have to work without a squeak while accommodating a wide tolerance for nonconformity, in the form of ego and aggressiveness.

An angular man, Sloan had a thin face with large features. He was one of the most sartorially stylish men ever to head a business, dressing like a matinee idol circa 1905. He favored high white collars and spats long after both of those had given way to duller days in men's clothes, and wore suits of uncommon quality and tailoring, often with a handkerchief billowing extravagantly out of the breast pocket. Meticulous in dress, Sloan was unruly in posture. He didn't bother to contain his stretching and fidgeting, and preferred to fold at least one foot onto a chair when he was sitting down.

Sloan had a sense of humor and a loud laugh when he heard something funny, but his overriding concern and stated priority was the business of General Motors. During the working day, diversions from that business were, at most, momentary.

In 1915, Billy Durant purchased the Hyatt Roller Bearing Co., and soon knit it—along with Alfred Sloan—into the fabric of General Motors. The deal made rich men of the Sloans. Alfred Sr. took his half ($6 million) in cash. Alfred Jr. took his in stock, and became an executive in Durant's growing empire. The situation there deteriorated after World War I, however. Two considerations kept Sloan in the carnival atmosphere at GM, despite his predilection for order. First, his fortune was tied up in the company and he was loath to sell out too abruptly. Second, he was as taken as everyone else with Billy Durant—a trying boss, perhaps, but one with blinding integrity and a disarming personality.

Trapped in his job—slightly bored with what he was supposed to do and more than slightly frustrated with what everyone else was doing—Sloan pondered GM and recognized the methods that could optimize its bigness even while accentuating the distinctiveness of its many parts. He gave Durant the reports that resulted from his ponderings. Each time, Durant thanked him sincerely before moving on to something more pressing.

In the summer of 1920, aware that Durant's financial dealings were more precarious than ever, Sloan went to London with his wife, Irene, on the long vacation that he had requested. While in England, he decided to quit and sell all his stock just as soon as he returned. The very moment that Sloan decided to become a former GM employee could probably be determined, because while in London he placed an order for a Rolls-Royce.

When Sloan returned to New York, he found that Billy Durant had overextended his credit, along with that of GM, in a falling market. On the memorable evening of November 18, 1920, Durant was informed that he owed no less than $34 million in obligations to various brokers. His wife later said that he was done in by bankers who had suddenly awakened to the potential of General Motors. J.P. Morgan & Co., the lead bankers in the affair, contended that they intervened only to stave off the general market panic that might have developed had Durant failed to make good on his debts. In any case, the crisis was averted. Durant ceded control of GM to a contingent of bankers led by Morgan and to the duPont family. Pierre duPont, who had already been serving GM as its rather distant chairman of board, was named president. He had recently retired from the same position in his family's chemical company. Alfred Sloan was named as one of duPont's two operating vice presidents. GM was to be reorganized—or fully organized for the first time, as it were. Sloan brought out his reports and sent copies to the new boss. DuPont enthusiastically approved of the ideas they contained.

Not only was Sloan's work read in the newly quietened atmosphere of GM, the reports became intracompany best-sellers—copies had to be privately printed to meet all the requests. One of Sloan's concepts, for example, was that divisions should stop selling components to each other at cost, because that practice made it hard to judge the true profitability of individual divisions. According to Sloan, the only standard by which individual divisions, or the whole corporation, could be judged was return on investment. Sloan didn't want to see any asterisks attached to that figure, such as, "We would have made more money, but we sold a big order of our axles to Buick at cost." Nor could Buick be evaluated in such a case, since part of its return would have been reaped from GM's investment in the axle division . . . which would have been another asterisk on the perception of GM operations.

Sloan's theory on interdivisional billing received particular praise from Donaldson Brown, who had been sent from the duPont Company to become GM's head of finance. Another executive later said of the enigmatic Mr. Brown, "He is the real brains at GM, but he doesn't speak any known language." That Brown approved of the new thinking was worthy of mention in Sloan's memoirs.

The best kind of control was Sloan's ultimate goal for GM management: control based on accurate information. And to him, accurate information emanated from order.

Sloan's most influential report was the one on organization. In his view, divisions had to remain sovereign entities, making nearly all decisions on their own. He wanted them to remain as vainglorious as ever they'd been in Durant's days: each division competing with other automakers, of course, but also competing with itself and its own true potential. One of the central executive staff's primary jobs was to set the goals that held forth that individual potential. It also offered advice in areas such as engineering and sales, but in Sloan's organization, central management only advised, except in emergencies. It did not dictate.

The organizational plan was sleek: complex, but taut. Pierre duPont made one or two minor changes and then, with the approval of the board, GM was pushed and pulled into a structure that mirrored Sloan's organizational chart.

In formulating "decentralized management with coordinated control" as the corporate structure of GM, Sloan initiated a new era in corporate administration. The nuances of his organization, along with its formulas for fact-gathering and control, have been widely emulated ever since.

Alfred Sloan was at the head of General Motors as president, chief executive officer, or chairman until 1956, and he still remained on the board until his death in 1966. Sloan was known as a rather remote leader, yet that was consistent with his notion that incentive should be derived from rewards embedded right into the corporate structure: A company leader should not have to be a cheerleader to achieve the same ends. Properly organized, the corporation would go a long way toward leading itself.

In the words that follow, Alfred Sloan describes how his management organization controlled General Motors' progress while leaving itself out of divisional activities as much as possible. Sloan was analytical by nature and preferred to consider problems in the abstract, testing merits and faults in a sort of vacuum before allowing exigencies of the moment to crowd his thinking. One can see in the quotes that follow that he had a lawyerly interest in constructing a system that would work consistently and smoothly in actual practice. Disdaining "seat-of-the-pants" business leadership, Sloan did not believe that a management system should have to be reinvented with each new business day.

Alfred P. Sloan, Jr.

Survival

We must recognize that irrespective of how well we may do or think we are doing our particular job today, it must be done better tomorrow. It must be done still better next week and again, still better next month. We must make continual progress if we are entitled to survive.

Competition

Companies compete in broad policies as well as in specific products.

Giving Orders

[*By the time Sloan was named president of GM in 1923, he was engaged in structuring GM according to his theories of "decentralization, with co-ordinated control."*]

Even when we make recommendations from the general corporation's office, the head of a division is at liberty to accept or reject—and once in a while he rejects.

At first many of our men believed that this was too good to be true. Some feared that although we meant it, we could not carry it out. They began tentatively unleashing their brains and making important decisions, but they kept one eye on the general corporation office, expecting at any moment to receive a veto of their decisions, or an order that would conflict with their decisions.

No such thing happened. We do not issue orders. I have never issued an order since I have been the operating head of this corporation.

Direction

Where do policies come from, if they are to be useful in the business? Out of the business itself. And that is where our policies come from. They must come from the men who are in daily contact with problems. They must handle activities of whatever sort, whether production, sales, service, or finance. Policies are not correct which do not fit such conditions. Our policies come from the bottom.

Everything possible in the organization starts from the bottom.

Work Flow

Of all business activities, 99% are routine. They do not require management attention except in the aggregate. Only the one exception in a hundred cases need come to a manager's attention.

The entire 100% can be handled by managing the 1% of exceptions. Deciding the symptomatic cases, the exceptional cases which emerge above routine, keeps routine flowing in its channels and, at the same time, allows for progress.

We get that 1% of exceptions managed as closely as possible to the men from whom they arise.

Work

My office force is very small. That means that we do not do much routine work with details. They never get up to us. I work fairly hard, but it is on exceptions or construction, not on routine or petty details.

It means also—and this is more important than any effect on me personally—that I do not bother the other man below me with a continual stream of questions about details, and requests for reports.

Cooperation

After forty years of experience in American industry, I would say that my concept of the management scheme of a great industrial organization, simply expressed, is to divide it into as many parts as consistently can be done, place in charge of each part the most capable executive that can be found, develop a system of co-ordination so that each part may strengthen and support each other part; thus not only welding all parts together in the common interests of a joint enterprise, but importantly developing ability and initiative through the instrumentalities of responsibility and ambition—developing men and giving them an opportunity to exercise their talents, both in their own interests as well as in that of the business.

Appraisal

It is impossible to get the measure of what an individual can accomplish unless the responsibility is given him.

Incentive

To make our theory work, our executives must have a definite financial interest in the success of the business as a whole. The equivalent of the rewards of private enterprise must be offered to men of this type; and it must be offered in the contingent form that would obtain if they were actually in private business, for it is exactly the sporting element of uncertainty as to the size of the reward that is a chief fascination of private enterprise.

Principles

[*In his book* Adventures of a White Collar Man, *Sloan made notes on the principles that developed into GM's operating philosophy.*]

Management: The collective effort of intelligence, experience and imagination.

The Facts: A constant search for the truth.

The open mind: Policy based upon analysis without prejudice.

Courage: The willingness to take a risk, recognizing the fact that leadership exacts a price.

Equity: Respect for the rights of others.

Confidence: The courage of one's convictions.

Loyalty: The willingness to make any sacrifice for the cause.

Progress: There must always be a better way.

And most important of all, for without it all else is of little avail: Work. The catalysis that energizes all these ingredients, so that they may take their respective parts in promoting the common cause.

Consistency

We could not follow one policy some of the time, and another policy the rest of the time.

Many times there were strong temptations to step in and do things the quick way, following my own opinion, but we used patience. If, at any time, I or any of our other officials from the general office had stepped in with a sudden order, it would have halted our progress. Men would have had their fears confirmed. They would not only stop short, but fall back. They would have left decisions altogether to us . . .

So it was necessary to choose absolutely our habits. We could have no middle ground. We could not follow one policy some of the time, and another policy the rest of the time. We could not follow one policy in the main, with exceptions to it once in a while.

Analysis

The only report we ask from all our units is one page a month.

This page summarizes essentials, however, such as the inventory on hand, the turnover or ratio of materials in process to a year's finished goods and sales.

Each month's page contains actual figures for the month just closed and estimates for each of the four following months. In writing the figures, each manager has to plan the big essentials of operations and profit and tell us his plans.

Each manager's past estimates are compared with his subsequent estimates and his present accomplishments to form what is called an accuracy report. Our men are becoming more and more accurate in their estimates of the future.

Accounting

I have been appalled at the utter lack of appreciation on the part of even our big organizations as to the fundamental factors upon which their profit and loss depends . . .

As I see the picture, business—and I believe that this applies quite generally to large business as well as small business and both to the production and distribution end—lacks an appreciation of the possibilities of what can be accomplished through accounting. The more popular conception of this subject is to enable us to know how we stand at the end of any period. In other words, it is a matter of history. Too many lines of business have established accounting systems because they recognize it as the right thing to do. They have not, however, an adequate appreciation of what its tremendous possibilities are. While it is important to know our status at any one time, it is still far more important to understand and appreciate the various factors and influences that underlie our whole structure to the end that we can look forward, by means of our accounting system, and can alter our procedures or policies to the end that a better operation results. In one case we are in principle, looking backward—in the other case, forward . . .

Financial Controls

It was on the financial side that the last necessary key to decentralization with co-ordinated control was found. That key, in principle, was the concept that, if we had the means to review and judge the effectiveness of operations, we could safely leave the prosecution of those operations to the men in charge of them. The means as it turned out was a method of financial control which converted the broad principle of return on investment into one of the important working instruments for measuring the operations of the divisions. The basic elements of financial control in General Motors are cost, price, volume, and rate of return on investment.

A word on rate of return as a strategic principle of business. I am not going to say that rate of return is a magic wand for every occasion in business. There are times when you have to spend money just to stay in business, regardless of the visible rate of return. Competition is the final price determinant and competitive prices may result in profits which force you to accept a rate of return less than you hoped for, or for that matter to accept temporary losses. And, in times of inflation, the rate-of-return concept comes up against the problem of assets undervalued in terms of replacement. Nevertheless, no other financial principle with which I am acquainted serves better than rate of return as an objective aid to business judgment.

Costs

We will sit around the conference table in General Motors and talk for hours about the influence of a dollar on the cost of a car. We know every dollar added to the cost means more than a dollar added to the consumer price. We know a higher consumer price means fewer consumer sales.

Inventory

The only way to cut back inventories—particularly in a time of declining business—is to reduce purchases and commitments for materials and supplies. Obvious? Not entirely. Anyway it took us a long time to learn this from experience. In those days the general managers tended to be optimists, as most executives in the selling end of the automobile business were and perhaps still are. They always expected that sales would increase and thereby bring the inventories in line. When the expected sales failed to materialize, a problem arose to which there could be no entirely pleasant solution. Hence we learned to be skeptical of expectations of increased future sales as a solution to a rising inventory problem.

Problem-solving

[*Sloan's earliest company, Hyatt Roller Bearing, supplied compo- nents to Weston-Mott Co., which produced axles. It became part of the GM palette at about the same time as Hyatt. The head of Weston-Mott was Charles S. Mott, whose own association with General Motors would last almost as long as that of Alfred Sloan.*]

I liked to work with Mott. His training had made him methodical. When he was confronted by a problem, he tackled it as I did my own, with engineering care to get the facts. Neither one of us ever took any pride in hunches. We left all the glory of that kind of thinking to such men as liked to be labeled "genius."

Sloan on Driving

[*In 1936, Sloan discussed automobile safety and driving with a reporter from* Good Housekeeping *magazine. In the course of the conversation, the reporter admitted that, despite having re- cently graduated from a $10 driving school, he didn't really know whether or not he should use the clutch when braking, and Sloan laughed—in a deep, rumbling way that the reported found unexpected for a man so slight.*]

Well, this isn't a driving course, it's an interview. Unless, of course, you want to pay me another ten dollars! But I'll tell you another thing gratis: leave that clutch in until the last minute any time you need quick braking power. You get an important extra retarding force from your engine that way.

[*Sloan continued the driving lesson:*]

I wish we could alter the scale we use to designate speeds. Instead of saying, "We are driving at 50 mph," we should say, "We are driving at 166-feet stopping distance." Then it might be more apparent that if you could see only 100 feet around the turn, you'd slow down to, say, 35 mph and leave yourself ample braking margin.

I have a friend who wrecked her car last winter by failing to do just that. She is a physician who has driven for years—one of these fast but apparently competent open-country drivers. She took a curve at good speed and went around fine until her wheels struck an unexpected wet spot and she skidded off the road.

She felt it was unfortunate that the pavement was wet. I feel it was more unfortunate that she should drive into a hidden hazard so fast as to lose control.

D e m a n d

The wants of man continue insatiable: what we call overproduction is merely a lack of distribution; a surplus is usually something men want and cannot buy—in effect a challenge to improve the system of distribution and increase the buying power until the one-time surplus has been used to sustain, dignify, or otherwise improve the lot of mankind. To destroy a surplus wantonly is to remove a strong incentive to social progress.

I n c e n t i v e

We have consolidated the cash assets of a great many plants and former independent companies into one pool for financial management, but we have never consolidated the various units of personnel. We have left each personnel unit to develop its own corps spirit and initiative. Our Cadillac unit today is not so much a matter of plant or equipment or even design and patents, as it is a matter of men. We could destroy the buildings of the Cadillac plant, and yet we would have the Cadillac car intact in the Cadillac organization, for they are used to making the car, skilled in the team-work of assembling it, and are held together by an enthusiastic belief in the supremacy of their product. They have been left free to develop it by their own initiative so that they feel it is theirs. Likewise with the Buick or any of our other cars.

Incentive

I believe strongly that those managing our great industrial enterprises should have a real stake in the business. I believe it is essential that corporate executives be placed as far as possible in the same position as the joint owners of a private business.

Power

[*Sloan's first management experience came at Hyatt Roller Bearing, then a very small outfit.*]

Every executive has to recognize sooner or later that he himself cannot do everything that needs to be done. Until he recognizes this, he is only an individual, with an individual's power, but after he recognizes it, he becomes, for the first time, an executive, with control of multiple powers. This necessary conversion happened to me while I was assisting John Hyatt to perfect his mechanism for making billiard balls . . .

Up to this time, I was an engineer, a designer, or a salesman—not a manager. Even an embryo manager must have learned how to arouse the individual initiative of the men working with him.

Naturally, the change in attitude of mind could not take place overnight. We floundered more or less, after the fashion of a boy thrown into the water to swim. But after a while, we thoroughly grasped the principle that the work must be done by other men. Granted that, we had to find a way to arouse their initiative.

That is still the most important thing I have ever learned about management—to make men think and act with individual zeal and initiative, yet cooperating with each other.

Shareholders

There frequently arise questions of policy and procedure affecting the position of one part of the Corporation as against another. In such instances, the raising of the question as to what the interest of the stockholders requires enables us to obtain the correct answer. No management can have a proper appreciation of its responsibilities as trustees should it approach the question from any other viewpoint.

Investing

I do not know whether many would agree with my philosophy on the subject of investing one's savings, but it grows out of my own experience. I have seen General Motors go from eighty-five dollars a share to seven dollars, but never sold a single share. Speculations never had any attraction for me. Other than a few professional operators, who has really got ahead by stock-market trading?

Placement

Never inject a man into the top if it can be avoided. In a big organization to have to do that, I think, is a reflection on management.

Debate

Differences in opinion are often differences in conception as to what is the vital point; one man argues for, another against, and all the time they are talking about different things.

Work

Irrespective of what our individual part may be in any organization, be it that of the humblest worker or the most important executive, our own success and the institution's success is dependent upon the willingness of each and every one of us to make the sacrifice of time, personal convenience and effort to give at all times all there is to give for the good of the cause.

David Packard in 1969, when he was appointed to Richard Nixon's cabinet as assistant secretary of defense. He served in the post three years, trying to reduce Pentagon bureaucracy. Once, asked what he had accomplished during his tenure in Washington, he dourly replied, "I quit smoking."

David Packard

1912–1996

David Packard cofounded Hewlett-Packard in Palo Alto, California, in 1938 and afterward presided over the high-tech frontier that grew up all around him in the Silicon Valley. The company that Packard started as a partnership with William Hewlett built electronic test equipment in its early years, but later branched out even more successfully into computers and printing equipment. Packard, who shouldered much of the financial management at HP, was notably wary in matters of finance and growth, giving HP its reputation as a solid company amid the volatile high-tech industry. For Packard, the basis of success at HP rested with employees at every level who thought for themselves—for the company's sake. A combination of corporate responsibility and individual incentive, the "HP Way" was widely emulated by new generations of executives in the Silicon Valley and elsewhere. Few were ever quite as modern as David Packard, though, in trusting good employees with a company to build.

$\mathcal{A}$nnual lists of most respected companies in the 1960s and 1970s included Hewlett-Packard as though the space had been ordained for it. The company was cited just as predictably as being among the nation's best in innovation, environmental practices, employee relations, and overall management excellence. For all of its achievement, though, the company didn't sparkle with delight at its own image, as some might, nor did it rumble with the tension of living up to that image, as some have done. In fact, Hewlett-Packard never seemed to gaze at itself at all. Its appeal was shirt-sleeved and plain-spoken, a frame of mind that became known early on as "the HP Way." Established on the day in 1938 when Bill Hewlett and David Packard formed their partnership, the HP Way was still intact 55 years later, when 105,000 people were sharing the employment roster with them.

The HP Way was a balance of attitudes that made Hewlett-Packard at once the most conservative and most progressive of companies, giving it a refreshing sense of proportion about matters well beyond bookkeeping. Profits were crucial—and abundant—at HP, but not at any cost. According to the HP Way, the company didn't take financial risks or accept outsize contracts in the interest of short-term gains, not when doing so could eventually necessitate cutbacks and displace loyal employees.

During the 1980s, Hewlett-Packard doubled in size as it became the nation's fourth-largest computer maker and its largest source for laser printers. By then, David Packard and Bill Hewlett were both in their late seventies. Largely distanced from company matters, they busied themselves with their families, hobbies, and community projects: typical retirees enjoying their spare time. But they were not entirely typical, of course. Between the two of them, they owned more than one-quarter of the nation's twenty-ninth-largest company.

The frenzied horde tearing into the computer market in the late 1980s truly admired Hewlett-Packard's peaceable kingdom. Nonetheless, they wanted nothing more than to lay waste to it, and they suddenly seemed ready to do so in 1990. The size of computers was shrinking, yet HP was lagging dangerously in the transition.

The company reported decreasing profits in 1990, and during the first six months of that year its stock price dropped by half. The prevailing wisdom was that it was too late for Hewlett-Packard to salvage its computer business. The leapfrogging technology of the computer industry was bruising enough, just as a matter of science, but combined with the rapaciousness of the young entrepreneurs who set the pace, the market was nothing less than "guerilla warfare," in the words of one competing CEO.

As it happened, though, the two most aggressive warriors in Silicon Valley were a couple of men who were nearing eighty years of age.

David Packard was born in 1912 in Pueblo, Colorado, where his father was a lawyer and his mother a teacher. "The most important thing about my career," he once said, "is that I decided I wanted to be an engineer when I was about 10 years old and never changed." The second most important thing was that as a teenager, Packard took a vacation to California with his mother and sister, making a polite detour to visit an acquaintance who was studying at Stanford University in Palo Alto.

Packard not only decided to attend Stanford, he made the school a part of his life for as long as he lived. A good athlete and a big one, at six-foot-four, Packard played football for his school, but distinguished himself on campus as an ardent ham radio operator.

At Stanford, Packard formed a fast friendship with Bill Hewlett, the son of the late dean at the university's medical school. Hewlett shared Packard's enjoyment of hiking, along with his interest in electrical engineering. By their senior year, the two also shared a resolve to start their own company as soon as conditions permitted. Neither of them felt insulated from the Depression, despite having had the good fortune to pass part of it in the idyll of a college campus. During one summer, Packard assisted his father in bankruptcy proceedings and learned firsthand that even a successful company can perish when debt serves to intensify economic conditions.

In 1938, Packard and Hewlett rented a house in Palo Alto and started Hewlett-Packard in the garage—a garage now revered, according to a historical marker, as "the start of Silicon Valley."

Nothing ever really starts from scratch, however, not even a company with listed assets of but $538 and two engineering diplomas. Whenever Packard and Hewlett needed to borrow a tool, they went to the nearby workshop where Charlie Litton had already started Litton Industries—in a small way, of course.

At first, Hewlett and Packard were inventors for hire. A handful of clients brought them concepts, such as one for a machine using radio waves to help people lose weight. However, they found a better niche with their own ideas, including one of Hewlett's for a resistance-tuned audio oscillator that could help engineers make clear recordings. (And perhaps even help people lose weight.)

After Hewlett left for duty with the Signal Corps during World War II, Packard tested his own potential as a businessman, overseeing one hundred employees and revenues of over $1 million by 1945. When Hewlett returned from the service, he concentrated on product planning, being a sharp engineer, while Packard developed into a professional manager.

Straightforward in demeanor, David Packard maintained an open-door policy and would see any employee who had a question or problem. His focus was intense, his curiosity about scientific and humanitarian subjects wide ranging. However, he had a peremptory way of interrupting people in midsentence if he thought he knew what they were going to say. It was probably a result of his intellectual bearing, rather than his business rank, for David Packard remained oblivious to most of the trappings of corporate power.

He enjoyed hard ranchwork and hunting; he also liked to ferret out jazz spots with his wife, Lucile, to hear the Dixieland music to which he said he was "addicted." Another interest was poetry. On one occasion, his remarks to a meeting of HP general managers were limited to a recitation of Oliver Wendell Holmes's poem "The One Horse Shay," about a carriage that had been designed and constructed without such a thing as a "weakest spot."

Serving in semiretirement as chairman of his company's board of directors, Packard carried himself as a sort of plenipotentiary for Hewlett-Packard in international business. However, in the spring of 1990, he and Bill Hewlett (then retired except as a board member) realized that vital opportunities in the computer business were slipping away from the company, dragging down its profits and its future. They returned to work on a daily basis.

"One of the reasons it's important for Bill Hewlett and me to be in on this," David Packard told a local newspaper, "is that we're probably going to have to make painful reductions in some places." At first, they did what they did best: They walked around. Touring as many of the company's plants and offices as they could, they talked with employees at all levels.

"We had too damn many committees," Hewlett concluded. In fact, decisions were made, or delayed, made by committees of committees: Just to think of a name for a new product, for example, one hundred people on nine committees conferred for seven months.

"Overhead is something that creeps in," Hewlett said, "It's not something that overtakes you overnight." But practically overnight, Packard and Hewlett did away with the excess overhead. Management was reduced, such that only four layers of administration separated David Packard, as chairman of the board, from nearly any worker on the production line. Moreover, Packard and Hewlett insisted on redrawing the lines around autonomous divisions, in keeping with the type of trim work teams that had once given HP its entrepreneurial thrust.

Every change carried the same intention: to make Hewlett-Packard move more quickly; to make it, in fact, move quickest. Regaining its balance, the company introduced a well-received workstation the following spring, launching two more within months. Development time for new products had been cut in half, and the response to arising problems was so quick that HP was outpacing the industry by 1992.

As a manager, David Packard was long practiced in his ways, the HP ways he'd developed with Bill Hewlett. The last of those ways was always the same. It may be the hardest to accept, but it was the one that built the company: Stay out of the way of people in pursuit of a goal.

In the words that follow, David Packard speaks about several of his concerns in his role as manager of a high-tech company, including the obligation to provide job security even in an unpredictable industry and the need for basic trust within the company. In excerpts from an early talk at the company, Packard explains the reasons for enunciating corporate objectives clearly and then does so, laying the groundwork for the system of values later known as the HP Way.

IN THE WORDS OF

David Packard

Organization

You've got to avoid having too rigid an organization.

When you get up to a certain size you need to have some sort of structure. So you work out an organization chart that gives people areas of responsibility. You make sure that all the areas are covered and relate properly to each other.

Actually, if an organization is going to work effectively the communications should be through the most effective channel regardless of the organization chart.

I've often thought that after you get organized you ought to throw the chart away.

Accessibility

Everyone at HP works in open-plan, doorless offices. This ready availability has its drawbacks in that interruptions are always possible. But at HP we've found that the benefits of accessibility far outweigh the disadvantages.

Walking Around

I learned that quality requires minute attention to every detail, that everyone in an organization wants to do a good job, that written instructions are seldom adequate, and that personal involvement is essential.

We have a technique at HP for helping managers and supervisors know their people and understand the work their people are doing, while at the same time making themselves more visible and accessible to their people. It's called MBWA—"management by walking around." The term, a good one, was coined many years ago by one of our managers . . .

Leadership

Once we promoted a man, a good worker, to be the manager of our machine shop. A few days later he came to see me. He said he was having a tough time managing and wanted me to come out to the shop and tell his people that he was their boss. "If I have to do that," I said, "You don't deserve to be their boss."

Motivation

I recognized pretty early that while I might be able to do something better than a few guys could, I certainly couldn't do it any better than 100, so I had better think about how to get our people to do their job right rather than think of how I could do it myself.

We figured that people would accomplish more if they were given an opportunity to use their talents and abilities in the way they work best.

How do you do this? You establish some objectives for them, provide some incentive, and try not to direct the detailed way in which they do their work. We've found you're likely to get a much better performance that way than if you have a more military-type procedure where somebody gives orders and expects them to be followed in every detail.

Command

[*Packard once delineated four primary elements of corporate management, including attention to human factors, organization, and community involvement.*]

There is always a fourth dimension added. It can best be described as the strong-minded man.

He may even be lacking in some of the other dimensions, but somehow he brings out the best in his people and his organization, and he brings out performance beyond the call of duty. He can do it, whatever his assignment. If he needs financial controls, or mathematical approaches, or computers, he will get them if he can. If he doesn't have them, he will get the job done anyway.

Management Attitude

What the employee conceives your attitude to be is more important than the actions you take on compensation and other things.

The most important element in our personnel policy is the degree to which we are able to get over to our people that we have faith in them and are more interested in them than someone else is.

Market Share

[*Packard felt that the company became reoriented after the success of the HP-35 handheld calculator, Hewlett-Packard's first high-profile product, in the early-1970s. He addressed his managers in 1974:*]

Somewhere we got into the idea that market share was an objective. I hope that's straightened out. Anyone can build market share, and if you set your prices low enough, you can get the whole damn market. But I'll tell you it won't get you anywhere around here . . .

Stability

During the war we had opportunities for some large contracts, but I decided we shouldn't take on anything larger than we could handle on our own. We didn't want to get overextended and do what many companies do when they take on big contracts—hire a lot of people, and when the contracts are over, let them go.

Our company philosophy started in that period and we've stuck with it—to grow as fast as we can with our own earnings and make every job we create a permanent one.

Debt

My philosophy goes back to the Depression. I don't want to be in debt if a downturn comes.

Expenditures

We don't believe in gold plating, such as plushing up executive offices. We find better uses for our profits.

Accomplishment

I think you get the most satisfaction in trying to do something useful. After you've done that, you ought to forget about it and do something else. You shouldn't gloat about anything you've done; you ought to keep going and try to find something better to do.

Projection

We've made mistakes in selling things before they were really developed. We've learned it never really pays.

We've learned the hard way that an engineer is often over-optimistic on how long it's going to take to develop a new product.

He quite often thinks all the main problems are solved when they aren't, so it's very important to produce a model and shake out the bugs before you sell it.

Trust

Keeping storerooms and parts bins open was advantageous to HP in two important ways. From a practical standpoint, the easy access to parts and tools helped product designers and others who wanted to work out new ideas at home or on weekends. A second reason, less tangible but important, is that the open bins and storerooms were a symbol of trust, a trust that is central to the way HP does business.

Work Reduction

Because of a downturn in the U.S. economy [in 1970], our incoming orders were running at a rate quite a bit less than our production capability. We were faced with the prospect of a 10 percent layoff. Rather than a layoff, however, we tried a different tack. We went to a schedule of working nine days out of every two weeks—a 10 percent cut in work schedule with a corresponding 10 percent cut in pay. This applied to virtually all our U.S. factories, as well as to all executives and corporate staff. At the end of a six-month period, the order rate was up again and everyone returned to a full work schedule. Some said they enjoyed the long weekends even though they had to tighten their belts a little. The net result of this program was that effectively all shared the burden of the recession, good people were not released into a very tough job market, and we had our highly qualified workforce in place when business improved.

The Hewlett-Packard Way

[*In his 1995 book* The HP Way, *David Packard outlined the corporate philosophy that came to be widely known by that name. Packard covered the subject with the benefit of his long experience in observing the HP Way under actual conditions, making the book a uniquely valuable memoir of the Hewlett-Packard Co. Some of the foregoing quotes in this section were drawn from it. In the book, Packard related how the HP Way had germinated at a company management meeting in January 1957. Introduced on the agenda as "Dave Packard presenting a discussion of corporate objectives and review of operations for 1956," the remarks made that day started an ongoing effort to define and abide by a set of specific values within the corporation. The following excerpts have been drawn from Packard's comments. As he noted in his book, the HP Way evolved in many respects after 1957, but the following are some of his original thoughts on the subject (the section headings are additions).*]

Objectives

There are many reasons why a business is founded and why a business continues to exist. Sometimes these reasons are not clearly understood or clearly stated at any particular time. They often change as the organization grows. It is desirable to clarify the objectives of a business and to state them from time to time so that all of the people in the organization will have a better understanding of the business and direct their efforts toward the common goal . . .

I believe such a restatement will help you to have a better

basis for making your decisions. I think a restatement of the objectives will help some of the younger people in the organization have a better understanding of what is going on.

Profitability

It is difficult to decide which is the most important objective of the company and in placing the one I have chosen first, I do so with the specific emphasis that I consider it to be the most important objective to guide your day-to-day thinking. It is the objective which makes all of the other objectives possible, but it alone is not a sufficient objective. It is as follows: TO OPERATE OUR BUSINESS SO THAT YEAR IN AND YEAR OUT, WE OBTAIN A PROFIT OF ABOUT 20% OF SALES BEFORE TAXES.

Our ability to obtain money from the market, from the prospective lenders or from any other source is greatly enhanced by the profit performance of the company. It is this which has enabled us to build a great deal of reserve strength in our whole structure and to do all of the other things which make for a good company. The more I have considered the matter, the more important I feel this objective to be, and I would venture to put it so strongly as to say that anyone who cannot accept this objective as one of the most important of all has no place either now or in the future on the management team of this company.

Focus

We have had our success in the field of instruments. It should be our objective to stay in that field almost to the exclusion of anything else. I say "almost to the exclusion," because I think all of our objectives should be somewhat flexible and in case there came to our attention the opportunity to do something important outside of the field of measuring instruments and techniques we should not automatically forgo that opportunity, but rather we should concentrate our main efforts as we have in the past and consider outside activities only when and if they offer unusual potential.

Quality

Early in the business we felt it was possible to design and manufacture good instruments at a lower cost than those which were then available. Historically we have done this. We have kept out the frills and held to the important aspects of the job. In the past I have described this as "inexpensive quality."

This inexpensive quality can come from engineering design, from clever and advanced production techniques and methods, or from better methods of sales and distribution.

I think it is important for you to keep this objective in mind lest we fall unknowingly into ways which will lead us astray. This objective I think is especially important because it involves decisions of compromise at every point. Perhaps we could restate this objective in another way: Cost is an important factor in everything you do from the design concept to servicing the instrument after the sale is made.

Employees

In the field of personnel it is my opinion that the general policies and the attitude of management people toward the employee are more important than specific details of the personnel program. Personnel relations will be good if the people have faith in the motives and integrity of the company. Personnel relations will be poor if they do not, regardless of all of the frills that we have. I think a statement of our personnel policy belongs in the list of objectives of the business: TO PROVIDE EMPLOYMENT OPPORTUNITIES FOR HP PEOPLE THAT INCLUDE THE OPPORTUNITY TO SHARE IN THE COMPANY'S SUCCESS WHICH THEY HELP MAKE POSSIBLE; TO PROVIDE FOR THEM JOB SECURITY BASED ON THEIR PERFORMANCE; AND TO PROVIDE THE OPPORTUNITY FOR PERSONAL SATISFACTION THAT COMES FROM A SENSE OF ACCOMPLISHMENT IN THEIR WORK.

We have stated a number of times that we believe it is important for people to enjoy their work at Hewlett-Packard Company. This does not mean that we expect them to sit around and play all day, but rather that they should have the opportunity to achieve a large degree of personal satisfaction through accomplishment. We are not always as successful as we might be in meeting this phase of this objective.

Social Responsibility

Many of the things which we are now using in our day-to-day work have come about because the frontiers of knowledge have been pushed forward by our universities. A large part of the training which our people are using in their everyday work has come from universities. Our churches and schools play a large part in the intellectual and moral training which we rely on every day without giving the matter a second thought. This points up the fact that the Hewlett-Packard Company as a business should include as one of its objectives a recognition of these facts. TO MEET THE OBLIGATIONS OF GOOD CITIZENSHIP BY MAKING CONTRIBUTIONS TO THE COMMUNITY AND TO THE INSTITUTIONS IN OUR SOCIETY WHICH GENERATE THE ENVIRONMENT IN WHICH WE OPERATE.

Growth

One of the very important problems in running a business has to do with growth. In the past we have speculated many times as to what is the optimum size of a company. I have heard other people do likewise. Some people feel that when a company has reached a certain size there is no point in letting it grow any further. Other people feel that they want to develop as big an empire as possible, and bigness seems to be one of their main objectives. There is actually quite a range over which growth can be controlled.

There is a saying that "a business must grow or die," but I am inclined to think this is more of a cliché than a fact. However, over the period of years we have developed a fairly well defined objective as far as growth for the Hewlett-Packard Company is concerned, and it is as follows: TO LET OUR COMPANY GROWTH BE DETERMINED PRIMARILY BY OUR PERFORMANCE, LIMITED ON THE ONE HAND BY THE RATE OF GROWTH WHICH WE CAN FINANCE FROM OUR CURRENT PROFITS AND ON THE OTHER HAND BY THE RATE AT WHICH WE CAN

BUILD UP OUR PRODUCT LINE AND OUR MARKET
THROUGH CUSTOMER ACCEPTANCE IN ACCOR-
DANCE WITH OUR OTHER OBJECTIVES.

Succession

Finally, I want to state an objective which I think is important,
and although it may not appear to be so, it is very important to
Bill [Hewlett] and me. That object is to build sufficient strength
into our organization so that the future of the Hewlett-Packard
Company is not dependent upon any one or any two or three
people, including Bill and myself.

PART V

No Matter What Everyone Else Is Doing: MAVERICKS

The maverick has to go through life constantly comparing two distinct images: the way an industry ought to be and the way it actually is. In between is a person with a lot of changes to make, either to image or to industry. The frustration of not only seeing potential clearly but of knowing it innately is a ringing impetus for business success. A level of lonely dissatisfaction, with a large measure of optimism regarding it, launched each of the people in this section.

Clarence Birdseye went so far as to feel sorry for anyone who had achieved a level of security in life. He believed that an individual way of looking at things is practically an obligation in business.

Herb Kelleher of Southwest Airlines insists that going against the tide of accepted wisdom has a valuable built-in advantage: It makes a business unique, for better or for worse. Margaret Rudkin made money during the Depression selling high-priced Pepperidge Farm bread. It couldn't work. But it did. And when Ted Turner built his television company, Turner Broadcasting System, he changed his industry far more than it changed him. The same could be said for any of the four mavericks in this section.

Herb Kelleher hands out peanuts, along with laughs, on a Southwest Airlines flight. On holidays, Kelleher has been known to dress up as a St. Patrick's leprechaun or a Halloween ghoul, as he takes his turn as an inflight steward.

Herb Kelleher

1931–

Herb Kelleher simplifies problems. In the airline industry, that alone has been enough to make him a maverick, if not an outcast. Kelleher has been with Southwest Airlines since its conception in 1966, and has been at the head of the company since 1980. The most common reason of all to do things a certain way—because they have always been done that way—has never cluttered Kelleher's thinking, and his thinking has carried Southwest to fifth place among American airline companies. With his own bounding personality, Herb Kelleher has established an improbable business atmosphere at Southwest, in which work and lighthearted fun are cultivated as a natural pair. Within the company, Kelleher's expectation is that each employee should be just as much a leader as Kelleher himself is, an estimable goal that might be unrealistic in some organizations. Kelleher backs it up, though, by gladly welcoming all the nonconformity it engenders at Southwest.

$\mathcal{T}$he airline industry grew up acting as though it wanted to be in the Air Force. Flight deck officers in gold-braided uniforms used clipped accents to make rather monotonous announcements, and a sense of authority prevailed. The glamor, such as it was, may have been borrowed, but airline fleets expanded on their military formula, deriving strength from regimentation and a certain comfort from conformity. Herbert Kelleher didn't spring from that tradition, though. He'd never been in the Air Force, he'd never worked in the air travel industry, and the airline he cofounded in 1971, Southwest, grew up acting as though it wanted to be in the Mardi Gras celebration.

Kelleher cultivated an atmosphere that made passengers feel less as though they were being deployed to another base and a little more like they were on a float in a parade. The silliness may be unrestrained, yet Kelleher's Southwest is nonetheless a crack outfit, as they might say in the Air Force, its staunch discipline arising not from regimentation, but from— oddly enough—humor. "Management by fooling around," Kelleher once called it.

Herb Kelleher is a funny man, one of the few CEOs who might be said to follow in the executive tradition of Benny Hill. The jokes that pop into his head are broad, topical, sometimes childish—usually childish, as a matter of fact. Yet to discuss Kelleher's humor is not merely to dwell on the times like the one in 1988 when he had an inquiry from a rival, Robert Crandall of American Airlines, as to how Southwest planned to clean up after the planes it had painted to look like whales—to which he responded by having a bucket of chocolate mousse delivered to Crandall, with a spoon. It is to look even further into the meaning of humor.

"We want to be interested in our employees as individuals and not as part of a profit-making machine only," Kelleher said. "Then we want to give them the latitude to be individuals in their jobs. We want them to be good-natured and have a good-humored approach to life and to have fun doing their job."

To the ancients who coined the word, *humor* meant the very stuff of life, as it flowed through the body. Embracing the individual (literally, as often as possible), the bear-hugging Kelleher has given humor something of that deeper meaning at Southwest. A major aspect of his work is to encourage the flow of initiative that makes the difference between life and decay in all things, corporate or animal.

Raised in New Jersey, Kelleher made good grades in high school, college, and then law school without seeming to try, participating in sports and an unfettered social life all the while. To a "grind," academic excellence required some sacrifice of one's humor; for Kelleher, the two were inseparable. Besides, he loved to have fun. In the summers he worked as a production worker at the Campbell's Soup Co., where his father was a general manager. Kelleher once said that the most important training or education he ever received was that his parents raised him to regard people strictly in an individual light.

After law school, Kelleher married Joan Negley, who was from San Antonio, Texas. In 1960 the couple moved to San Antonio and Kelleher established himself as one of the city's most aggressive lawyers.

The idea for Southwest Airlines coalesced in a bar in 1966. The magna carta of the whole enterprise, a cocktail napkin blotted with a proposed flight pattern, is now on display in the corporate offices. In the course of conversation, a client of Kelleher's, an entrepreneur named Rollin King, suggested that Texas needed a simple, inexpensive airline service covering its biggest cities: Dallas, San Antonio, and Houston. Kelleher thought it was a great idea. Texas's three largest airlines, Braniff, Trans Texas, and Continental, thought it was a despicable idea.

Charging that the proposed airline was unnecessary, the established airlines fought successfully to keep Southwest from receiving certification from the Texas Aeronautics Commission. Over the course of four years, Southwest's initial investment group spent over a half-million dollars in legal fees in order to prove the merit of a new commuter airline for Texas, only to lose over and over again. It was a rather sickening way to fritter away money to which higher hopes had once been attached. Others in the "Air Southwest" camp were for quitting, but Kelleher insisted on representing the proposed airline in a final appeal to the Texas Supreme Court. Pouring effort into the case—which he ultimately won through a series of decisions—Kelleher emerged with the feeling that Southwest Airlines was more than a business opportunity. To him, it became a cause, a chance to prove something.

Southwest started flying in 1971. At the time, Kelleher was named chief legal counsel; a veteran airline executive named Lamar Muse was president. Muse and a team of experienced executives guided the company through its early days, when its rivals were as determined as ever to quash it. One day, when prospects seemed especially bleak, Kelleher was gratified to hear his sister-in-law speak glowingly of all the attention she'd received from the stewardesses on a Southwest flight.

"It turned out she had been the only passenger on the plane," Kelleher said. The company eventually started to fill up the other seats, though, and turned a profit in its third year. In 1978, when Muse resigned over a dispute with the board of directors, Kelleher was named as his replacement.

Herb Kelleher had no experience as a manager, but proceeded on the assumption that if costs were low and customers were happy, the airline would succeed under any economic conditions. Further, if the company books were strong, and debt was managed conservatively, Southwest could withstand any type of competition.

As an outsider, Kelleher was oblivious to fads within the industry; every new idea was weighed against the effect it would have on costs as he understood them. When other airlines adopted the "hub" system for funneling passengers through centrally located airports, Southwest clung to its point-to-point system for the sake of customer convenience, cost efficiency, and the uniqueness that Kelleher considers an automatic asset to any business.

Kelleher's own formula for running the airline efficiently depends on sharing responsibility as fully as possible with employees. At the same time, no one could work much harder than the boss (who gives the company sixteen-hour days and seven-day weeks), but employees seem inclined to try. They frequently work extra hours without pay for the sake of the company, and have racked up long-standing records within the industry for customer satisfaction, safety, and on-time performance. However, the success of the company didn't hinge on Kelleher hiring his equals in silly humor or even in hard work, but in caring about the airline as a cause, a chance for each to prove something.

In the words that follow, Herb Kelleher discusses the working atmosphere at Southwest, though his first point is that there is no "plan" or "program" behind it. Creating the type of morale that puts an extra player on the field is a matter of spontaneous and sincere details, according to Kelleher, and he relates several to show what he means. He also describes why it is demonstrably cost effective to care about employees in a service corporation. The business points are serious, but the jokebook isn't, with a bit of Kelleher's humor (but no peanuts).

IN THE WORDS OF

Herb Kelleher

Employees

Southwest has its customers, the passengers; and I have my customers, the airline's employees. If the passengers aren't satisfied, they won't fly with us. If the employees aren't satisfied, they won't provide the product we need.

Spontaneity

If it's a plan, it ain't sincere and it doesn't work.

It's interesting when folks come to Southwest Airlines from some other company. They visit us, and then they want to establish a culture similar to ours. When you tell them it's just treating people right, that's too simplistic for them. They want something far more complex. They want a program. We always felt that making it a program murders it.

Perspective

Think small and act small, and we'll get bigger. Think big and act big, and we'll get smaller.

Costs

There's no organization of any size that can't reduce its costs if they really get serious about it. There's always some slippage wherever you are. It's a bottom-up thing, not a top-down thing. It's looking at each item individually—why do you need this person, why do you have to buy these supplies? That causes you to be a cost-effective organization.

Preparedness

We realized that, on an average of twice a decade, you're going to be faced with difficult times. I tell the people here that we must always manage so that we do well in bad times.

In all the battles we've fought—and there have been a tremendous number of them—we've had the lowest costs and the best customer service. And that prevails every time if you have the wherewithal to fight for a prolonged period of time.

Procedure

Before you implement an idea that's been generated in the office, you should always take it to the field and ask for their criticisms. Pretty soon the idea will look like Swiss cheese—full of holes. They know what they're doing and we don't. We may supply the idea, but they know how to implement and execute it. That's why we keep specifications as short as possible, why we use no elaborate guidelines.

Support

The front office is there to support the working troops, not vice versa. We want to know what they need and then supply it.

Communication

There's a lot being said about the importance of communication. But it can't be rigid, it can't be formal. It has to proceed directly from the heart. It has to be spontaneous. "Communication" is not getting up and giving formal speeches. It's saying, "Hey Dave, how you doing? Heard the wife's sick—she okay?" That sort of thing.

Remembering the Employee

[*Southwest devotes a considerable budget to celebrating its employees with parties, banquets, gifts, birthday cards, and outings.*]

If you were a statistician, you wouldn't do these kinds of things, because you'd say, "Well, we could save money if we didn't do it." Southwest Airlines has the best customer-complaint record in the American airline industry, and who can say how much that's worth?

Leadership

I think leadership is valuing the time you spend with your people more than anything else that you do.

Direct Exposure

Say there's a problem with anything. I—or somebody—goes out and experiences the problem. Someone says the bin doors don't work. I want to see them not work, to feel them. How can I talk to Boeing about it if I haven't actually had the experience of it malfunctioning? How can I call Boeing and say, "There's something wrong with the bin doors." They'd say, "Oh, really, what?" And I'd have to say, "Well, I don't know. I just heard that they're not working."

Change

You can innovate by not doing anything, if it's a conscious decision.

[*In the 1970s, every major airline in the country adopted the hub system, whereby flights transferred through a central airport.*]

We said we would continue what we had been doing. As a consequence, we wound up with a unique market niche: We are the world's only short-haul, high-frequency, low-fare, point-to-point carrier.

By not changing, we wound up with a market segment that is peculiarly ours, and everything about the airline has been adapted to serving that market segment in the most efficient and economical way possible.

Market Share

Market share says we just want to be big; we don't care if we make money doing it. That's what misled much of the industry for fifteen years, after deregulation. In order to get an additional 5 percent of the market, some companies increased their costs by 25 percent. That's really incongruous if profitability is your purpose.

Identifying the Competition

[*In some cases, Southwest priced flights to compete not with other airline fares, but with the cost of ground transportation. In fact, one of the reasons it has been impervious to the recessions that have periodically stabbed the revenues of other airlines is that it is positioned in a slightly different way.*]

We've created a solid niche—our main competition is the automobile. We're taking people away from Toyota and Ford.

324   No Matter What Everyone Else Is Doing: Mavericks

Positioning

Sometimes the best way to fight is on the flank, not in the center of the activity where your opponent masses its own force.

Planning

We don't even do one-year plans. When we bump up against some benchmark that requires us to make a major decision, we review our strategic definition of the airline and decide whether we should depart from it.

Salaries

We don't need to skimp on pay, just get a good day's work out of employees.

Hiring

What we are looking for, first and foremost, is a sense of humor.

We don't care that much about education and expertise, because we can train people to do whatever they have to do. We hire attitudes.

[*Southwest rejects approximately ninety-seven applications for every three accepted.*]

Individuality

There's a hundred roads to Rome; the important thing is to get there, not to use the same road.

We tell our people that we value inconsistency. By that, I mean that we're going to carry 20 million passengers this year and that I can't foresee all of the situations that will arise at the stations across our system. So what we tell our people is, "Hey, we can't anticipate all of these things, *you* handle them the best way possible. *You* make a judgment and use *your* discretion, we trust you'll do the right thing. If we think you've done something erroneous, we'll let you know—without criticism, without backbiting."

Firing

People will write me and complain, "Hey, I got terminated or put on probation for purely subjective reasons." And I'll say, "Right! Those are the important reasons. We believe in taking subjective people." It's not enough to just show up at 8:00 each morning and say, "Oh, I've done a wonderful thing." Very often, the most valuable things in life aren't quantifiable. Let's stop trying to be little scientists and putting everything in a little box and weighing and measuring it.

Business Law

[*For decades, Southwest Airlines found itself constricted by a special federal law, called the Wright Amendment, forbidding carriers from flying out of Dallas's Love Field to any destination except those in Texas or states immediately adjoining it. Southwest, which considers Love Field its home, fought the amendment for decades. As Kelleher said in 1995, "Everytime you think it's gone to Transylvania and climbed into a coffin and had a silver stake rammed through its heart, it comes up again." Finally, the company gave up its fight and has adopted a neutral stance on the issue.*]

The Wright Amendment is a pain in the ass, but not every pain in the ass is a constitutional infringement.

Performance Appraisal

Customers provide you with the most accurate barometer of what's right and wrong.

Receptiveness

I have a naive and childlike mind when it comes to ideas. If you get crusty and keep backing away from risks, you're never going to try anything new.

Manager Education

The more time I spend with our people, the more I learn about our company.

Uncle Herb's Jokebook

[*Herb Kelleher, known to all of his employees as "Herb," or "Uncle Herb," was named president of Southwest Airlines in 1978. A practicing lawyer until the age of forty, he had served in other capacities at Southwest, but none in management.*]

I was apprehensive, just as I expect everyone was, so I got everybody together for a meeting. And the first thing I told them was not to worry because I had the most important executive ability down cold . . . I've always been able to make erroneous decisions very quickly.

In a 1943 photo, Clarence Birdseye experiments on a process for dehydrating food, a goal he realized before the end of World War II. Among the other inventions that drew Birdseye's interest in the years after his work in frozen food were the kickless whale harpoon, industrial lighting, infrared lamps, and paper made from sugar cane husks.

Clarence Birdseye
1886–1956

Clarence Birdseye considered unabashed self-indulgence to be his own personal business strategy. He was a hardworking man, but throughout his career, he took orders only from his own warm sense of curiosity, which led by a circuitous route to his founding of the frozen food industry in the 1920s. Birdseye was an inventor by nature: He was also an inventor in nature, one who found much of his inspiration in the outdoors. After living in Labrador as a young man, he developed a small business around a process to bring foods ranging from flounder to strawberries to the table year-round, via the freezer. History is rife with examples of inventors who died poor, robbed of their rightful gains, but Birdseye was not one of them. Protecting all of his inventions tightly through patents, he sold his company to General Foods in 1929 and moved on to other inventions, wherever it was that his inclinations took him.

*W*hen Clarence Birdseye was five years old, he came across a dead mouse and felt the thrill of opportunity, right at his feet. He skinned the little body and dressed the fur, such as it was, and gave it to his mother as a present. Mrs. Birdseye wasn't necessarily the sort of person who needed a mouse fur; she was a well educated and otherwise well dressed resident of Brooklyn. But she accepted the pelt with all the gratitude she could muster, and pleased her son no end.

No one deeded Clarence Birdseye the universe, but once he found out that it was free, he helped himself to it. He started with mice—they were free—and for the rest of his life, he kept looking around at all the rest that there was, just for the taking. It made for a ramble, early in his career. To him, opportunities were never all in one place; they were lying on the ground or trotting over it, wherever he looked.

Birdseye's father was a respected legal scholar, the author of treatises and books of standardized forms. He didn't earn a large or steady income and the family moved often in and around New York.

At high school in Montclair, New Jersey, Birdseye was a bright student, and an unusual one. Not because he took his wilderness ways into class: quite the opposite. He was noted, instead, as the only boy to attend home economics classes. Following in his father's footsteps, he attended Amherst College, joining the class of 1910. By then, though, his parents couldn't contribute anything at all toward his tuition, and he had to earn his way through.

Birdseye did what he always did when he needed money. He went outside.

One afternoon, Birdseye was passing the time, as only

Birdseye would, snooping around in the bone shed behind a local butchershop, when he came across a nest of rats. Not common rats—he recognized them as a relatively rare strain and sold them by the crate to genetic scientists at Columbia University.

"I ain't afeer'd o' bugs, or toads, or worms, or snakes, or mice, or *anything*," the editors wrote teasingly next to Clarence Birdseye's picture in the Amherst yearbook. At Amherst, Birdseye's life became an equation by which he made relatively easy money as a naturalist—selling things he never quite owned—only to spend it on studies that did not interest him at all by comparison. Just before his senior year, he quit. For a few weeks over the summer, he had a real job as an office boy on Wall Street. Then he got an even more real job: He announced his plan to become a trapper in Labrador.

From his initial venture in fur trading, Birdseye realized a profit of $6,000, which he brought home in 1915. His ability to astonish his family was still far from spent, though. After he and Ida Underwood were married in Washington, D.C., they remained there long enough to have a son. Then, only five weeks after the baby was born, they left to make a home for him in a three-room shack in Labrador, 250 miles from the nearest doctor.

The overeducated trapper, bundled against Atlantic gales, was in the peculiar position of having the same basic concerns as the modernizing American housewife: Each was cooking for the whole family, looking for ways to introduce variety into the menu, and making a life that depended above all else on ingenuity.

In lieu of trips to the grocery store, Clarence caught animals, butchered them, and stored the meat in a shed. It was well-known among trappers that food stored during the dead of winter remained fresh, while that put up in early spring or late fall cooked up as a mushy pulp. Birdseye examined samples of each type, recognizing that the primary difference was that the fresh-tasting food had been frozen almost instantly in winter temperatures, while the mushy stuff had frozen much more slowly in the milder seasons.

Even in Labrador, Birdseye could speculate that at frigid temperatures, all of the liquid contained within a foodstuff froze at the same time — or close enough to it to protect the cell structure and the distinctive qualities of the food. His initial discoveries were not new. There were those in America and Europe who already knew in 1916 that food tasted better if it was fast-frozen. However, as a practical matter, there were only a couple of packers in Germany who knew how to chill it at exactly the right temperature, and within a scant hour. Slow-frozen food, on the other hand, was very well known in America, especially in the countryside, where farm families stored vegetables and meats outdoors during the winter. And that was precisely the problem: Slow-frozen in America's milder winters, food did not retain its character or taste.

The prime factor discouraging any industrial development in the field of frozen food was that slow-frozen food was already known and it was disgusting. Birdseye moved back to Brooklyn with the idea of perfecting quick-freezing equipment. After initial experiments using a home icebox, he continued his work in one corner of an ice cream factory in New Jersey. He developed a deep-freeze process along a conveyer belt, using steel plates both on top and below to subject food to frigid temperatures of 45 degrees below zero.

Birdseye's development budget started with an outlay of $7

and crawled up as slowly as possible from there. In 1922, he moved his family to Gloucester, Massachusetts, where he set himself up in business as Birdseye Seafoods, Inc., buying fish and freezing it fast. The process was a success and the company was a total failure.

The Birdseyes were just about to give up, when they cashed in their life insurance and tried again. The company was still tiny, yet it was trying to broaden into the name it would soon adopt: General Foods, Inc. Birdseye kept experimenting with his process until he learned to fast-freeze vegetables and berries. In fact, his first minor business success was in selling fresh-packed strawberries to restaurants for use year-round.

The development of the restaurant trade served, if only by contrast, to illustrate the two reasons that Birdseye foods were not being accepted in the household market. While large restaurants were likely to have electric freezers as part of their regular kitchen equipment, most households required only iceboxes. Even more important, restaurants ordered food in advance; individual consumers picked it out at stores. But stores didn't have freezers, either.

Birdseye was attempting to create a massive new food chain, despite the fact that his product represented just one link. He couldn't sell food to consumers who didn't own freezers . . . and not through grocery stores that didn't have freezer cases. It seemed an excellent time for a tiny, unwanted company to go out of business.

However, Birdseye remained in his lab in Gloucester, piling up patents until they numbered over 150. The son of a lawyer, he was careful to protect every slight variation in his process, until his filing cabinet bulged with the makings of an entire industry. Only then did Birdseye start to look for a giant, one that could construct an industry from scratch. The prime candidate was the Postum Co., a cerealmaker that was then vigorously branching out. In a matter of three years in the mid-1920s, Postum had absorbed such companies as Jell-O, Baker's Chocolate, Calumet Baking Powder, and Diamond Salt. It was as if Postum executives were wandering around a grocery store, tossing whole companies into a shopping basket.

Meanwhile, Clarence Birdseye, back in Gloucester, had added corn on the cob and oysters to his roster of freezable foods. He couldn't get lettuce or tomatoes onto his list, but he was still working on them when he happened to meet one of his most enthusiastic customers, an established businessman named Wetmore Hodges. Wetmore was convinced that frozen food had a spectacular future—which brought the number of people who felt that way up to at least a dozen, all of them living in Gloucester, and most of them named Birdseye.

Cultivating a number of potential bidders, Birdseye and Wetmore set their sights on Postum, which asked Goldman, Sachs to examine Birdseye's company and issue a report. The conclusion was that the company itself was worthless, but that the patents it held were immensely valuable. "Frosted foods have a sales potential of at least $1,000,000,000," the report predicted. Goldman, Sachs even volunteered to participate in the purchase. Between them, Postum and Goldman entered the successful bid of close to $25,000,000.

Postum Co. lost no time in changing its own name to General Foods Corp, while the line of frozen products was named Birds Eye (two words). Clarence Birdseye remained under contract as director of research, but pursued his own projects as well.

"There are at least 20 times as many opportunities as there were when I was 21," Birdseye wrote when he was 67. The following year, he proved it, leaving for Peru on a long-term project to turn sugar cane husks into paper. He worked out a process, but recurring heart trouble forced him to return home after two years in the higher altitudes. In 1956, Clarence Birdseye died from heart failure at the apartment he kept at the Grammercy Park Hotel in New York.

In the words that follow, Clarence Birdseye encourages people to follow his lead—not in moving to Labrador or even in inventing things, but in being a "gambler." Birdseye admonishes anyone against placing a greater value on security than on the adventure of the unknown in business. He gives a lesson in curiosity, which he considers the most important element of the human mind, and recommends that by exercising curiosity freely, almost anyone can find a way to improve upon something in a world always ripe for change. Birdseye, a respected gourmet cook, also gives a recipe, but only in fun. It is definitely not worth trying.

IN THE WORDS OF

Clarence Birdseye

Go around asking a lot of damn-fool questions and taking chances.

Versatility

Inventing is only one of my lines. I am also a bank director, a president of companies, a fisherman, an author, an engineer, a cook, a naturalist, a stockholder, a consultant, and a dock-walloper. Whenever anyone asks me what I am, I become rather confused, because I don't know which one of these occupations to give.

"To be perfectly honest," I told a young friend, "I am best described as just a guy with a very large bump of curiosity and a gambling instinct."

Stick-to-itiveness

Enthusiasm and hard work are indispensable ingredients of achievement. So is stick-to-itiveness.

Worthwhile success is impossible in a 40-hour week.

Risk

The dice will fall against the risk-taker more often than not, but his chances of ultimate success are far greater than those of the man who seeks merely security. And, whether he wins or not, he will find life much more interesting than if he always plays safe.

Curiosity

I do not consider myself a remarkable person. I did not make exceptionally high grades when I went to school. I never finished college. I am not the world's best salesman. But I am intensely curious about the things which I see around me, and this curiosity, combined with a willingness to assume risks, has been responsible for such success and satisfaction as I have achieved in life.

I am never bored, because I am always prying into something or other which fascinates me.

If I see a man skinning a fish, for example, a host of questions pop into my mind: Why is he skinning the fish? Why is he doing it by hand? Is the skin good for anything? If I am in a restaurant and get biscuits which I like, I ask the chef how he made them: What did he put in the dough? How did he mix it? How long did the biscuits bake? At what temperature? When I visit a strange city, I go through the local industrial plants to see how they make things. I don't care what the product is. I am just as interested in the manufacture of chewing gum as of steel.

Commercial Insight

I did not discover quick-freezing. The Eskimos had used it for centuries before I came along, and there were scientists in Europe who had made experiments along the same lines that I had. What I accomplished with the direction and cooperation of many other men and a lot of other folks' money, was merely to make packaged quick-frozen foods available to the general public.

Fads

Food tastes are principally psychological. We judge foods by our prejudices instead of with our taste buds. Americans, above all other nationalities, are notorious for the number of things they won't eat. That, of course, is because we have always had a superabundance to choose from, both as to quantity and variety.

Only a half a dozen years ago, ocean perch, a delicious salt-water cousin of the well-known fresh-water family, was caught in large quantities, along with other fish, only to be shoveled overboard as unprofitable to handle. Recently popularized, however, by a progressive Boston company, it is now shipped throughout the country and, more than any other one variety, is responsible for the present almost fabulous prosperity of New England fishermen.

✻

[*In the face of food shortages during World War II, Birdseye vouched for the delectability of wild animals, naming young whales, muskrats, porpoises, lynx, prairie dogs, and starlings as being among his favorite dishes. He also displayed his sense of fun with the following recipe.*]

Coots [sea ducks] furnish grand shooting along the north Atlantic seaboard, but many hunters don't consider them fit to eat. In fact, around Gloucester, a favorite recipe goes like this: Pluck the bird, cut it in sections, and soak it overnight in salt water. Wash in fresh water and place in an iron pot with a quart of granite pebbles. Boil until the pebbles are tender. Then throw away the coot and eat the pebbles . . .

Wealth

[*Birdseye realized a fortune of several million dollars in 1929 when Post, Inc. purchased his fledgling General Foods Corp. — and adopted the name to boot.*]

I was in my forties when this transaction made me financially independent for the first time in my life. A good many of my friends advised me to retire and take it easy. I had no more intention of doing so than I have today. Following one's curiosity is much more fun than taking things easy and I continued to ask questions and take chances.

Opportunity

Two qualities—curiosity and chance-taking spirit—are inherent in all of us, and I strongly recommend them to every ambitious youth who is starting out today. He should develop them through constant exercise, just as an athlete develops his muscles. Otherwise, his chances of doing big things will be small. Only through curiosity can we discover opportunities, and only through gambling can we take advantage of them.

Birdseye at Work:
Fifty Fish per Minute

[*In mid-July 1925, Birdseye wrote to a potential investor named Isaac Rice, keeping him apprised of developments in Gloucester. The following is excerpted from the letter, in which Birdseye reported on a fish filleting machine he needed for his total fast-freezing system.*]

I have delayed answering your letter of June 25 because, although we have been constantly working on our line of dressing apparatus, there was nothing completed and no practical tests have been made . . .

The filleting machine has done remarkably well under practical tests, although we look for still better results when we put on the new knives which we received last week, as the old ones are pitted and dull and cannot be adjusted as finely as they should be. So far I have myself done all the filleting and this morning put through one lot of 500 pounds of haddock at the rate of 23½ fish a minute, which is the full capacity of the machine with the present motor and gearing, although this speed can probably be increased to 40 or 50 fish a minute with a different motor.

The yield of fillets on various kinds of fish is at present about the same as is obtained by good hand filleters and there seems a good chance that we will be able to better this materially with further experience and adjustment . . .

Balanced Thinking

Mix your knowledge with imagination and apply both.

Opportunity

Change is the very essence of American life, and change brings with it an ever-increasing complexity of human wants.

Resiliency

Anyone who attempts anything original in this world must expect a bit of ridicule. I have long since learned to take it in my stride.

Tradition

Just because something has always been done in a certain way is never a sufficient reason for continuing to do it that way. Quite the contrary.

Margaret Rudkin, at fifty-eight, poses with a loaf of her Pepperidge Farm bread. To produce the bread to her pioneering all-natural standards, Rudkin had to commission farmers to grow high-quality wheat, and then arrange for stone grinding at vintage mills throughout the northeast.

Margaret Rudkin

1897–1967

Margaret Rudkin proved that an astute customer could be the smartest marketer of all. After noting that supermarkets were stocking only one type of bland white bread, she founded Pepperidge Farm in her own kitchen in Connecticut in 1937. Flying in the face of accepted wisdom in every way, Mrs. Rudkin was nonetheless besieged by customers, even in some of the dimmest years of the Depression. Her success helped to open grocery stores to niche brands in all food categories. While educating consumers of her day to the merits of healthy, all-natural products, Rudkin established Pepperidge Farm as one of the most recognizable of all food industry brands. After just over twenty years, she sold her company to Campbell's Soup. Margaret Rudkin never left the place where she began, though, and remained true to the way of life that had launched her business in the first place, at the house on Pepperidge Farm.

*L*ife in its episodes came rather easily to Margaret Rudkin. Bright and energetic, she grew up in a proper Irish home in New York and had a career at a firm on Wall Street in the early 1920s, before leaving to marry Henry Rudkin, a partner in the firm. In 1929, the Rudkins built a horse farm in Connecticut, where Henry was the neighborhood polo star. The Rudkins raised three sons at the farm (with the help of a governess), and made a hobby for themselves out of living off their own land as much as possible, doing everything from churning butter to raising a pig. Then, as something to do next, Margaret Rudkin revolutionized marketing in the grocery business.

She started without fanfare by baking a loaf of bread one afternoon at the farm, which she and her husband had named Pepperidge Farm after a stand of trees on the property. Rudkin's recipe was old-fashioned and very high in quality—and one other thing, after she started to sell it in supermarkets in 1938: wildly expensive. But Pepperidge Farm bread became a sales phenomenon, even at two-and-a-half times the prevailing price for bread.

Concepts intrinsic to supermarkets today—the niche for premium products, the demand for all-natural, healthy ingredients, the response to brands perceived as comfort food—were pioneered by Margaret Rudkin with Pepperidge Farm.

As the supermarket developed in the late 1920s, stores were not very big, and choices in product categories were limited to the brands with the best distribution, which was, in turn, limited to those brands with the widest appeal. As convenience rose, the common denominator of quality sank: That is usually the case. It was especially the case in bread.

"What she wants," said a representative at a national baking company, referring to the average American housewife, "is something in the nature of an edible piece of paper she can use to push peanut butter and jam into her kids three times a day, seven days a week." Supermarkets didn't offer anything but soft white bread of that type, at 10 cents a loaf.

To improve her family's diet, Margaret Rudkin baked a whole wheat bread in 1937. "I had never baked bread in my life," she later said. "They say life begins at forty—well, that's how old I was when I baked that first loaf. I just turned to the reliable *Boston Cookbook*, and started following directions. And then, suddenly, I seemed to remember the way my grandmother did it when I was six years old." Once she had perfected a recipe, she was taken aback by how delicious the bread was. Moreover, so was everyone else who tried it. Almost no one had tasted anything like real bread in a long, long time.

For all her urbane sophistication, Margaret Rudkin's distinguishing quality was pluck. Any person who sends for a government brochure on how to slaughter a pig—and then does it—has pluck in great reserve. In 1938, she started to sell her bread to local supermarkets, and then she went to New York to make sales calls there. In each case, the grocer's best wisdom was that whole wheat bread at a quarter a loaf wouldn't sell next to white bread at a dime: not in a Depression just then settling into a second dip.

All that Rudkin asked, though, was to leave a few loaves on trial. And in each case, the bread sold within hours, if not minutes. During the first days of the foray into New York, Margaret would bake the bread in her own kitchen and Henry would deliver it on his way to his office. However, that system placed obvious limits on expansion. A freight company soon contracted for deliveries, while Rudkin renovated the polo pony stable at Pepperidge Farm into a custom bakery, hiring her first employee at the same time.

Within a year of entering business, Margaret Rudkin had to move the bakery off the farm to even bigger quarters in town, with room for fifty employees. That same year, Rudkin hired a press agent, from whom *Reader's Digest* heard that a society woman in Connecticut was selling homestyle bread in supermarkets—so unusual a notion that the magazine printed an article about Pepperidge Farm. Demand shot up as a result (and Rudkin gave the press agent five percent of her company out of gratitude). By 1942, five years after baking her first loaf, Margaret Rudkin was selling two million loaves a year, with a small fleet of her own trucks for deliveries.

Rudkin became a popular subject for magazine articles. *The New Yorker* noted with delight that all of her great success was based on the fact that 99.9 percent of the public didn't want her bread. "Few other commercial bakers can make that claim," the magazine marveled. Yet that is exactly why Rudkin was such an important new force: She introduced supermarkets to her highly profitable 0.1 percent, and kept them from catering exclusively to the mass market. What she was purveying was old-fashioned American goodness, and if that is a cliché, Rudkin nonetheless cornered the market on it for well over a decade. When others began to think that they could follow her example simply by charging high prices for old-fashioned American goodness, she tightened her grip on that corner of the market. Perhaps that sounds untoward: Actually, what Rudkin did was go on vacation to Europe in 1948.

In every city she went to, she discovered delicious cookies. She was glumly aware, however, that she was not about to find the recipes for them in her reliable *Boston Cookbook*. Eventually, she contracted with a Belgian bakery to supply the recipes for a new line of cookies named after cities and resorts in Europe. The cookies, introduced in 1956 (and still in production), identified the same type of connoisseur as had the bread: the extraordinary customer in the ordinary supermarket.

Margaret Rudkin led the industry to the realization that practically every customer at the grocery store is an extraordinary customer—in the 0.1 percent—where one food category or another is concerned.

The Rudkins, who owned just over eighty percent of Pepperidge Farm, Inc., sold the company to Campbell's Soup in 1960, for stock valued at $28 million. At the time of Margaret's death in 1967, the recipe and the ingredients for Pepperidge Farm whole wheat bread were still exactly the same as those she had used in the very first loaf she made at the farm.

In the words that follow, Margaret Rudkin relates some of her experiences in transforming a hobby into a business, and then building Pepperidge Farm into a nationally recognized corporation. She credits her marketing acumen to the fact that she never lost the perspective that made her launch the business in the first place. Rudkin also relates how her insistence on using high-quality ingredients turned purchasing for her company into something of an adventure in living history.

IN THE WORDS OF

Margaret Rudkin

Salesmanship

[*Margaret Rudkin made her first sales call on August 17, 1937. She approached a neighborhood grocer and asked him if he would care to stock her bread, priced at 25 cents a loaf. At the time, every other bread on the market was a dime. The grocer said so, and asked if she were daft.*]

I had thought that might be his reaction, however, so I had come prepared with some butter and a bread knife. I sliced a loaf and buttered the slices and he and his clerks sampled my product. The look on their faces told the story. They all reached for more and said, "Well, that's bread!" I then gave my well-rehearsed sales talk about the ingredients I used and the high quality of the product and left my loaves.

[*Rudkin said that by the time she got home, the grocer had already called to say that the loaves she left were sold out.*]

Start-up Marketing

- Be sure your product will fill a definite need. Avoid fads, for they have no future.
- Learn all that can be learned about your product, at the start.
- Sell your product on its merits.
- Little cash doesn't mean small capital. Integrity, ability, and ambition are priceless assets and cannot be borrowed at the bank.

Recognizing Opportunity

I believe that success is often the result of an accidental circumstance and an opportunity to take advantage of it. My accidental circumstance was my interest in proper food for children, and the opportunity to take advantage of it lay in the fact that we had space and facilities to work with, and a ready-made name for products from Pepperidge Farm.

Business Appraisal

[*As the company grew, Rudkin resisted the temptation to discuss its standing in terms of sales figures.*]

Figures change and the growth of this business rests on a permanent and fundamental basis—on the expansion of a household art that people cherish, but seldom practice, and on persistent maintenance of quality. All that I have done is to make more and more loaves of the same bread that I have given my family ever since I started housekeeping and to sell them for a price that allows me to keep up the quality.

Respect for Figures

[*Margaret Rudkin attended public schools in New York, graduating first in her class from high school on Staten Island. Her first job was helping keep the books at a bank.*]

There were just three of us in the bookkeeping department—two elderly gentlemen, who wore alpaca jackets and sleeve garters, and this upstart redhead. The books were too heavy for me to carry, so the old gentlemen hauled them out of the vault and put them on a high bench every morning, and I sat there all day on a stool making entries. At the end of the day, you had to add up the debits and credits—the bank didn't have an adding machine—and if they didn't balance, you had to sit there until you found the mistake. I remember several times, when I had to stay late, my mother came down with her knitting to sit with me. I was a bookkeeper for two years, and then I was made a teller. I liked that. It gave me a good background for business. Of course, figures have always been easy for me. Right this minute, I can go out to Cliff—he's the Comptroller—and say "What's the balance?" and I can tell offhand if it's correct.

Resourcefulness

There was no planning, no theory, just: What is necessary to do next? Well, let's do it and see what happens.

Standards

[*At first, Rudkin ground her own flour in a coffee grinder, because stores did not sell a variety of flours in the 1930s. When she entered commercial production, she still found it hard to locate properly ground flour. In 1938, she told a reporter:*]

I have my flour ground in the old stone mill in Farmington [Connecticut]. It was owned by Winchell Smith [a playwright], who ran it for many years. Calvin Coolidge was one of his customers. When Mr. Smith died, he stipulated in his will that the mill should continue under the direction of the same miller and it is from him that I get my flour. It is the pure wheat grain, merely ground down with none of its live germ removed.

This is the element of the business which gives me greatest satisfaction. I am glad to have succeeded in putting it on a business basis, but I should never sacrifice the health aspects of my bread, no matter how I might be tempted to expand.

Growing

[*Rudkin launched Pepperidge Farm by baking the bread in her own kitchen. When orders outgrew its capacity, she transformed an empty stable on the property into a bread bakery.*]

I didn't spend a dollar if I could avoid it, and just used odds and ends I had in the house.

Knowing the Niche

I am only trying to please the minority who want a good loaf of bread and are willing to pay for it.

Ted Turner in his office in Atlanta holding a special cane made for him out of wood from Costa Rica. Turner not only influenced television as it is now known, but sports, as well. His bold decision to televise every Braves baseball game in 1976 changed the economics of sports teams, which are now valuable as components of entertainment conglomerates.

Ted Turner

1939–

Ted Turner helped to steer the communications revolution of the 1980s and was for a time the most influential person in broadcasting, as the head of the Turner Broadcasting System and its pioneering Cable News Network. In expanding his reach from a single local station into a veritable network of cable networks, Turner perceived that the basic market was changing profoundly, from a narrowly banded television audience to a shifting international populace. Technology changed viewership, spawning new needs as television infiltrated people's lives even more deeply than ever before. Ted Turner, a man singularly unafraid to be first in anything, filled demands even while they were still imperceptible to others. The industry followed in the wake of the man responsible for the Cable News Network—but then, for many years, there was no choice in television but to follow Ted Turner.

$\mathcal{A}$ person would have to love television inordinately to fall for WTCG, Channel 17, in Atlanta, a station with such a weak signal that it hardly mattered what it broadcast. Those few who managed to find it on the UHF dial usually couldn't make out the picture, anyway. Ted Turner, who had traded part of a thriving billboard business for WTCG in 1970, suavely assured potential advertisers that his station drew the most intelligent viewers in Atlanta: Who else, he asked, could figure out how to tune it in?

Six months after buying the Atlanta station, Turner bought one in Charlotte, North Carolina, where things were even worse. To stay in business, he staged a "Beg-a-Thon," in which the station asked viewers to send donations, lest the city lose it as a cultural asset. Some people actually mailed checks, a sort of early experiment in pay TV. Turner used the money and then returned it when he was able, with interest.

Perhaps it was events like the Beg-a-Thon that made Ted Turner love television—the jaunty freedom of it, along with the power to reach something good in people. At the same time, though, the bitter necessity of begging all day long, in one way or another, left him with a deep resentment of TV's three commercial networks, anointed with all of the medium's power and most of its money. Giving the subject a little thought, Turner realized that what he especially hated was what passed for entertainment on the networks. "They make heroes of criminals and glamorize violence. They've polluted our minds and our children's minds. I think they're almost guilty of manslaughter," he said.

The more Ted Turner thought about television from his new vantage within the industry, the more certain he was that its potential was being wasted. He developed a healthy disrespect for rest of the industry, its "sleaziness" on screen and its inefficiencies in business. Perhaps he had to hate it in order to surpass it, but in the early 1970s, Ted Turner was not able to do very much more than brood. According to his understanding of the industry, he lacked two things necessary to turn the might of little WTCG against the commercial networks: programming and distribution.

However, in 1973, Turner began to remedy his weakness in programming by buying the rights to broadcast Atlanta Braves baseball games. Three years later, he demonstrated a fresh understanding of his two sports—television and baseball. To own a station is merely to sign purchase papers for it. To truly own a channel, as Turner meant to, is to own the programming behind it.

Ted Turner grew up in Cincinnati, though his family later moved to Atlanta. He was expelled from Brown University after repeatedly breaking school rules, and served a short time in the Coast Guard before taking over his father's billboard company in 1963 at the age of twenty-four. His father, who had committed suicide, left the company in ruins, but Ted rebuilt it with boyish energy and pressing desperation, neither of which he ever lost.

For a long time, the excesses of Turner's behavior masked his insight, as he became known early on for episodes of public drunkenness and a rogue's reputation around women. Even people who considered Turner to be uncouth at times admitted that there was a mesmerizing charm about him, an immediacy found in few others, as his thoughts spewed forth, unedited and rather exuberant, in his peculiarly loud voice.

Only occasionally did a question leave Turner silent. In

1977, by then the owner of the Atlanta Braves, he was suspended from baseball for breaking rules regarding recruitment and for generally rejecting the traditional role of an owner (one of his lesser misdemeanors was acting occasionally as the Braves' batboy; one of his greater ones was suiting up as manager for a game). Confronted with Turner's rebellious antics, Commissioner Bowie Kuhn called him and asked, "Why can't you be like everybody else?"

In some ways, Ted Turner was exactly like everybody else or he wouldn't have been such a success in his self-appointed role—watching television for a growing audience. But he wasn't like many other people in business. No one else could have become as obsessed as he did with making WTCG an important entity: There was nothing important about it, a little station in a neglected market. However, in 1976, Turner invested $750,000 in equipment that would allow a newly launched RCA satellite to supply WTCG's signal to the nation's cable systems. Turner changed the call letters of the station to WTBS and labeled it a "superstation." No one knew what that meant, but then, not many people knew what cable TV was, in 1976.

Cable television had been invented in 1949 by a television retailer in rural Pennsylvania, who planted an antenna on a mountaintop and promised to send its crystal-clear signal by special wire to anyone in the area who bought a TV set from him. Other cable systems followed in rural areas, but they were locally oriented, depending as they did on various types of antennas.

With the launch of RCA's satellite, antennas were obviated. Moreover, distances were obliterated. Turner was the first to recognize that if cable TV proliferated nationally, then even the most humble television station could rival a network. He nominated WTBS to be that station. Offering an evening mix of major league sports and high-quality movies, in sharp contrast to network series, WTBS was instrumental in helping newly established cable systems attract subscribers.

By the time WTBS was being seen nationally on cable television, Turner Broadcasting owned the Atlanta Hawks basketball team in addition to the Braves baseball team. Almost year-round, Turner could depend on programming from those two sources. As to movies, he had made a policy of purchasing them outright rather than leasing them for limited broadcast. While known for penny-pinching ways around the office, he was a veritable impulse buyer in the acquisition of programming. He didn't haggle, he didn't hesitate, and by 1976, he owned over 3000 movies. The buying spree culminated one decade later, when Turner purchased MGM for $1.5 billion, $500 million more than it was thought to be worth. Selling off the studio's production facilities, he was left with 3650 movies from the MGM library, including his own all-time favorite, *Gone With the Wind*. Others scoffed, totting up the length of time it would take to run 3650 movies on WTBS. But that was a moot point. The following year, Turner initiated a new cable channel, Turner Network Television; six years later, he launched Turner Classic Movies. Both depended on programming in the form of movies, and Turner already owned them in perpetuity. It was the kind of deal he liked, and in 1994, he repeated it, starting the Cartoon Network after purchasing the extensive Hanna-Barbera library. He had the channels and he owned the programming.

Turner had one other source for programming in mind: It couldn't be bought, but as he proved, it might just be owned. In June of 1980, Ted Turner started the Cable News Network.

After a slow start, CNN grew to as be as profitable as it was influential. With its adjunct, Headline News, it made more money by itself in a typical year during the 1990s than did any of the three broadcast networks overall, including their entertainment and sports divisions. In the mid-1990s, their news departments were cutting back drastically, ceding whole aspects of television journalism to CNN, which was then assuming worldwide scope as the first global television channel. By some law of transference, by some dash into opportunity, Ted Turner owned the news to an extent no one ever had before.

Turner oversaw the sale of Turner Broadcasting to Time-Warner in 1997. He emerged from the deal with $3.2 billion, and afterward devoted more and more of his time to ambitious environmental rehabilitation projects on over one million acres that he owns in the Western Hemisphere.

"I want to live five lives," Ted Turner once told a friend, "I have to hurry to get them all in." In cable television, he found the way to live at least five and all at once.

In the words that follow, Ted Turner expresses the independence that allowed him to become a force in broadcasting without ever quite falling into step with the rest of the industry. Widely credited with possessing vision, a phenomenon he tries to explain, Turner was very often written off after launching some risky new venture in television or sports. He reveled in such derision, he claims, and let it underscore whatever determination he already had. Ted Turner probably cares far more about the environment and other people around the world than the average, yet some part of his appeal as a leader is bright and shiny egotism that he can display, as when a reporter asked him who in history he would most like to be, and why.

IN THE WORDS OF

Ted Turner

Challenge

I just love it when people say I can't do something. There's nothing that makes me feel better, because all my life people have said I wasn't going to make it.

Pioneering

In the case of WTBS we had a huge initial advantage because we were first. But just as the AM radio stations were first, that doesn't guarantee you in today's world. You constantly have to stay ahead.

Leadership

When I bought the Braves, I didn't know what a balk or an infield fly was, but I've got the ability to inspire people. What makes me a successful sailboat racer is that I've got executive ability, I can make 11 guys work harder and longer than anybody else. And baseball players are the same way. They just want someone who really cares.

Talk

I couldn't do any sport, but I learned to speak on my feet and that's a hell of a lot better than being a high school quarterback. I went into debating in my sophomore year in high school and ended up winning the state championship my senior year. I've got a virtually limitless supply of bullshit.

[*The transcripts of a taped interview Turner gave* Playboy *magazine in 1978 ran to 800 pages.*]

Wealth

[*In 1986, Turner explained in a speech that:*]

It's not how much you earn, but how much you owe.

I'll owe $2 billion, more than some smaller Third World countries, and I'm pretty proud of that. Today it's not how much you earn, but how much you owe.

[*Turner's 1986 debt load, resulting largely from his acquisition of MGM, proved unwieldy, however, and he was forced to accept help from a group of cable system operators, who became partners in the management of Turner Broadcasting.*]

V i s i o n

[*Many observers scoffed at Turner's 1986 $1.5 billion acquisition of MGM, saying that he had paid too much by at least $500 million.*]

Anybody who says this was a foolish move doesn't understand. They're probably the same people who said CNN wasn't going to work. Right? And I haven't heard that many people say that this was a bad deal, either. I mean, by now people have had so much egg on their face by saying Turner's done it this time, and it always comes out. I just think things through carefully, that's all. I'm no genius. I'm not at all; I just happen to look five or 10 years ahead and think things through, that's all. And I discuss it with other people, too. This was a carefully calculated move. Just like CNN was. I thought about it for years. I thought about putting WTBS on satellite for years. It takes that long to do it.

I m a g i n a t i o n

I fantasize about everything; being a fireman, an Indian chief, climbing mountains. Anything is possible.

T r o u b l e

What is "trouble?" Trouble is what makes life interesting—that's why everybody is in broadcasting. Everybody in broadcasting likes trouble because you've got to worry about the ratings and stay on top of the thing, make sure the transmitters work. If you wanted an easy job, you could be a grave digger or run a graveyard. All you do is plant the people once and then leave them there, right? Or sell the cemetery lots, if you want something that moves slowly. But everybody in broadcasting likes action.

Accounting

I've always believed in cash flow rather than stated profits, because when you state profits, you've got to pay 50% to the government. And if you look back at our company over the last 30 years, we've only paid a few million dollars in corporate income tax the entire time. We kept expanding fast enough . . . I've been doing that for 30 years and my father did it before me with the billboards. He was always trying to keep the depreciation up so he didn't have to pay taxes, and he was able to use his whole cash flow to retire debt. But he wasn't a public company. But even when we went public, we stuck with that. We tried to build values and build real values rather than make it look like you're making a lot of money by paying taxes.

Universality

We are trying to eliminate the word, "foreign," at CNN. We have done away with the foreign desk . . . we call them "international," because foreign is extraterrestrial . . . If you think of foreigners, it is a lot easier to say, "Oh, that foreigner, let him starve to death," but when you think of everybody as your neighbors and your brothers and sisters, then it is another story.

Poverty

[*WTBS underwrote the research of oceanographer Jacques Cousteau starting in 1983, after Turner accompanied him on a voyage up the Amazon River.*]

Captain Cousteau told me years ago—I will never forget it: "I cannot enjoy my own life fully knowing that so many people have nothing." I feel that way too.

Information

Back in the Dark Ages, only the Church and politicians had knowledge, and the people were kept in the dark. Information is power. I see CNN as the democratization of information.

Influences

You know, you can take children. And you can either turn them into eagle scouts or Hitler Youth. What you've got today are a trashy, snotty bunch. Television determines their central character.

Economizing

In deciding on a headquarters for a new network, I chose Atlanta. The industry hooted. But I said, "Why not?" Those who watch our programs know we have a Southern-Midwest look about them. We emphasize family values a bit more. And in Atlanta it's a whole different ball game. People are friendly; they don't try to run over you with taxi cabs. It's not as crowded as New York, nor are we dying like they are out there in Los Angeles, where the air is so polluted. And being in Atlanta has worked. It costs a lot less to operate there. I mean, the rent's a third as much, lunches are $30 in New York and we have a lunch down there in Atlanta for $2.50. Another thing, we're not unionized. That's the bad thing about those big networks. They have a lot of people just standing around. If you want an electric light plugged in, you've got to call an electrician, and everybody has to wait for him to come and plug in the light.

Accessibility

[*On attending ball games:*]
All the owners sit up there behind their bulletproof glass and they're afraid to meet the fans. I sit down front and I have to give about three dozen autographs during every game. Anyway, I figure the best seats are in the front row.

Work

I can quit whenever I want to. I am not worried about what people think. But I am the right man in the right place at the right time, not me alone, but all the people who think the world can be brought together by telecommunications.

Politics

[*Turner was asked by a* Maclean's *magazine reporter in 1988 whether he was tempted to enter politics.*]

I'm in politics—I vote.

Power

I can do more in communications than any conqueror could have done. I want to be the hero of my country. I want to get it back to the principles that made us good. Television has led us, in the last 25 years, down the path of destruction. I intend to turn it around before it is too late.

Money

[*In 1997, Turner said in a speech before a group of newspaper editors:*]

I bet you're all wondering what it feels like to be a billionaire. It's disappointing, really. I remember when it happened to me. I'd been watching the value of my stocks climb, and I realized that when they hit a certain point, I'd become a billionaire. On the day they hit, I was so excited. I wanted to tell someone. But who? I couldn't tell my employees. They'd say, "Great. Now pay me more money." I couldn't tell my friends. They weren't nearly as wealthy as I was. So that evening I told my wife as the kids were running around. She said, "That's great, but I have to deal with the kids right now."

Extremes

One of the human traits is to make too much of it when someone is doing a good job and make too much of it when people
are having a bad streak of luck.

Self-respect

[*In 1984, a reporter for the* Saturday Evening Post *asked Turner
who in all of history he would most like to be.*]

That's easy. Ted Turner.

I'm in history and I like myself. I wouldn't want to be anyone else.

SOURCES

Thomas J. Watson Sr.

12. Thomas J. Watson, *Men-Minutes-Money* (International Business Machines, 1934), p. 422.

12. Speech by Thomas Watson before the freshman convocation of the New York University School of Commerce, Accounts and Finance; September 21, 1932; quoted in *Men-Minutes-Money*, p. 690.

13. Speech by Thomas Watson before the IBM Manufacturing School, April 16, 1925; quoted in *Men-Minutes-Money*, p. 73.

13. Thomas J. Watson, "To Make a Business Grow—Begin Growing Men!" *System*, August 1926, p. 151.

13. Talk by Thomas Watson to IBM executives, September 25, 1933; quoted in *Men-Minutes-Money*, p. 853.

13–14. Speech by Thomas Watson to the Binghamton, New York Chamber of Commerce, January 12, 1932; quoted in *Men-Minutes-Money*, p. 572.

14. Speech by Thomas Watson at a company banquet, January 19, 1917; quoted in *Men-Minutes-Money*, p. 34.

14. Thomas J. Watson, "To Make a Business Grow—Begin Growing Men!" *System*, August 1926, p. 151.

14. Company speech by Thomas Watson, January 25, 1915; quoted in *Men-Minutes-Money*, p. 24–27.

15. Company speech, January 25, 1915; quoted in *Men-Minutes-Money*, p. 24–27.

16–17. Company speech, January 25, 1915; quoted in *Men-Minutes-Money*, p. 24–27.

17. *Men-Minutes-Money*, p. 228.

17–18. Sales convention speech by Thomas Watson, January 1916; quoted in *Men-Minutes-Money*, p. 30–31.

18. Sales convention speech, January 1916; quoted in *Men-Minutes-Money*, p.33.

18–19. Sales talk at a company conference, October 26, 1921; quoted in *Men-Minutes-Money*, p. 57.

19. Sales talk, May 16, 1928; quoted in *Men-Minutes-Money*, p. 154.

19. Speech by Thomas Watson at a company convention, January 17, 1917; quoted in *Men-Minutes-Money*, p. 35.

20. Speech by Thomas Watson at a company convention held January 29–February 3, 1917; quoted in *Men-Minutes-Money*, p. 38.

20. Speech by Thomas Watson to the Salesmanship Club of New York, November 23, 1917; quoted in *Men-Minutes-Money*, p. 41.

20–21. Company speech by Thomas Watson, August 1929; quoted in *Men-Minutes-Money*, p. 253.

21. *Men-Minutes-Money*, p. 405.

21. Sales convention speech by Thomas Watson, January 1926; quoted in *Men-Minutes-Money*, p. 81.

21–22. *Men-Minutes-Money*, p. 208.

22. Speech by Thomas Watson for the company Executive School, October 27–November 7, 1924; quoted in *Men-Minutes-Money*, p. 69.

22. Company sales convention speech, January 1926; quoted in *Men-Minutes-Money*, p. 79.

22. Company speech by Thomas Watson during a convention held January 27–February 3, 1927; quoted in *Men-Minutes-Money*, p. 113.

22–23. *Men-Minutes-Money*, p. 227.

23. *Men-Minutes-Money*, p. 462.

23. *Men-Minutes-Money*, p. 594.

24. Speech by Thomas Watson before the sales staff of the Dayton Scale Division of IBM; quoted in *Men-Minutes-Money*, p. 594.

24. Speech by Thomas Watson to the Sales Executives Club of New York; September 15, 1932; quoted in *Men-Minutes-Money*, p. 682.

25. *Men-Minutes-Money*, p. 131.

25. Speech by Thomas Watson at a company banquet in Germany, July 22, 1930; quoted in *Men-Minutes-Money*, p. 391.

25. Company speech by Thomas Watson, July 18, 1928; quoted in *Men-Minutes-Money*, p. 162.

25–26. Speech before the Sales Executives Club of New York, September 15, 1932; quoted in *Men-Minutes-Money*, p. 679.

26. Company speech by Thomas Watson, May 8, 1929; quoted in *Men-Minutes-Money*, p. 246.

26. *Men-Minutes-Money*, p. 418.

26. *Men-Minutes-Money*, p. 430.

26–27. Speech by Thomas Watson before the New York Advertising Club course on Advertising and Selling, November 17, 1932; quoted in *Men-Minutes-Money*, p. 721.

27. Company speech by Thomas Watson, January 1933; quoted in *Men-Minutes-Money*, p. 774.

27. Speech at a company convention held January 29–February 3, 1917; quoted in *Men-Minutes-Money*, p. 39.

William Wrigley Jr.

37. S.J. Duncan-Clark, "Make a Good Product for a Fair Price—Then Tell the World," *Illustrated World*, March 1922, p. 45.

37. Neil M. Clark, "The Low-Down on Salesmanship," *American Magazine*, October 1929, p. 22.

37–38. "The Low-Down on Salesmanship," p. 23.

38. "The Low-Down on Salesmanship," p. 22.

38–39. "The Low-Down on Salesmanship," p. 129.

39–40. William Wrigley Jr., "Why We Are Pushing Sales Now—and Getting Them," *System*, October 1921, p. 397.

40. William Wrigley Jr., as told to Forrest Crissey, "Owning a Big-League Ball Team," *Saturday Evening Post*, September 13, 1930, p. 24–25.

40–41. "Owning a Big-League Ball Team," p. 24.

41. "Make a Good Product for a Fair Price—Then Tell the World," p. 44.

41. Merle Crowell, "The Wonder Story of Wrigley," *American Magazine*, March 1920, p. 191.

41. "The Low-Down on Salesmanship," p. 124.

42. "The Low-Down on Salesmanship," p. 124.

42–43. "The Low-Down on Salesmanship," p. 23.

43. William Wrigley Jr., reported by Neil M. Clark, "Spunk Never Cost a Man a Job Worth Having," *American Magazine*, March 1931, p. 162–163.

43–44. "Spunk Never Cost a Man a Job Worth Having," p. 163.

44. "The Low-Down on Salesmanship," p. 129.

45. "Make a Good Product for a Fair Price—Then Tell the World," p. 46.

45. "Make a Good Product for a Fair Price—Then Tell the World," p. 46.

46. "Make a Good Product for a Fair Price—Then Tell the World," p. 44.

46–47. "The Low-Down on Salesmanship," p. 130.

47. "The Low-Down on Salesmanship," p. 126.

47–48. "Spunk Never Cost a Man a Job Worth Having," p. 164.

48. "Spunk Never Cost a Man a Job Worth Having," p. 63.

48. "Chewing Gum Is a War Material," *Fortune*, January 1943, p. 99–100.

49. "Spunk Never Cost a Man a Job Worth Having," p. 163.

49. "William Wrigley Jr., American," *Fortune*, April 1932, p. 86.

49. "Make a Good Product for a Fair Price—Then Tell the World," p. 47.

Andrew Carnegie

62. Charles M. Schwab, "How Carnegie Dealt with His Men," *System*, June 1922, p. 729.

62–63. Charles M. Schwab, "What I Learned about Business from Andrew Carnegie," *System*, May 1922, p. 528.

63. Andrew Carnegie, *Autobiography* (Boston: Houghton Mifflin, 1920), p. 55.

63. *Autobiography*, p. 129.

64. *Autobiography*, p. 170.

64. Memo Carnegie wrote to himself, December 1868; quoted in *Autobiography*, p. 152–153.

64. *Autobiography*, p. 130.

65. "How Carnegie Dealt with His Men," p. 681.

65. A.B. Farquhar, "Carnegie's Ideas on What Makes a Business Pay," *System*, April 1923, p. 470.

65. *Autobiography*, p. 118–120.

65–66. *Autobiography*, p. 118–120.

66–67. *Autobiography*, p. 118–120.

67. *Autobiography*, p. 118.

67–68. *Autobiography*, p. 70.

68. *Autobiography*, p. 55.

68. Speech by Andrew Carnegie in Glasgow, September 24, 1888; quoted in "Current Foreign Topics," *The New York Times*, September 25, 1888, p. 1.

68–69. Speech by Andrew Carnegie before the British Iron and Steel Institute; printed as Andrew Carnegie, "The Secret of Business Is the Management of Men," *World's Work*, June 1903, p. 3523.

69. *Autobiography*, p. 217.

69. Speech before the British Iron and Steel Institute; printed as "The Secret of Business is the Management of Men," p. 3526.

70. *Autobiography*, p. 148.

70. Charles M. Schwab, "Carnegie's Theory of Business," *System*, August 1922, p. 142.

70. Andrew Carnegie, "The Advantages of Poverty," *The Nineteenth Century*, March 1891, p. 378.

70–71. Speech by Andrew Carnegie before the Lotos Club, January 27, 1900; printed as "Mr. Carnegie Guest of the Lotos Club," *The New York Times*, January 28, 1900, p. 2.

71. Andrew Carnegie, "What Would I Do with the Tariff If I Were the Czar?" *Forum*, March 1895, p. 24.

71–72. Speech by Andrew Carnegie at the 26th anniversary of the Railroad branch of the Young Men's Christian Association, January 14, 1902; printed as "Advice of Mr. Carnegie," *The New York Times*, Jan. 15, 1902, p. 2.

72. Andrew Carnegie, "Britain's Appeal to the Gods," *The Nineteenth Century*, April 1904, p. 504.

73. "A Millionaire Socialist," *The New York Times*, January 2, 1885, p. 1.

74. Speech by Andrew Carnegie at Cooper Union, March 8, 1904; quoted as "Carnegie's Views on Wealth Distribution," *The New York Times*, March 9, 1904, p. 3.

74. Speech at Cooper Union, New York City, March 8, 1904; quoted as "Carnegie's Views on Wealth Distribution," p. 3.

74. "The Advantages of Poverty," p. 370.

75. "The Advantages of Poverty," p. 371.

75. *Autobiography*, p. 35.

75. Speech by Andrew Carnegie at Cornell University Founder's Day, January 11, 1896; quoted in *The New York Times*, Jan. 12, 1896, p. 16.

75. "The Advantages of Poverty," p. 373.

Sam Walton

85. Todd Mason, "Sam Walton of Wal-Mart: Just Your Basic Homespun Billionaire," *Business Week*, October 4, 1985, p. 142.

85. Sam Walton and John Huey, *Made in America* (New York: Doubleday, 1992), p. 217.

85. Comment made by Sam Walton in July 1974; quoted in *Discount Store News*, June 15, 1992, p. 51.

86. Isadore Barmash, "The Hot Ticket in Retailing," *The New York Times*, July 1, 1984, p. 4.

86. "Wal-Mart: The Model Discounter," *Dun's Business Month*, December 1982, p. 60.

86. *Made in America*, p. 203.

86–87. Comment made by Sam Walton in October 1985; quoted in *Discount Store News*, June 15, 1992, p. 50.

87. *Made in America*, p. 221.

87. *Made in America*, p. 231.

87–88. Letter from Sam Walton in *Wal-Mart World*; quoted in Jennifer Lawrence, "Adman of the Year," *Advertising Age*, December 23, 1981, p. 14.

88. *Made in America*, p. 224.

88. Comment by Sam Walton, in *Discount Store News*, Aug. 12, 1974; reprinted in *Discount Store News*, June 15, 1992, p. 69.

89. "The Hot Ticket in Retailing," p. 4.

89. *Made in America*, p. 63.

89–90. Sam Walton, quoted in *Discount Store News*, June 15, 1992, p. 52.

90–91. Sharon Reier, "CEO of the Decade: Sam M. Walton," *Financial World*, April 4, 1989, p. 62.

91. *Made in America*, p. 128.

91. "The Super Stars of Selling," *Sales & Marketing Management*, March 1991, p. 49.

91. Comment made by Sam Walton in February, 1985; quoted in *Discount Store News*, June 15, 1992, p. 54.

Mary Pickford

100. Mary Pickford, as told to Campbell McCulloch, "Stay Away From Hollywood," *Good Housekeeping*, January 1930, p. 226.

100. Mary Pickford, "My Own Story," *Ladies Home Journal*, August 1923, p. 118.

100–101. "My Own Story," p. 121.

101. "Mary Pickford Turns to Radio," *The New York Times*, September 16, 1934, IX, p. 11.

101. "My Own Story," p. 16.
101. "My Own Story," p. 7.
102. "My Own Story," p. 122.
102–103. "My Own Story," p. 16.
103. Mary Pickford, as told to Charles D. Rice, "Stars Have to Shine," p. 9, clipping file, New York Public Library.
103–104. Mary Pickford, *Sunshine and Shadow* (New York: Doubleday, 1952), p. 194.
104–105. Tino Balio, *United Artists* (Madison, Wisconsin: University of Wisconsin, 1976), p. 176–177.
105–106. *Sunshine and Shadow*, p. 234–235.
106. *United Artists*, p. 196.
106–107. Mary B. Mullet, "Mary Pickford Describes Her Most Thrilling Experience," *American Magazine*, May 1923, p. 34.
107. Looking back . . .

Edwin Land

116. Interview with Edwin Land, "As I See It," *Forbes*, June 1, 1975, p. 49.
116. Michael Jacobs, "The Physicist as Entrepreneur," *Physics Today*, January 1982, p. 40.
116. "As I See It," p. 49.
117. "As I See It," p. 49.
117. "On Some Conditions for Scientific Profundity in Industrial Research," Charles F. Kettering award address by Edwin Land, June 17, 1965; reprinted in *Selected Papers on Industry by Edwin Land* (Polaroid Corp., 1983), p. 22.
117–118. Polaroid Corp. stockholders' report, 1978; reprinted in *Selected Papers on Industry by Edwin Land* (Polaroid Corp., 1983), p. 31.
118. "Research by the Business Itself," paper presented at the Standard Oil Development Co. Forum, October 5, 1944; reprinted in *Selected Papers on Industry by Edwin Land* (Polaroid Corp., 1983), p. 5.
118–119. Edwin Land, "Thinking Ahead," *Harvard Business Review*, September-October 1959, p. 148–150.
119. Interview with Philip Taubman, "The Most Basic Form of Creativity," *Time*, June 26, 1972, p. 84.
119. "On Some Conditions for Scientific Profundity in Industrial Research"; reprinted in *Selected Papers on Industry by Edwin Land*, p. 19–20.

120. "The Second Great Product of Industry: The Rewarding Working Life," paper presented at the fiftieth anniversary of the Mellon Institute, May 1963; reprinted in *Selected Papers on Industry by Edwin Land* (Polaroid Corp., 1983), p. 14–15.

121. "On Some Conditions for Scientific Profundity in Industrial Research"; reprinted in *Selected Papers on Industry by Edwin Land*, p. 22.

121–122. Polaroid Corp. stockholders' report, 1978; reprinted in *Selected Papers on Industry by Edwin Land*, p. 29.

122–123. "The Physicist as Entrepreneur," p. 35.

123–124. "The Second Great Product of Industry: The Rewarding Working Life"; reprinted in *Selected Papers on Industry by Edwin Land*, p. 15.

124. "The Most Basic Form of Creativity," p. 84.

124. "Polaroid: Turning away from Land's One-Product Strategy," *Business Week*, March 2, 1981, p. 110.

124. "On Some Conditions for Scientific Profundity in Industrial Research"; reprinted in *Selected Papers on Industry by Edwin Land*, p. 21.

125. "Polaroid: Turning away from Land's One-Product Strategy," p. 109.

William Paley

134. John K. Hutchens, "Radio Showman," *Theatre Arts*, November 1943, p. 660.

134. William S. Paley, "Radio and the Humanities," *American Academy of Political and Social Science*, January 1935, p. 94.

135. Broadcast by William Paley over CBS Radio; reprinted in *Literary Digest*, January 1, 1938, p. 23.

135. Tony Schwartz, "A Talk with William Paley," *The New York Times Magazine*, December 28, 1980, p. 18.

136. "A Talk with William Paley," p. 46.

136. "Radio Showman," p. 659–660.

136. "Radio Showman," p. 657.

136–137. "A Talk with William Paley," p. 46.

137–138. William S. Paley, *As It Happened* (New York: Doubleday & Co., Inc., 1979), p. 76–77.

138. Speech by William Paley before the National Association of Radio and Television Broadcasters, May 25, 1964; reprinted in Harry J. Skornia and Jack W. Kitson, eds., *Problems and Controversies in Television and Radio* (Palo Alto, California: Pacific Books, 1968), p. 36–37.

139. "Radio Showman," p. 657.

139. *As It Happened,* p. 381.

139–140. Speech by William Paley before the National Association of Broadcasters convention, October 1946; quoted in *The New York Times,* October 27, 1946, II, p. 9.

140. *As It Happened,* p. 90.

140–141. Speech by William Paley before the Associated Press Broadcasters Convention, June 6, 1980; reprinted in *Vital Speeches,* August 15, 1980, p. 670.

141. William S. Paley, "International Broadcasting: Now and in the Future," *Annals of the American Academy of Political and Social Science,* July 1930, p. 40.

John D. Rockefeller

155. John D. Rockefeller, *Random Reminiscences of Men and Events* (Garden City, New York: Doubleday, Doran & Co., 1909), p. 132.

155–156. "Rockefeller Tells of Spurning Temptation," *The New York Times,* September 12, 1905, p. 1.

156. *Random Reminiscences of Men and Events,* p. 132.

156. *Random Reminiscences of Men and Events,* p. 132.

156. Transcript of conversations of John Rockefeller with William Inglis (Rockefeller Archives), p. 126.

157. John D. Rockefeller, *Mr. Rockefeller's Ledger: The First He Kept and What Was in It, an address by John D. Rockefeller before the Young Men's Bible Class* (New York City: privately printed by the class, March 17, 1897), p. 9–10.

157. *Random Reminiscences of Men and Events,* p. 21.

157–158. *Random Reminiscences of Men and Events,* p. 38–39.

158. Original typewritten manuscript of Rockefeller speech to "The Club," May 7th, 1904 (Rockefeller Archives), p. 5.

158–159. *Random Reminiscences of Men and Events,* p. 44–45.

160. *Random Reminiscences of Men and Events,* p. 132.

160–161. Transcript of conversations with William Inglis, p. 199.

161. *Random Reminiscences of Men and Events,* p. 119.

162. Letter from John Rockefeller to Frederick Gates, May 13, 1906 (Rockefeller Archives).

162. Transcript of conversations with William Inglis, p. 126.

162–163. Transcript of conversations with William Inglis, p. 50.

163–164. *Random Reminiscences of Men and Events,* p. 73.

164. *Random Reminiscences of Men and Events,* p. 60.

164–165. Transcript of conversations with William Inglis, p. 1222.

165. Transcript of conversations with William Inglis, p. 126.

166. *Random Reminiscences of Men and Events*, p. 132.

166. *Random Reminiscences of Men and Events*, p. 88.

166–167. Transcript of conversations with William Inglis, p. 115.

167. Letter from John Rockefeller to Frederick Gates, April 3, 1905 (Rockefeller Archives).

167–168. *Random Reminiscences of Men and Events*, p. 46.

168. *Random Reminiscences of Men and Events*, p. 64.

168. *Random Reminiscences of Men and Events*, p. 57.

168. *Random Reminiscences of Men and Events*, p. 6.

169. *Random Reminiscences of Men and Events*, p. 136.

169. Transcript of conversations with William Inglis, p. 115.

169–170. *Random Reminiscences of Men and Events*, p. 87–88.

170–171. Letter from John Rockefeller to Frederick Gates, September 21, 1904 (Rockefeller Archives).

171–172. Letter from John Rockefeller to Charles F. Lang, September 19, 1904 (Rockefeller Archives).

172. *Random Reminiscences of Men and Events*, p. 132.

172–173. *Random Reminiscences of Men and Events*, p. 74.

173. *Mr. Rockefeller's Ledger: The First He Kept and What Was in It, an address by John D. Rockefeller before the Young Men's Bible Class*, p. 5.

Henry Ford II

183. Speech by Henry Ford II before the National Association of Purchasing Agents, May 3, 1966; reprinted as "The Common Thread," *Vital Speeches of the Day*, June 1, 1966, p. 497.

183–184. Speech by Henry Ford II at Yale University, February 19, 1959; reprinted as "Big Labor—Boon or Menace? How a Top Industrialist Sees It," *U.S. News & World Report*, March 9, 1959, p. 89.

184. Speech by Henry Ford II at the University of Chicago School of Management, March 5, 1964; reprinted as "How High Are Profits?" *Vital Speeches of the Day*, May 1, 1964, p. 435.

184–185. Henry Ford II, "Choosing a Business Career," *Saturday Evening Post*, October 20, 1962, p. 34, 38.

185. Interview by Tom Lilley, "Henry Ford II Speaks Out," *Atlantic Monthly*, December 1947, p. 32.

185. Speech by Henry Ford II before the Society of Automotive Engineers, January 9, 1946; reprinted as "The Challenge of Human Engineering," *Vital Speeches of the Day*, February 15, 1946, p. 274.

185–186. "The Challenge of Human Engineering," p. 274.

186. "The Hidden Revolution," p. 567.

186–187. Speech by Henry Ford II at Los Angeles Regional banquet, National Conference of Christians and Jews, June 5, 1969; reprinted as "The Hidden Revolution," *Vital Speeches of the Day*, July 1, 1969, p. 568.

187. Speech by Henry Ford II in New York City, January 12, 1967; reprinted as "Government and Business—Must They Be Enemies?" *U.S. News & World Report*, January 22, 1967, p. 85.

187–188. Speech by Henry Ford II before the Society of Automotive Engineers, January 15, 1964; reprinted as "Technological Exploration," *Vital Speeches of the Day*, February 1, 1964, p. 248.

188. "Technological Exploration," p. 247.

188. Speech at Los Angeles Regional banquet, National Conference of Christians and Jews, June 5, 1969; reprinted as "The Hidden Revolution," p. 567.

188–189. Ford Motor Co. "blue letter," sent by Henry Ford II; reprinted in Booton Herndon, *Ford* (New York: Weybright and Talley, 1969), p. 108.

189. Speech before the Society of Automotive Engineers, January 9, 1946; reprinted as "The Challenge of Human Engineering," p. 272.

189–190. Speech before the Society of Automotive Engineers, January 15, 1964; reprinted as "Technological Exploration," p. 246.

190. "How Henry Ford II Sees the Outlook in Autos," *U.S. News & World Report*, August 19, 1963, p. 74.

190. Henry Ford II, "Henry Ford's Idea: More Planning," *Time*, February 10, 1975, p. 71.

190. Henry Ford II, "The Crisis-Crash Syndrome," *Newsweek*, August 6, 1973, p. 7.

191. Henry Ford II, "The High Cost of Regulation," *Newsweek*, March 20, 1978, p. 15.

191. Speech at Yale University, February 19, 1959; reprinted as "Big Labor—Boon or Menace? How a Top Industrialist Sees It," p. 89.

191–192. "Big Labor—Boon or Menace? How a Top Industrialist Sees It," p. 92.

192. "Big Labor—Boon or Menace? How a Top Industrialist Sees It," p. 91.

192–193. Speech before National Association of Purchasing Agents, May 3, 1966; reprinted as "The Common Thread," p. 497.

Madame C.J. Walker

200. "Wealthiest Negro Woman's Suburban Mansion," *The New York Times Magazine*, November 4, 1917, p. 6.

200. "Wealthiest Negro Woman's Suburban Mansion," p. 6.

201. "Wealthiest Negro Woman's Suburban Mansion," p. 6.

201. A'Lelia Perry Bundles, *Madame C.J. Walker: Entrepreneur* (New York: Chelsea House, 1991), p. 63.

201. "Wealthiest Negro Woman's Suburban Mansion," p. 6.

201. "Wealthiest Negro Woman's Suburban Mansion," p. 6.

201–202. *The Madame C.J. Walker Schools Text Book of Beauty Culture* (Indianapolis: Madame C.J. Walker Co., 1924), p. 207.

202. "Wealthiest Negro Woman's Suburban Mansion," p. 6.

202. *Report of the Thirteenth Annual Convention of the National Negro Business League* (Washington, DC: William H. Davis, 1912), p. 154–155.

203. *Report of the Fourteenth Annual Convention of the National Negro Business League* (Washington, DC: William H. Davis, 1913), p. 210.

203. *Report of the Fourteenth Annual Convention of the National Negro Business League*, p. 210.

203. *Report of the Thirteenth Annual Convention of the National Negro Business League*, p. 154–155.

203–204. *Report of the Fourteenth Annual Convention of the National Negro Business League*, p. 210.

204–205. *Report of the Thirteenth Annual Convention of the National Negro Business League*, p. 154–155.

205. Floyd J. Calvin, "A Brown Cinderella's Dream Come True!" *The Pittsburgh Courier*, September 1, 1928; clipping file, New York Public Library.

205. Remarks by Madame C.J. Walker to the National Association of Colored Women, 1912; quoted in *Madame C.J. Walker: Entrepreneur*, p. 105.

A.P. Giannini

214. B.C. Forbes, "Giannini—The Story of an Unusual Career," *Forbes*, November 10, 1923, p. 169.

214. Interview with A.P. Giannini in *Coast Banker*, June 1924; quoted in Marquis James and Bessie R. James, *Biography of a Bank* (New York: Harper, 1954), p. 163.

214–215. "Giannini—The Story of an Unusual Career," p. 173.

215. "Giannini—The Story of an Unusual Career," p. 143.

215–216. A.P. Giannini, "Methods," *System*, August 1926, p. 163.

216. "Methods," p. 163.

216. *Biography of a Bank*, p. 163.

216–217. Matthew Josephson, "Big Bull of the West," *Saturday Evening Post*, September 20, 1947, p. 16.

217. "Big Bull of the West," p. 31.

217. Communication from A.P. Giannini to the board of directors of the Bank of Italy, November 1914; quoted in *Biography of a Bank*, p. 69.

218. Richard Dempewolff, "The Bank That Youth Built," *Reader's Digest*, September 1947, p. 128.

218. "Giannini—The Story of an Unusual Career," p. 173.

218. "Giannini—The Story of an Unusual Career," p. 176.

219. *The Citizen*, October 1926; Bank of America Archives clipping file.

219. G. Marvin, "Debunking Banking: Bank of Italy," *Sunset*, February 1928, p. 14.

219. "Big Bull of the West," p. 31.

220. Newspaper interview, 1924; quoted in *Biography of a Bank*, p. 271.

220–221. George Creel, "My Hardest Job Is to Keep from Being a Millionaire," *American Magazine*, January 1931, p. 25.

221. "How 22 Executives Tackle Their Business Problems," *System*, June 1925, p. 747.

221–222. *Biography of a Bank*, p. 68.

222. "Big Bull of the West," p. 135.

222–223. "Giannini—The Story of an Unusual Career," p. 176.

223. Gertrude Atherton, *My San Francisco* (Indianapolis: Bobbs-Merrill, 1946), p. 227.

223. "Giannini—The Story of an Unusual Career," p. 169.

223–224. "Giannini—The Story of an Unusual Career," p. 173.

224. "Giannini—The Story of an Unusual Career," p. 173.

224. "Big Bull of the West," p. 31.

224. "A.P. Giannini," *Fortune*, July 1949, p. 18.

Harvey Firestone

234. Harvey Firestone with Samuel Crowther, *Men and Rubber* (Garden City, New York: Doubleday, Page & Co., 1926), p. 115.

234. *Men and Rubber*, p. 112.

234–235. *Men and Rubber*, p. 116.

235. *Men and Rubber*, p. 2.

235. *Men and Rubber*, p. 70.

235–236. *Men and Rubber*, p. 17.

236. *Men and Rubber*, p. 5.

236–237. *Men and Rubber*, p. 176–177.

237. H. S. Firestone, "What I Have Learned about Men," *American Magazine*, p. 138.

237. "What I Have Learned about Men," p. 138.

237. *Men and Rubber*, p. 64.

237–238. *Men and Rubber*, p. 94–95.

239. *Men and Rubber*, p. 114.

239–240. *Men and Rubber*, p. 113.

240. *Men and Rubber*, p. 169.

240–241. *Men and Rubber*, p. 65.

241. *Men and Rubber*, p. 125.

241. *Men and Rubber*, p. 100.

241–242. *Men and Rubber*, p. 9–11.

243. *Men and Rubber*, p. 172.

243. *Men and Rubber*, p. 170.

243–244. *Men and Rubber*, p. 165–166.

244. Alfred Lief, *The Firestone Story* (New York: Whittlesey House, 1951), p. 128.

244–245. *Men and Rubber*, p. 56–57.

245–246. *Men and Rubber*, p. 59.

246. *Men and Rubber*, p. 15.

246. *Men and Rubber*, p. 46–47.

247. *Men and Rubber*, p. 42.

247. *Men and Rubber*, p. 47–48.

247. *Men and Rubber*, p. 18, 19.

248. "What I Have Learned about Men," p. 16.

248. *Men and Rubber*, p. 72–73.

248. *Men and Rubber*, p. 21.

248–249. *Men and Rubber*, p. 39.

249. *Men and Rubber*, p. 6.

249. *Men and Rubber*, p. 111.

J. Paul Getty

257. J. Paul Getty, *How to Be Rich* (Chicago: Playboy Press, 1965), p. 40.

257–258. *How to Be Rich*, p. 89.

258. J. Paul Getty, *My Life and Fortunes* (New York: Duell, Sloan and Pearce, 1963), p. 99.

258–259. *How to Be Rich*, p. 64–65.

259. J. Paul Getty, *How to Be a Successful Executive* (Chicago: Playboy Press, 1971), p. 108.

260. *How to Be Rich*, p. 50.

260. *How to Be a Successful Executive*, p. 66–67.

260–261. *How to Be a Successful Executive*, p. 68.

261. *How to Be a Successful Executive*, p. 146–147.

262. *How to Be Rich*, p. 52.

262–263. *How to Be Rich*, p. 66.

263–264. *How to Be Rich*, p. 106–107.

264. *How to Be Rich*, p. 109–110.

264–265. *How to Be a Successful Executive*, p. 180, 185.

265. J. Paul Getty, *As I See It* (Englewood Cliffs, New Jersey: Prentice-Hall, 1976), p. 293.

265–266. *As I See It*, p. 325–326.

266–267. *How to Be Rich*, p. 141.

267. *How to Be a Successful Executive*, p. 201.

267. *How to Be a Successful Executive*, p. 201.

Alfred Sloan Jr.

277. Alfred P. Sloan Jr., "Millions of Automobiles," *Technology Review*, April 1929, p. 380.

277. Alfred P. Sloan Jr. edited by John McDonald with Catharine Stevens, *My Years with General Motors* (Garden City, New York: Doubleday & Co., 1964), p. 65.

277–278. Alfred P. Sloan Jr., "The Most Important Thing I Ever Learned about Management," *System*, August 1924, p. 138.

278. "The Most Important Thing I Ever Learned about Management," p. 138.

278–279. "The Most Important Thing I Ever Learned about Management," p. 195.

279. "The Most Important Thing I Ever Learned about Management," p. 195.

279–280. Alfred P. Sloan Jr., *Adventures of a White Collar Man* (New York: Doubleday, Doran & Co., 1941), p. 135.

280. "A.P. Sloan, Jr. — Prosperity Depends upon Ambition," *World's Work*, March 1928, p. 562.

280. Alfred P. Sloan Jr. as described to French Strother, "Modern Ideals of Big Business," *World's Work*, October 1926, p. 699.

280–281. *Adventures of a White Collar Man*, p. 205–206.

281. "The Most Important Thing I Ever Learned about Management," p. 138.

282. "The Most Important Thing I Ever Learned about Management," p. 196.

282–283. "Millions of Automobiles," p. 334.

283–284. *My Years with General Motors*, p. 140.

284. *Adventures of a White Collar Man*, p. 165.

284. *My Years with General Motors*, p. 125.

285. *Adventures of a White Collar Man*, p. 50.

285–286. Paul W. Kearney, "Horse Sense vs. Horse Power," *Good Housekeeping*, February 1936, p. 161.

286. Alfred Sloan Jr., "The Forward View," *Atlantic Monthly*, September 1934, p. 259.

286–287. "The Most Important Thing I Ever Learned about Management," p. 137–138.

287. *Adventures of a White Collar Man*, p. 154.

287–288. "The Most Important Thing I Ever Learned about Management," p. 137.

288. "Millions of Automobiles," p. 378.

288–289. *Adventures of a White Collar Man*, p. 103.

289. *Adventures of a White Collar Man*, p. 137.

289. "We Never Give an Order Says Sloan, of General Motors," *Business Week*, March 4, 1931, p. 28.

289. "Millions of Automobiles," p. 380.

David Packard

298. "David Packard of Hewlett-Packard," *Nation's Business*, January 1974, p. 42.

298–299. David Packard, *The HP Way* (New York: HarperCollins, 1995), p. 158.

299. *The HP Way*, p. 156, 155.

299. *The HP Way*, p. 129.

299–300. "David Packard of Hewlett-Packard," p. 41.

300. "A Very Rich Man for the Pentagon," *Business Week*, January 11, 1969, p. 83.

300–301. "David Packard of Hewlett-Packard," p. 41.

301. "Hewlett-Packard: Where Slower Growth Is Smarter Management," *Business Week*, June 9, 1975, p. 50.

301. "David Packard of Hewlett-Packard," p. 39–40.

302. "Hewlett-Packard: Where Slower Growth Is Smarter Management," p. 52.

302. "David Packard of Hewlett-Packard," p. 42.

302. Judy Erkanat, "Hewlett-Packard Co-founder Dies," *Electronic News*, April 1, 1996, p. 1.

302. "David Packard of Hewlett-Packard," p. 42.

303. *The HP Way*, p. 136.

303. *The HP Way*, p. 133–134.

304–309. David Packard, *Objectives of Hewlett-Packard Company*, original typescript, January 1957 (retyped 1984), Hewlett-Packard Company Archives.

Herb Kelleher

319. David A. Brown, "Southwest Airlines Gains Major Carrier Status by Using Go-It-Alone Strategy," *Aviation Week & Space Technology*, March 5, 1990, p. 84.

319. Leigh Strope, "Kelleher; Southwest Will Stay on Top," *Dallas Business Journal*, April 21, 1995, p. 2.

319–320. Dan Reed, "Flying Like a Madman," *Sales & Marketing Management*, October 1996, p. 94.

320. Kathleen Melymuka, "Sky King," *Computerworld*, September 28, 1998, p. 68.

320. "Kelleher; Southwest Will Stay on Top," p. 2.

320. Subrata N. Chakravarty, "Hit 'Em Hardest with the Mostest," *Forbes*, September 16, 1991, p. 48.

320. "Flying Like a Madman," p. 94.

321. Interview with Bill Lee, "Southwest Airlines' Herb Kelleher: Unorthodoxy at Work," *Organizational Dynamics*, Fall 1994, p. 11.

321. David A. Brown, "Southwest Airlines Gains Major Carrier Status by Using Go-It-Alone Strategy," p. 84.

321. "Southwest Airlines' Herb Kelleher: Unorthodoxy at Work," p. 9.

321–322. Stephanie Gruner, "Have Fun, Make Money: How Herb Kelleher Parties Profitably at Southwest Airlines," *Inc.*, May 1998, p. 123.

322. "Sky King," *Computerworld*, September 28, 1998.

322. "Southwest Airlines' Herb Kelleher: Unorthodoxy at Work," p. 10.

322. Charles A. Jaffe, "Moving Fast by Standing Still," *Nation's Business*, October 1991, p. 58.

323. "Moving Fast by Standing Still," p. 58.

323. Kevin Freiberg and Jackie Frieberg, *NUTS!* (Austin, Texas: Bard Press, 1996), p. 49.

323. Richard Woodbury, "The Prince of Midair," *Time*, January 25, 1993, p. 55.

324. "Hit 'Em Hardest with the Mostest," p. 49.

324. Anthony L. Velocci, Jr., "More City Pairs Await Southwest," *Aviation Week & Space Technology*, August 7, 1995, p. 42.

324. Michael Verespej, "Flying His Own Course," *Industry Week*, November 20, 1995, p. 23.

324. Kenneth Labich, "Is Herb Kelleher America's Best CEO?" *Fortune*, May 2, 1994, p. 50.

325. "Southwest Airlines' Herb Kelleher: Unorthodoxy at Work," p. 12.

325. "Moving Fast by Standing Still," p. 59.

325. "Southwest Airlines' Herb Kelleher: Unorthodoxy at Work," p. 11.

326. "Is Herb Kelleher America's Best CEO?" p. 52.

326. Vivian Pospisil, "Best Barometer," *Industry Week*, January 8, 1996, p. 11.

326. Dan McGowan and Tim Searson, "The Making of a Maverick," *Southwest Spirit*, June 1991, p. 38.

327. "Moving Fast by Standing Still," p. 59.

327. "Moving Fast by Standing Still," p. 57.

Clarence Birdseye

336. Clarence Birdseye, "If I Were Twenty-one," *American Magazine*, February 1951, p. 19.

336. "If I Were Twenty-one," p. 19.

337. "If I Were Twenty-one," p. 112.

337. "If I Were Twenty-one," p. 112.

337. "If I Were Twenty-one," p. 19.

337–338. "If I Were Twenty-one," p. 112.

338. "If I Were Twenty-one," p. 114.

338–339. Clarence Birdseye, "We Can Always Eat Crow," *American Magazine*, July 1943, p. 32.

339. "We Can Always Eat Crow," p. 33.

339. "If I Were Twenty-one," p. 114.

340. "If I Were Twenty-one," p. 19.

340–341. "The Unpublished Letters of Clarence Birdseye On Freezing," *Quick Frozen Foods*, March 1960, p. 322.

341. Clarence and Eleanor Birdseye, *Growing Woodland Plants* (Oxford University, 1951), p. v.

341. "If I Were Twenty-one," p. 19.

341. "If I Were Twenty-one," p. 113.

341. "If I Were Twenty-one," p. 112.

Margaret Rudkin

348. Margaret Rudkin, *The Margaret Rudkin Pepperidge Farm Cookbook* (New York: Grosset & Dunlap, 1963), p. 202.

349. Ruth Millett, "Cooking Hobby Started by Fairfield Society Woman," *Bridgeport* [Connecticut] *Post*, March 13, 1938; clipping file, Bridgeport, Connecticut, Public Library.

349. *The Margaret Rudkin Pepperidge Farm Cookbook*, p. 201.

349–350. Elizabeth Richey Dessez, "Ten Thousand Loaves a Day—But Still a Home Industry" *Christian Science Monitor*, January 3, 1940; clipping file, Bridgeport, Connecticut, Public Library.

350. John Bainbridge, "Striking a Blow for Grandma," *The New Yorker*, May 22, 1948, p. 40.

350. *The Margaret Rudkin Pepperidge Farm Cookbook*, p. 204.

351. Emma Bigbee, "Son's Illness Put Broker's Wife into Home-Made Bread," *New York Herald-Tribune*, March 21, 1938.

351. *The Margaret Rudkin Pepperidge Farm Cookbook*, p. 201.

351. "Striking a Blow for Grandma," p. 40.

Ted Turner

359. Hank Whittemore, *CNN: The Inside Story* (Boston: Little, Brown, 1990), p. 14.

359. "Neither Broke nor Broken," *Broadcasting*, August 17, 1987, p. 50.

360. "Ted Turner," *Playboy*, August 1978, p. 73–74.

360. "Ted Turner," p. 74.

360. speech by Ted Turner in Davos, Switzerland; quoted in Cynthia Crossen, "Shop Talk," *The Wall Street Journal*, February 10, 1986, p. 23.

361. "Ted Turner's Quantum Leap," *Broadcasting*, March 31, 1986, p. 52.

361. Steven Koepp, "Captain Outrageous Opens Fire," *Time*, April 29, 1985, p. 61.

361–362. "Ted Turner's Quantum Leap," p. 42.

362. "Neither Broke nor Broken," p. 62–63.

362–663. Jacqueline Trescott, "CNN's Ted Turner: Front and Center," *The Washington Post*, July 18, 1988, p. B-4.

363. "CNN's Ted Turner: Front and Center," p. B-4.

363. Subrata N. Chakravarty, "What New World to Conquer?" *Forbes*, January 4, 1993, p. 86.

363. Peter W. Kaplan, "Ted Turner, Station-to-Station," *Esquire*, February 1983, p. 100.

363–364. Maynard Good Stoddard, "Cable TV's Ted Turner: Spirited Skipper of CNN," *Saturday Evening Post*, March 1984, p. 46.

364. "Ted Turner," p. 74.

364. William A. Henry III, "Shaking Up the Networks," *Time*, August 9, 1982, p. 56.

365. Julia Bennett, "Adventurer in Cable TV," *Maclean's*, April 11, 1988, p. S6.

365. Harry F. Walters with others, "Ted Turner Tackles TV News," *Newsweek*, June 16, 1980, p. 66.

365. Speech by Ted Turner before the American Society of Magazine Editors, February 5, 1997; reprinted in George Gendron, "I'll Bet You're All Wondering What It Feels Like to Be a Billionaire," *Inc.*, April, 1997, p. 11.

366. "CNN's Ted Turner: Front and Center," p. B-4.

366. "Cable TV's Ted Turner: Spirited Skipper of CNN," p. 44.

ACKNOWLEDGMENTS

Material on the business leaders in this book came from a variety of places. While many people were helpful, none read the material in advance of publication, with the result that I am the only one responsible for the conclusions in the book, and for the facts as they are presented. It should also be noted that none of the companies cited here tried in any way to influence the content of this book; they gave their help generously, without conditions.

Dawn Stanford of IBM sent the picture of Thomas Watson with such efficiency, she might have been sitting there waiting for my call. The Chicago Historical Society responded to a request for a picture of William Wrigley having fun at the ballpark. Linda Hanrath and Anne Marie Vela of the Wm. Wrigley Jr. Company sent material on the company founder; their offices are still in the building he built in 1924. Gil Pietrzak and Marilyn Holt of the Carnegie Library of Pittsburgh sent a terrific selection of Andrew Carnegie pictures; come to think of it, their offices are still in the building that *he* built.

The Rockefeller Archive Center in North Tarrytown, New York, is the most important source of material on John D. Rockefeller, and granted permission to quote from his letters and interviews. Over the years, the RAC has escorted me in my abiding interest in the career of John Rockefeller. Ann Sindelar of the Western Reserve Historical Society in Cleveland sent the photo of Rockefeller, which I think shows his face in balanced concentration.

A'Lelia Bundles is related to Madame C.J. Walker and has amassed a rich collection of material, some of which she generously sent me for use in this book. Bundles is the author of two books on Madame Walker, including *My Mother's Mothers: The Legacy of Madame C.J. Walker* (Scribner/Lisa Drew). It also tells the story of Madame Walker's daughter, who was a major figure on the cultural scene of the 1920s. Kathleen Collins and Nancy Whitten Zinn of the Bank of America were especially encouraging in supplying material related to A.P. Giannini. Janet Lorenz of the Academy of Motion Picture Arts and Sciences supplied me with a selection of Mary Pickford photos, and Elaine Archer of the Mary Pickford Foundation graciously gave permission to use one in this book. Several of the Pickford quotes were used with the permission of the State Historical Society of Wisconsin, which maintains extensive archives on United Artists. Nancy Childs of the Polaroid Corp. sent valuable material on Edwin Land. Richard Thomas of Bridgestone/Firestone kindly sent the photograph of Harvey Firestone building a tire.

Karen Lewis of Hewlett-Packard assisted David Packard on his memoir, *The HP Way* (HarperCollins, 1995), and related her impressions of him to me in a very enlightening conversation. Carol Parcels of HP located just the photo I had wanted of David Packard. Nancy Steffes of General Motors was helpful and enthusiastic in finding just the photo I wanted of Alfred P. Sloan Jr. Cami Simonis of Southwest Airlines sent a selection of photographs of Herb Kelleher. True to the company's unwritten edict, she did so with great cheer.

Personally, I am ever grateful to Karl Weber, the best possible literary agent. Ruth Mills, the editor at Wiley, made the chapters into a book with insight and suggestions that uncovered new potential at every turn. Everyone at Wiley deserves my gratitude, notably Kirsten Miller, Ruth's assistant, who worked closely on many details. Stephanie Landis, the copy editor, of North Market Street Graphics, made an enormous contribution to the text, as well as entertaining me with oldtime baseball stories. For a stretch of many months, my parents, sister-in-law Terriruth Carrier, and my cousin Randi Roth all helped in any way they could. Last and most, I'd like to mention Neddy.

INDEX